*Palgrave Advances in Language and Linguistics*
Series Editor: Christopher N. Candlin, Macquarie University, Australia

*Titles include:*

Charles Antaki (*editor*)
APPLIED CONVERSATION ANALYSIS

Mike Baynham and Mastin Prinsloo (*editors*)
THE FUTURE OF LITERACY STUDIES

Noel Burton-Roberts (*editor*)
PRAGMATICS

Susan Foster-Cohen (*editor*)
LANGUAGE ACQUISITION

Monica Heller (*editor*)
BILINGUALISM: A SOCIAL APPROACH

Juliane House (*editor*)
TRANSLATION: A MULTIDISCIPLINARY APPROACH

Barry O'Sullivan (*editor*)
LANGUAGE TESTING: THEORIES AND PRACTICES

Martha E. Pennington (*editor*)
PHONOLOGY IN CONTEXT

Mastin Prinsloo and Christopher Stroud (*editors*)
EDUCATING FOR LANGUAGE AND LITERACY DIVERSITY

Steven Ross and Gabriele Kasper (*editors*)
ASSESSING SECOND LANGUAGE PRAGMATICS

Ann Weatherall, Bernadette M. Watson and Cindy Gallois (*editors*)
LANGUAGE, DISCOURSE AND SOCIAL PSYCHOLOGY

*Forthcoming:*

Ann Hewings, Lynda Prescott and Philip Seargeant (*editors*)
FUTURES FOR ENGLISH STUDIES

Paul Baker and Tony McEnery (*editors*)
CORPORA AND DISCOURSE STUDIES

Fiona Copland, Sara Shaw and Julia Snell (*editors*)
LINGUISTIC ETHNOGRAPHY

---

**Palgrave Advances in Language and Linguistics**
**Series Standing Order ISBN 978–1–1370–2986–7   hardcover**
**978–1–1370–2987–4   paperback**
(*outside North America only*)

You can receive future titles in this series as they are published by placing a
standing order. Please contact your bookseller or, in case of difficulty, write to us
at the address below with your name and address, the title of the series and the
ISBN quoted above.

Customer Services Department, Macmillan Distribution Ltd, Houndmills,
Basingstoke, Hampshire RG21 6XS, England

*Also by Mastin Prinsloo*

LITERACIES, GLOBAL AND LOCAL (*co-edited*)

LITERACY STUDIES (*co-edited, 5 vols*)

THE FUTURE OF LITERACY STUDIES (*co-edited*)

THE SOCIAL USES OF LITERACY
Theory and Practice in Contemporary South Africa (*co-edited*)

*Also by Christopher Stroud*

STYLE, IDENTITY AND LITERACY
English in Singapore (*co-authored*)

# Educating for Language and Literacy Diversity

## Mobile Selves

Edited by

Mastin Prinsloo
*University of Cape Town, South Africa*

and

Christopher Stroud
*University of Western Cape, South Africa*

First published 2014 by
PALGRAVE MACMILLAN

Palgrave Macmillan in the UK is an imprint of Macmillan Publishers Limited, registered in England, company number 785998, of Houndmills, Basingstoke, Hampshire RG21 6XS.

Palgrave Macmillan in the US is a division of St Martin's Press LLC, 175 Fifth Avenue, New York, NY 10010.

Palgrave Macmillan is the global academic imprint of the above companies and has companies and representatives throughout the world.

Palgrave® and Macmillan® are registered trademarks in the United States, the United Kingdom, Europe and other countries.

ISBN 978–1–137–30983–9 hardback

ISBN 978–1–137–30984–6 paperback

This book is printed on paper suitable for recycling and made from fully managed and sustained forest sources. Logging, pulping and manufacturing processes are expected to conform to the environmental regulations of the country of origin.

A catalogue record for this book is available from the British Library.

A catalog record for this book is available from the Library of Congress.

Typeset by MPS Limited, Chennai, India.

# Contents

# List of Figures

# List of Tables

# Acknowledgements

Figure 8.1 has been reprinted with kind permission of City Lights Books, and Figures 8.3, 8.4 and 8.5 have been reprinted with kind permission of Grass Roots Press.

# Notes on the Contributors

**Elsa Auerbach**, Professor Emerita, taught in the Applied Linguistics and English departments at the University of Massachusetts Boston for 30 years. She has written extensively about critical and participatory approaches to adult language and literacy education for English language learners. Her research and publications focus on curriculum development, family literacy, worker education, and teacher education; she has participated in various adult education and literacy initiatives in South Africa since 1995. She currently works with Jewish Voice for Peace, a US organisation engaged in the struggle for a just peace in Israel/Palestine, and is part of the editorial collective of *Amandla! Magazine*.

**Kathleen Heugh** teaches English to international students at the University of South Australia, using pedagogical practices informed by research and theories of multilingualism and multilinguality emerging from Africa and South Asia. Her research has focused on language policy and planning and multilingual education in sub-Saharan Africa, particularly South Africa. More recently she has engaged in collaborative research in India and among migrant communities in Australia. She has conducted classroom-based research in a number of countries, and has led several small, medium and large-scale countrywide and multi-country studies of: literacy, mother-tongue and multilingual education; and large-scale assessment of students in multilingual settings.

**Hilary Janks** is a Professor in the School of Education at the University of the Witwatersrand, Johannesburg, South Africa. She is the author of *Literacy and Power* (2010) and the editor and author of *Doing Critical Literacy* (2014). Her teaching and research are in the areas of language education in multilingual classrooms, language policy and critical literacy. Her work is committed to a search for equity and social justice in contexts of poverty. Her current research focuses on the use of mobile phones for teaching literacy in poor schools.

**Michael Joseph** joined the University of Natal (Pietermaritzburg, now UKZN) as head of the Department of Second Language Studies and then moved to the Molteno Project in Johannesburg to head the Adult Literacy Unit. After two years as a research scholar at Wits, he moved with his partner Esther Ramani to the University of Limpopo to start up a new bilingual degree: BA in Contemporary English and Multilingual Studies. Michael is currently an Associate Professor in Education at Rhodes University where he helps develop undergraduate and postgraduate courses, which foreground multilingual education. He has helped to set up study groups at Rhodes on bilingual education and is involved with two colleagues in mapping the use of Vygotsky-inspired teaching and research at Rhodes.

**Kimberly Lenters** is an Assistant Professor at the Werklund School of Education, University of Calgary, Canada. Situated within a sociocultural perspective on literacy, her work examines productive spaces in which children engage in multimodal composition: in classrooms, in out-of-school spaces, and across home–community–school boundaries. Using assemblage theory to examine children's literacy practices as enacted in networks of people and objects, this work focuses on the complexity of children's meaning-making practices, taking into consideration a range of communicational modalities and texts, embedded and circulating within personally meaningful contexts.

**Constant Leung** is Professor of Educational Linguistics in the Centre for Language Discourse and Communication, Department of Education and Professional Studies at King's College London. He also serves as Deputy Head of Department. He was the founding chair of the National Association for Language Development in the Curriculum (NALDIC), a national subject association for teachers of English as an Additional Language in UK. His research interests include additional/second language curriculum, language assessment, language policy, and teacher professional development. He is Senior Associate Editor for *Language Assessment Quarterly* and Editor of Research Issues for *TESOL Quarterly*. He is an Academician of Social Sciences (UK).

**Carolyn McKinney** has a PhD from the University of London and is Senior Lecturer in the School of Education, University of Cape Town, South Africa. Drawing on linguistic ethnography, sociolinguistics and sociology of education, she conducts interdisciplinary research on the intersections of language, subjectivity, power and inequality in education. Her publications have focused on critical literacy and student subjectivity; language ideologies and discursive practices in multilingual classrooms and language and subjectivity among youth in a changing South Africa. She runs a Masters programme in Applied Language and Literacy studies and contributes to pre-service teacher education.

**Mastin Prinsloo** is an Associate Professor in Applied Language and Literacy Studies at the School of Education at the University of Cape Town and former Director of the Centre for Applied Language and Literacy Studies. He was founding Editor of *Reading and Writing*, the journal of the Reading Association of South Africa. His research in literacy studies is currently focused on young people's engagement with electronic media, particularly in low socio-economic contexts. As Director of the Social Uses of Literacy research project and the Children's Early Literacy Learning research project, his earlier research has included studies of unschooled adults' literacy engagement and children's early literacy learning.

**Esther Ramani** arrived in South Africa in 1992, to help establish the department of Applied English Language Studies at Wits and then moved to the University of Limpopo, where with Michael Joseph, she set up the Academic Development Unit, and an MA programme in English Language Education. They also launched the dual-medium undergraduate degree, BA in Contemporary English and Multilingual Studies (BA CEMS), taught and assessed in Sesotho sa Leboa and English in 2003, which continues to attract growing numbers of students. Professor Ramani moved to Rhodes University in 2013, and has taken up a part-time position at the Institute for the Study of English in Africa to develop an Honours module in Bilingual Education to be offered in 2015.

**Robert Serpell** is Professor of Applied Developmental Psychology and Coordinator of the Centre for Promotion of Literacy in Sub-Saharan Africa at the University of Zambia. His publications include numerous journal articles, *The significance of schooling: life-journeys in an African Society* (Cambridge, 1993) and *Becoming literate in the city: the Baltimore Early Childhood Project* (Cambridge, 2005, with Linda Baker and Susan Sonnenschein). Born and raised in England, he joined the University of Zambia (UNZA) in 1965 and became a naturalised citizen of Zambia in 1979. At UNZA he has served as Head of the Psychology Department (1974–77, 1987–89), Director of the Institute for African Studies (1977–83) and Vice-Chancellor (2003–6).

**Crain Soudien** is formerly the Director of the School of Education at the University of Cape Town and currently a Deputy Vice-Chancellor. His research is in the areas of social difference, culture, education policy, comparative education, educational change, public history and popular culture, including books and studies on District Six, Cape Town; youth identities; and studies of race, culture and schooling in South Africa.

He is chairperson of the Independent Examinations Board, the former chairperson of the District Six Museum Foundation, a former President of the World Council of Comparative Education Societies and was the chair of the Ministerial Committee on Transformation in Higher Education in South Africa.

**Brian Street** did anthropological fieldwork in Iran during the 1970s, from which he developed theoretical approaches to literacy in cross-cultural perspectives. He then taught social anthropology at Sussex University for over 20 years and is now Professor Emeritus of Language in Education at King's College London and Visiting Professor of Education at the University of Pennsylvania. He has worked and lectured in the USA, Australia, Brazil and South Africa, among others, applying cross-cultural perspectives to educational issues around literacy, language and development. He is also involved in the international project Learning Empowerment through Training in Ethnographic Research (LETTER) and is President of the British Association for Literacy in Development.

**Christopher Stroud** is a Senior Professor of Linguistics at the University of the Western Cape, Director of the Centre for Multilingualism and Diversities Research, and Professor of Transnational Multilingualism at Stockholm University, Centre for Research on Bilingualism, He has researched and written widely on multilingualism, language planning and policy and language education in contexts as diverse as Papua New Guinea, South East Asia, Scandinavia and Southern Africa.

**Virginia Zavala** has a PhD in sociolinguistics from Georgetown University. She is currently Professor in the Linguistics section of the Department of Humanities at the Pontificia Universidad Católica del Perú and director of the Masters Programme in Linguistics at the same university. Her research revolves around intercultural bilingual education, language policies, racism and racialisation and literacy as a social practice from an ethnographic and discourse analytic perspective. Her most important books are: *Desencuentros con la escritura. Escuela y comunidad en los Andes Peruanos* (2002), *Decir y Callar: Lenguaje, equidad y poder en la universidad peruana* (with Gavina Córdova, 2010) and *Qichwasimirayku: Batallas de una política lingüística* (in press, 2014). She has published many articles in Spanish, English and Portuguese.

# Introduction

*Mastin Prinsloo and Christopher Stroud*

Attention to language and literacy diversity in education is both timely and challenging. Our focus in this introductory chapter is on what to make of this diversity and its impact on education systems and practices. We conclude by introducing the chapters in this volume, pointing out the particular contributions they make to this collection.

We start from the common observation that educators and researchers in very many different locations around the world (though not everywhere) increasingly encounter linguistically and socioculturally diverse groups of students in their classrooms and lecture halls (Gardner and Martin-Jones, 2012; Creese and Blackledge, 2010). Fundamentally, this is due to the changes in recent years in the core dynamics of social, cultural and economic life, one indication of which is the changing language dynamics in particular settings, another the rise in translocal and transnational communication that takes place through electronic media. These dynamics raise concerns of a specifically linguistic and sociolinguistic kind: for example, what happens when people with diverging language histories share the same social or educational space, when their communication involves 'crossing', mixing or 'meshing' of language resources, or where they use 'colloquial' or local versions of standard languages? How do we understand everyday talk and writing in relation to schooling expectations under conditions of heightened linguistic and sociocultural diversity? Not surprisingly, such developments pose a range of social, cultural and material challenges to educational systems, where growing sociocultural and linguistic student diversity is accompanied by intensifying standardisation of assessment practices and often by institutional insistence on monolingual instruction through the medium of a standard national or international language. On the other hand, educational institutions also comprise vibrant sites of innovation and breakthrough that attempt to address the concerns of this diverse population – a healthy counterpoint to systems that all too easily tend towards resisting change.

Evidence of such diversity would seem to require more dynamic and mobile concepts around language and literacy than is often the case in educational discourse (Makoni and Pennycook, 2007; Blommaert, 2010; Blommaert and Rampton, 2011). It is also a question of interest and concern as to whether trends towards an increasing sociolinguistic diversity are happening uniformly across diverse settings across the world or themselves are subject to diverse manifestations: are there important differences between, for example, the nature of the diversities in neighbourhoods and schools in, say, West or East European or North American cities, on the one hand, and African, South American or other cities in the 'South', on the other. And what are the conceptual resources that best help us to make sense of these differences?

In what follows, we review key arguments on globalisation, language and literacy that serve to contextualise the contributions in the present volume. We discuss ideas, first, about sociolinguistic scales, hierarchy, social complexity and systemic views of the global. Then we examine competing models of complexity and scale, and develop a view on how global resources of language and literacy are distributed, assembled and adapted in distinctive ways in particular contexts; how they are 'placed' or territorialised in assemblages that combine mobile and widely circulating forms and resources with locally developed categories and practices, in shifting and often unpredictable combinations.

## Globalisation at large

It has become commonplace in recent times to situate research on language, literacy and diversity in educational and wider social contexts by way of references to globalisation as the source of the flows of migrants into local communities, and across nations and regions of the world. These dynamics present 'quotidian and formal public challenges to inherited Western assumptions about linguistic uniformity, cultural homogeneity, and national membership' (Blommaert et al., 2005: 201). However, while globalisation is widely seen as the source of increased cultural contact and linguistic diversity, it is also, in an apparent paradox, the source of centripetal processes of centralisation and homogenisation (Lo Bianco, 2010). In educational contexts, this takes the form of intensifying high-stakes testing of standardised language and knowledge forms in education institutions. Such testing, a spin-off of the quality assurance resources and processes that were developed for the reorganisation of work in multinational companies around the world, reminds us that globalisation, however we understand it, is more than simply about increasing diversity but also about changing forms of regulation and attempts at regulation, in schools and in social life.

Seen as a multifaceted agent which causes economic, political, cultural and environmental changes in the world, globalisation is primarily and commonly theorised as the global spread of socio-economic processes that Western capitalism has triggered. Globalisation is said to have gathered pace in the late 1980s with the deregulation of markets (Castells, 1996; Collier, 2006; Featherstone, 2006), where marketisation, or the rise of neo-liberalism as 'a logic of governing' (Ong, 2007: 3) becomes the defining characteristic of reorganised social life on a world scale, evident in the ease with which capital investments flow around the world in a supranational world economy. Although these dynamics are in many respects similar to earlier versions of world trade, developments in telecommunications infrastructure and transportation of goods and people (Castells, 1996; Jacquemet, 2005) have made possible a greater level of market coordination than previously. This has allowed an extensive interconnectedness of trade, investment and particularly finance. Sophisticated technologies for rapid human mobility and global communication are also transforming the communicative environment of the globalised social world, allowing the economy to operate as a unit with 'real-time' transactions happening at a global level.

But while the world economy may be global in the production and distribution of goods and services, only a very small fraction of work is skilled work in the multinational companies that account for close to half of the gross world product and two-thirds of international trade (Castells, 2009). Labour, therefore, has not been globalised and many regions, or places within those regions, are outside of the new economic order. This imbalance leads to movements of people, in particular, from parts of the world that are left out of the global network to those areas that are part of it, as well as movements of people across world centres and to different parts of the global periphery. Thus, this broad socio-economic model of globalisation provides an entry point into understanding phenomena such as increasing skilled and unskilled migration and the resulting linguistic diversity in many places as well as the dominance, for example, of particular language resources in others.

## Scales theory, superdiversity and language-in-education

Now a ubiquitous term, globalisation is also a central theme of contemporary social theory, but questions remain as to how 'global' and 'local' relate to one another with what kinds of results for language and literacy in education. One influential and productive approach in sociolinguistics for understanding linguistic diversity in relation to globalisation is by way of scales theory (Blommaert, 2007, 2010; Collins et al., 2009) which provides a set of conceptual resources for understanding the way power relations on a global scale shape the uptake of language resources in specific local contexts. This approach pursues the difficult task of integrating sociolinguistics, discourse analysis and social theory to address questions of power, social inequalities, language diversity and social interactions in their situated occurrence while taking account of the interconnectedness of social life across spaces and regions. This work offers a language, a framework and a set of constructs to talk about the remarkable movements of people, language and texts in recent times. The scales model suggests that each context (local, regional, national, global) has its own 'orders of indexicality' which assign meanings, values and statuses to diverse codes. Blommaert and Rampton (2011: 7) explain the concept of indexicality as follows:

the denotational and propositional meanings of words and sentences lose their preeminence in linguistic study, and attention turns to *indexicality*, the connotational significance of signs. So for example, when someone switches in speaking and/or writing into a different style or register, it is essential to consider more than the literal meaning of what they are saying. The style, register or code they have moved into is itself likely to carry associations that are somehow relevant to the specific activities and social relations in play.

These values or indexicalities are organised hierarchically at a global level in a world that is systemically organised in terms of scales from top to bottom. While local scales are momentary, situated and restricted, the codes and literacies of dominant groupings are valued at a translocal level because they are resilient, highly mobile and they can 'jump scales' (Blommaert, 2010: 36).

World systems analysis or WSA (Wallerstein, 1974, 1991), which this model draws on for a model of the global, argues that a world system and not nation states is the defining feature of contemporary social life and should be the primary focus of social analysis. In this model, the modern world system, essentially capitalist in nature, emerges out of European capitalism and operates as a social unit that consists of, primarily, core and peripheral regions, as well as semi-peripheral regions which act as a periphery to the core and a core to the periphery. Core countries, or sites within countries, focus on high-skill, capital-intensive production and peripheral sites and regions focus on low-skill production and resource exports to the core. A key point in WSA is that events and processes move and develop on a continuum of layered scales, with the strictly local (micro) and the global (macro) as extremes, and with several intermediary scales (for example the level of the state) in between, with varying degrees of impact and status (Blommaert, 2007). A sociolinguistics of globalisation (Blommaert, 2010) working with this model of the social as systemic pays attention to language hierarchy and processes that are seen as holding across situations and transcending localities. Scales theory thus provides a productive metaphor to analyse the way language resources retain or lose social value depending on where they are placed along spatio-temporal lines within social contexts, where power relations shape the uptake of language resources. Interaction between different scales is a crucial feature for understanding the sociolinguistic dimensions of such events and processes, because language and literacy practices are subject to social processes of hierarchical ordering. This analysis aims to account for large-scale features of language and literacy in particular, for example on institutional, national and transnational levels, as well as their impact on the dynamics of face-to-face interaction (Blommaert, 2007, 2010).

Blommaert (2007: 2) suggests that scales theory helps us to understand how children and adults can become inarticulate and deficient when they move from a space in which their linguistic resources are valued and recognised to a classroom or workplace closer to the economic and political centre, because these processes happen in a way that is shaped by the world system at a global scale. He cites the case of migrant children who possess complex and developed language and literacy skills but who nevertheless are declared illiterate in Belgian immersion classes, where Dutch language and literacy are the only recognised linguistic capital. Such processes of ordering are seen as happening not only at an interregional or cross-state level but also at a national and local level. Societies with pronounced levels of social inequality correspondingly devalue the diverse language and literacy resources of their citizens the further they are from national and local centres of power and authority. In this approach sociolinguistic and discursive phenomena are 'essentially *layered*, even if they appear to be one-time, purely synchronic and unique events' (Blommaert, 2007: 3), and social settings are seen as polycentric and stratified, with a multitude of centres of authority, local as well as translocal, cohering within a layered and hierarchical systemic global order. Thus, in this model social and linguistic 'norms' are the outcomes of local centres of authority which are 'stratified complexes' that are hierarchically located. Sociolinguistic scales are often both 'nested' within and overlapping with another, reflecting the criss-crossing complexities that constitute social and human organisation, with different linguistic values attaching to different languages in different scales of consideration. From this perspective, scales provide a tool with which to understand the way power relations shape the uptake of language resources.

## Competing models of sociolinguistic and socio-material complexity

There is a question to be asked, however, about the appropriateness of the fit between WSA, on one hand, and social and linguistic complexity on the other. One starting point amongst alternative views to WSA is that social life has become too complex and diverse for analysis that employs overarching narratives, such as the concept of a world system. Whatever globalisation is in contemporary times, it might be said to have unfolded in different ways, with a non-linearity about contemporary processes of global integration at least partly because of the ways people intercede in ways that disrupt systemic dynamics. If globalisation does have systemic features, it is not a closed system and, as a system 'open to the environment' it is *not* 'its own sweet beast' (Law, 2003: 13). In this criticism, Wallerstein also overstates the centrality of European capitalism in the new global economic order. His is a diffusionist model in which the significant changes were produced in one place, at the expense of other kinds of influences from elsewhere in the world (Featherstone, 2006).

Indeed, one of the troubling problems about conceiving of globalisation as systemic and hierarchical is the assumption that complexity is synchronous and scaled, that higher scales are more complex and that lower scales and peripheries are simpler forms of social organisation, with developments at the 'top' or the core of the world system having effects at the 'bottom', for example, observations that developments in the field of sophisticated, multimedial and multimodal Internet communication have effects on other, 'less sophisticated' forms of literacy in the periphery. The problem with such observations is that they do not take account of how these socially constructed resources are 'taken hold of' or refigured as 'placed resources' and as 'global assemblages' in 'peripheral' contexts and within particular networks of association. The suggestion that sophistication is a characteristic of one site and not the other would appear to be a judgement made from 'the centre', based on the assumption that sophistication (which we might read here as a synonym for complexity) is intrinsically an upper-scale phenomenon.

A case in point is the notion of 'grass-roots literacy' (Blommaert, 2008, 2010), a scaled view of writing across low socio-economic sites in Africa. Blommaert describes grass-roots literacy as a 'genre', a characteristic form of writing across poor communities in Africa, describing it as a non-elite form characterised by what he calls 'heterography' – the deployment of graphic symbols in ways that defy orthographic norms: words spelled in different ways, often reflecting the way they are pronounced in spoken vernacular varieties rather than following conventional orthographic norms or prestige language forms. Such texts, he says, will have local value but examined from beyond the local, they appear as inferior examples of writing, pointing to the low status of these persons on a larger stage. This analysis, accurate as it might seem from one perspective, deflects our attention from how these texts might well have a complexity in their uses and meanings which is not apparent from a distance or from a perspective which is not attentive to the complex networks of practice that shape these textual practices in specific ways. Attention to some familiar text features by the researcher such as orthography/heterography does not provide a sufficient account of these texts as literacy practices. To label such practices as forms of 'peripheral normativity' (Blommaert et al., 2005) might deflect our attention from the particularities and complexities at that site, and within those socio-material networks.

Canagarajah (in press), in contrast, argues that while particular communities might display characteristic writing forms, they might not necessarily be 'stuck' at 'one scale-level' or 'locked' into peripheral modernity. Canagarajah's study in a Cape Town school setting, in contrast with Blommaert et al.'s (2005) study in a similar setting, finds in the texts of the students a *recognition* of different norms from outside the local. In their writings on a school Facebook site students' heterography is evident in their mixing of English and isiXhosa, abbreviations and icons. Canagarajah identifies their writing here as a hybrid form of literacy activity, combining spoken, literate and visual resources and diverse languages. In their classroom written work, however, students do not mix codes in the same way and Canagarajah suggests they have shifted to a translocal norm, approximating to Standard Written English and with an emerging sense of the genre requirements of school essay writing. While student writing displays the types of grammatical problems that Blommaert identified, Canagarajah sees teachers as striving to correct these as they work to help students to develop their translocal English-language writing resources, albeit from a strongly constrained starting point. The scaled and hierarchical view of teachers' and students' struggles emphasises the structural constraints that situate them in a regime of norms and standards that is pre-given as a function of the assumed nature of social complexity. Canagarajah, on the other hand, presents an approach where the emphasis is more on the agentive dynamics that characterise the 'contact zones' between the language and literacy resources that students bring to school and the resources, discourses and practices of schooling in that context.

The view that complexity is produced systemically, that sophistication happens at higher-scale levels and that persons on the periphery are somehow 'stuck' with restricted language and writing resources because of their fixed place in the periphery of the world system offers a view that has been identified as 'romantic complexity' by Law (2003) and Kwa (2002). The researcher or theorist 'looks up' here to make sense of what is observed by examining its place in the larger complex system. Law offers an alternative view, closer perhaps to the ethnographic intentions of Blommaert and colleagues. Drawing on work on a material semiotics (Law, 2009) that treats everything in the social and natural worlds as a continuously generated effect of the webs of relations within which they are located (see e.g. Callon and Latour, 1981; Latour, 1990), Law finds complexity by 'looking down', at specificity and detail in the concrete and the specific. Our predominant understandings of complexity, he suggests, including the size or scale assumptions that we make, assume that the whole emerges as a result of the interconnectedness of its component parts. One of the outcomes of this sense-making strategy is that located complexity is passed over because, for the researcher who is looking up, the system may be of more interest than the components. Where the romantic intuition is that the global is necessarily large, with the local inserted somewhere down the hierarchy of emergence, Law prefers a view of the global as situated, specific and constructed in the practices included in each specificity. 'There *is* no system, global order or network', he suggests, 'these are, at best, partially enacted romantic aspirations' (Law, 2003: 9). The distinction between big and small is a relational effect, he insists, where scale is tenuous and precarious. Heterogeneous elements need to play their part moment by moment or it all comes unstuck. This is a view of the global as something that is poorly formed and elusive, that changes size and shape and only travels uncertainly. It is also close to the view that Street (2004) offered in his discussion of literacy practices and whether they are globally shaped or locally produced. Street's point was that the global only exists as substantiated in the local.

Collier's (2006) and Collier and Ong's (2005) discussion of 'global assemblages' is relevant here: seeking an alternative to the categories of global and local, they develop the notions of global forms and global assemblages. They see the idea of global assemblage as 'an alternative to the categories of local and global, which serve to cast the global as abstraction, and the local in terms of specificity' (Collier, 2006: 380). Global forms are seen as widely distributed conceptual and organisational resources that are assembled and adapted in distinctive ways at local and regional levels so as to work in those contexts, articulated in specific situations – or territorialised in *assemblages*. These assemblages define new material, collective and discursive relationships. Collier and Ong (2005) restrict this term to material technology and specialised social expertise, such as ISO standards in the workplace (international standardised quality-assessment criteria) as they are applied in particular locations), but we can certainly think of schooling assessment practices and high-stakes testing as constituting this kind of assemblage, and we can also think of language resources in this way when they become articulated and networked in particular settings – for example, English or Englishes when thought of as a world language or an 'English language complex' (Mesthrie and Bhatt, 2008) where particular mobile resources become 'placed'. These global forms interact with other resources and elements in particular contexts, in contingent, uneasy, unstable interrelationships. In the space of assemblage, a global form is simply one among a range of elements. An assemblage is the product of multiple determinations that are not predictable by a single logic. These interactions might be called the *actual* global, or the global in the space of assemblage. The assemblage is not a 'locality' to which broader forces from the global are counterposed. Nor is it the structual effect of such forces (Collier, 2006: 380). The term 'global asemblage' suggests inherent tensions, forms that are shifting, in formation, or at stake, heterogeneous, contingent, unstable, partial and situated (Collier and Ong, 2005). In this light, as an illustrative example here, Ong (2007: 3) conceptualises neo-liberalism 'not as a fixed set of attributes with predetermined outcomes, but as a logic of governing that migrates and is selectively taken up in diverse political contexts', including South

American and African contexts. The product of these interactions might be called the *actual* global, or the global in the space of assemblage. The point is that in the space of the 'global', heterogeneous things combine in ways that are hard to pin down with diagnostic resources which stress a global logic. Similarly, Featherstone (2006: 370), drawing on the arguments of Knorr Cetina, refers to such phenomena as major imbalances between cause and effect, unpredictable outcomes, and self-organising, emergent structures as features of globalisation. He suggests that 'the management of uncertainty, task predictability and orderly performances were much easier to facilitate in the "relatively complex" organizations of modern industrial societies'. A global society, on the other hand, he writes, 'entails a different form of complexity: one emanating more from microstructural arrangements that institute self-organizing principles and patterns'. In conclusion, perhaps such a concept of 'the global' is a productive way to think of language, literacy and diversity rather than via a scaled, systemic view of the social as comprising macro and micro dimensions and, indeed, closer to the ethnographic orientations of those scholars who have been using scale as a metaphor for understanding social complexity. Wortham (2012) similarly argues against the macro/micro conceptual frame that is familiar in the sociolinguistic field and suggests that researchers attend to multiple scales with no single scale treated as foundational or determinant. Wortham (2006) studied how students and teachers socially positioned each other in a single classroom over an academic year by drawing upon widely circulating sociohistorical models as well as locally developed categories of identity (such as 'loud black girls', 'disruptive students'), and the curriculum itself. What such an orientation leads to is a concern less with grand theorising but with small and focused research into the *actual* global in particular settings, as presented in the range of studies in this collection.

## Concepts of mobility, language and literacy

The chapters gathered in this collection offer a series of case studies or vignettes of the *actual* global in a diverse range of settings and they address a varied but complementary set of topics, from studies of the challenges presented to education by societal multilingualism and social inequalities in Zambia, South Africa, Ethiopia, London, Peru, the USA and Mexico. They examine questions of migration, transnationalism and the relationships between minority and dominant linguistic resources in particular contexts. They draw on and elaborate on recent work in interactional sociolinguistics and literacy studies that has questioned prevailing views from recent decades on language, literacy and bilingualism. This work has sought to develop alternative concepts for conditions of linguistic diversity (e.g. Makoni and Pennycook, 2007; Heller, 2007, Blommaert, 2010). We provide a short introduction to some of these debates here, before introducing the individual studies.

Widdowson (2010: 10) makes the point that linguists make statements and claims about language in general or languages in particular but 'these statements are necessarily abstractions from the actuality of language as experienced by its users'. Assumptions around the connectedness of language and ethnicity (Errington, 2008: 9) have encouraged linguists to look past the variability and complexity of the language resources they observed to name languages that identified groups of people and helped to construct or legitimate linguistic hegemony around the notion of national or ethnic languages. In doing so, they drew on highly naturalised and questionable assumptions about language–race–nation unity.

In contemporary contexts of language diversity these approaches to languages as boundaried constructs that are closely identified with situated, homogeneous speech communities are seen to be increasingly problematic in contexts of increasing diversity and multilingualism, and with regard to studies of bilingualism in social and educational contexts. Heller (2007: 1) described prevalent views on bilingualism as offering 'a "common-sense" but in fact highly ideologised view of bilingualism as the coexistence of two linguistic systems'. She argued against the notion that languages are objectively speaking whole, bounded systems and for the notion that speakers draw on linguistic resources which are organised in ways that make sense under specific social conditions. She supported a focus on language as a resource and languages as practices which are socially and politically embedded. We might say, with reference to the preceding discussion on global assemblages that, in this view, while they have been thought of before as forms which are autonomous, languages, in this view, are always assembled in actual contexts, where they receive shape and purpose.

A view of language as practised offers a perspective on language practices as socially embedded, of speakers as social actors and of boundaries between particular resources as products of social action. Indeed, literacy has been studied from this perspective for some time since the shaping work in literacy studies of Street (1984), Heath (1983), Scribner and Cole (1981) and Barton and Hamilton (1998). In this tradition, literacy is studied not as a single entity but as a complex of communicative practices and historically influenced attitudes to these practices (see also Prinsloo and Baynham, 2013; Baynham and Prinsloo, 2009). From this literacy studies perspective, literacy in school is produced by the practices of the classroom, providing not just technical skills but also a set of prescriptions about what knowledge is and how to display its use. These classroom practices include particular kinds of interaction amongst teacher and students, and literacy is produced through group activity, informally communicated judgements, as well as standardised tests and all the other evaluative apparatus of schooling (Cook-Gumperz, 2006). Such an approach to language and literacy as situated practices is better able to account for the varied ways that speakers draw on their resources when social or linguistic boundaries are no longer essentialised and are crossable. From an ideological perspective, however, we can recognise that language and literacy are resources and practice both in the fluid sense intended by Heller and Blommaert above, but also in more reified or institutionalised forms, as statements and understandings about the value or necessity of some rather than other of these available resources. Thus, for example, Lin (1997) pointed to both the grave educational consequences following from English language dominance in Hong Kong schools but also the urgent need to pay attention to the right of access to English by children of disadvantaged groups (for example, children whose parents speak little English and who live in communities where there is little access to English). She argued that curricular reforms are needed to help these disadvantaged children to acquire the dominant English capital while also affirming and building on their indigenous linguistic and sociocultural identities and resources. How such contradictory objectives are to be achieved, though, is not clear. In this light, Stroud and Wee (2012) present a nuanced view of youths in Singapore struggling with the effects of the dominance of standard English and Mandarin Chinese along with government's somewhat hollow insistence that 'heritage languages' should be maintained at home. Zavala (this volume) shows similar tensions between literacy classes in one site in Peru that associate Quechua literacy with an 'essential' Quechua culture and classes in another site where Spanish language and literacy resources are produced and shaped by teachers and students as skills for standardised testing within the schooling system.

## Bilingualism, education and heteroglossia

Critical interpretive sociolinguistics makes the case for research into the interactional and textual fine grain of everyday life in educational settings with attention to specific institutional regimes, including wider processes of political economy and change in contemporary society (Martin-Jones, 2007; Heller, 2007; Creese and Blackledge, 2010). Martin-Jones (2007) calls for attention to the everyday communicative practices of teachers and learners in schools as well to the wider policy discourses as they are articulated in policy documents, and this is indeed what Leung and Street (this volume) and Serpell (this volume) undertake. A starting point in this research is a recognition of the potential fluidity of language resources and attention to their often more rigid construction in educational policy and practice. As Creese and Blackledge (2010) put it,

> Schools operate as institutions (linked to the state) where specific languages (national official languages) and specific linguistic practices (ways of speaking, reading and writing) come to be inculcated with legitimacy and authority.

They draw our attention to the ways in which schools function as spaces to select and categorise students, for assessing performance (including linguistic performance) and providing credentials tied to positioning in the world of work. Bailey (2007) suggests that 'processual and socially infused constructs such as heteroglossia and indexicality' are useful for directing attention to the historical and ideological dimensions of language meanings and identity construction. We can then study the ways in which educational policies *and* classroom practices contribute to the reproduction of asymmetries of power between groups with different social and linguistic resources in specific places. Heller (1999) coined the term *parallel monolingualism*, to describe 'bilingual' language teaching strategies in schools where two or more standard languages are taught as if in separate silos, and Martin-Jones (2007: 167) pointed to a 'container metaphor of competence' in prevailing discourses around 'mother tongue' education and bilingual education, with a common preference for the construction of parallel monolingual spaces for learning, including strict monitoring of those spaces for their monolingualism. Such approaches manifest in terms like 'balanced bilingualism', 'additive bilingualism' and 'subtractive bilingualism', in effect all conceiving of languages and linguistic competencies as separate containers, side by side, that are more or less full or empty. Creese and Blackledge (2010) question understandings of bilingual pedagogy which keep languages rigidly separate in what they call a 'two solitudes' approach and describe instead a flexible bilingual approach to language teaching and learning in which two or more languages are used alongside each other, in an approach they call *translanguaging*. Canagarajah (2006: 58) advocates a similar strategy of 'code-meshing' where 'students bring in their preferred varieties' of a language into a conventional text in 'rhetorically strategic ways resulting in a hybrid text'.

In the light of the earlier discussion presented here, we might consider such concepts as translanguaging, code-meshing and heteroglossia as global forms for developing studies and instructional approaches to language and literacy in education under conditions of diversity or 'superdiversity' (Vertovec, 2007; Blommaert and Rampton, 2011). The next stage would be to study them as assemblages, as they are taken up in distinct and less or more coherent ways by researchers at particular sites. We see this work happening in a variety of ways in the chapters that follow, which we now introduce briefly. The book is divided into two parts: the first focuses on studies of diversity in educational settings, the second on methodologies and resources for pedagogy and research in contexts of language and literacy diversity.

## Part I: Studying diversity in education settings

1. Leung and Street's school-based study takes place in the context of 'high and rising levels of ethnic, linguistic and social diversity in British schools'. Their study of classroom work shows how everyday diversity and heterogeneity in particular contexts are at odds with the understandings and intentions embodied in central policies and also with teaching practices. Calls to 'improve achievement in literacy' in schools are reflected in 'return to basics' approaches, emphasising phonics teaching within a monolingual English perspective. They focus on how literacy is constructed and enacted in the classroom, against policy prescriptions and intentions. While the curriculum emphasises content, and referential uses of language, Leung and Street's observation of interaction, social relations, texts and practices shows that much more is going on, and they consider these classroom performances with regard to questions of social inequality, pedagogy and multilingualism. In seeing literacy, language and other modalities as sociocultural phenomena or as social practices, they see them as particular resources produced within the communicative framework of schooling.

2. Virginia Zavala's chapter focuses on 'intercultural' bilingual education and she examines two schools in Peru which are considered to be successful, but which present contrasting ways of reading in Quechua and reading in Spanish. Her study of this variability in what counts as reading draws on resources for the study of literacy as a social practice

and her attention is again on the performance of diverse types of actions which produce these differences. She identifies an ideological dilemma in Peruvian education where different interpretive repertoires about literacy education produce strategies that differently promote homogeneity and diversification. On one hand neo-liberalism as a 'strategy of governing' is taken up in schooling to promote an approach to education as technical and socially neutral, with results shown through standardised test scores. One critical result of this approach is a shared emphasis on testing on the part of students. While the orientation in school policy is towards the production of competitive, flexible and functional graduates, a gap is produced where there is a demand for education that produces critical, ethical and political citizens. Alternative indigenous movements and non-government organisations orient towards ideas on postcoloniality and interculturality as well as recovery of local cultural practices. However, some of these strategies index Quechua culture and language as ancestral cultural practices and promote a type of ethnic separatism as political action. In this way Quechua becomes identified as signalling a static site that is resistant to change and mobility. Zavala suggests that Quechua literacy remains a field of struggle where dominant interpretative repertoires construct it as an invisible language or as an ancestral language anchored in the rural world.

3. Robert Serpell's chapter examines research that assesses children's communicative competence in Zambia and questions the bias towards standard languages. He questions the colonial era survey of tribes and language that identified 73 languages and ethnicities indigenous to Zambia. Colonial linguists ignored the great deal of commonality in the language resources that they counted, Serpell suggests. He identifies a monolingual bias in Zambian education, in a setting where children grow up with adults who are competent in three or more language varieties, where the varieties have a strong core of grammatical and lexical commonalities and where the borders between varieties are porous. This diversity produces problems for tests of children's cognitive abilities, when children do not always easily switch from a vernacular language to the official local Zambian language that is used for instruction. It remains unclear how the boundaries should be drawn between 'cognate languages', here as elsewhere in Southern Africa. Along with these complexities, there are problems around superficial categorisation along the lines that this child is a speaker of that language. In fact, children growing up in multilingual African contexts are likely to encounter multiple strands of language before entering school that are seldom

explicitly labelled as an utterance in a particular language or dialect before schooling, and children's repertoires in designated languages seldom match the officially expected repertoire. He concludes that, if initial literacy is to be taught effectively to children enrolled in multilingual multidialectal classroooms, it seems essential to respect their prevailing patterns of communication.

4. Carolyn McKinney's chapter similarly draws on a school-based study to examine the complexities of social mobility and schooling with regard to linguistic resources. Her study of a desegregated suburban school shows the complexity of emerging and solidifying language practices around the production of an 'expanding "black" middle class'. Her study shows how close study of complex everyday language practices can offer us insights into changing sociocultural practices.

5. Kathleen Heugh's chapter shows Afar pastoralists resisting Amharic, the 'working regional language' of the Ethiopian federal centre, in their schools because of its historical associations for them with both Coptic Christianity and oppressive administrative regimes, but they embrace English-language instruction because of the perceived wider connectivity which English affords. From the perspective of the Ethiopian centre they are regarded as 'anti-school' but close up a different, more complex picture emerges.

## Part II: Teaching and research with diverse students

6. Michael Joseph and Esther Ramani's chapter focuses on a methodology to teach university students in the north of South Africa through the medium of Sesotho sa Leboa, a dominant language of the Limpopo province in the northernmost region of South Africa but not used officially to date as a medium of instruction beyond the early years of schooling. Learners are encouraged to draw on local knowledges in narratives that provide the grounds for further learning of an academic kind. The engagement with local as well as dominant language resources contributes to an in-depth understanding of the relation between language and thought in this setting.

7. Kimberley Lenters' chapter offers a close engagement with Shirley Heath's well-known accounting of the literate practices of three culturally diverse groups living in close proximity to one another in *Ways with Words* which was ground-breaking in its redefinition of the study of literacy. Lenters is concerned to update the methods Heath used to make them relevant for contemporary times and she shows how a greater sense of how the 'local' is a historically and politically networked site

is needed to complement the depth of Heath's engagements with local sociolinguistic and cultural specificities.

8. Elsa Auerbach's chapter offers an orientation towards a pedagogy of 'glocalization' that is aimed at benefiting the migrants who are the subjects of research on mobility. What does research about global, transnational and translocal processes mean for students and teachers as they work with each other inside and outside the classroom, she asks. She goes on to suggest ways of recontextualising research so that it might be used to enable people to participate in organising for change as part of global networks, in what she identifies as 'glocalised' action for change. She offers examples of initiatives that recontextualise language and literacy pedagogy in the service of transformation processes.

9. Hilary Janks offers an approach to critical language and literacy pedagogy through the example of engaging with xenophobia in the South African context. She examines the link between apartheid discourses and contemporary xenophobic Othering through a close and critical reading of *District 9*, the science fiction movie that was set in South Africa but widely distributed elsewhere. Following an engagement with the film as text and narrative, she concludes by offering an example of critical literacy activities relating to *District 9* and 'the role of movies, language and discourse in the construction of the dangerous Other'.

10. In a conclusion to the collection, Crain Soudien offers a reflection on language and the politics of social difference. He treats South Africa as an ontological hotspot for both the production and undoing of racialised forms of difference. He draws attention to language's role in allowing and prohibiting engagement with new identity practices in conditions of diversity. He identifies what he describes as the new embodied spaces in post-'formal apartheid', where people are having to learn how to manage their historically inscribed bodies in new ways and says that one of our quests should be to examine further how languages have become attached to racial identity in this setting.

## References

Bailey, B. (2007). Heteroglossia and boundaries. In M. Heller (ed.), *Bilingualism: a social approach* (pp. 257–74). Basingstoke: Palgrave Macmillan.

Barton, D. and Hamilton, M. (1998). *Local literacies: reading and writing in one community*. London: Routledge.

Baynham, M. and Prinsloo, M. (eds) (2009). *The future of literacy studies*. Basingstoke: Palgrave Macmillan.

Blommaert, J. (2007) Sociolinguistic scales. *Intercultural Pragmatics*, 4(1): 1–19.

Blommaert, J. (2008). *Grassroots literacy.* London: Routledge.

Blommaert, J. (2010). *The sociolinguistics of globalization.* Cambridge: Cambridge University Press.

Blommaert, J., Collins, J. and Slembrouk, S. (2005). Spaces of multilingualism. *Language & Communication,* 25: 197–216.

Blommaert, J. and Rampton, B. (2011). Language and superdiversity. *Diversities,* 13(2): 1–20.

Callon, M. and Latour, B. (1981). Unscrewing the Big Leviathan: how actors macrostructure reality and how sociologists help them to do so. In K. D. Knorr-Cetina and A. V. Cicourel (eds), *Advances in social theory and methodology: toward an integration of micro- and macro-sociologies* (pp. 277–303). London: Routledge & Kegan Paul.

Canagarajah, A. S. (2006). The place of world Englishes in composition: pluralization continued. *College Composition and Communication,* 57(4): 586–619.

Canagarajah, A. S. (in press). Negotiating mobile codes and literacies at the contact zone: another perspective on South African township schools. In C. Stroud and M. Prinsloo (eds), *Language, literacy and diversity: moving words.* London: Routledge.

Castells, E. (1996). *The rise of the network society.* Oxford: Blackwell.

Castells, E. (2009). *Communication power.* Oxford: Oxford University Press.

Collier, S. (2006). Global assemblages. *Theory, Culture & Society,* 23(2–3): 379–81.

Collier, S. and Ong, A. (2005). Global assemblages, anthropological problems. In A. Ong and S. Collier (eds), *Global assemblages: technology, politics, and ethics as anthropological problems* (pp. 3–21). Malden, Mass.: Blackwell.

Collins, J., Slembrouck, S. and Baynham, M. (eds) (2009). *Globalization and language in contact: scale, migration, and communicative practices.* London: Continuum.

Cook-Gumperz, J. (2006). The social construction of literacy. In J. Cook–Gumperz (ed.), *The social construction of literacy* (2nd edn) (pp. 1–18). Cambridge and New York: Cambridge University Press.

Creese, A. and Blackledge, A. (2010). Translanguaging in the bilingual classroom: a pedagogy for learning and teaching? *The Modern Language Journal,* 94(i): 104–15.

Errington, J. (2008). *Linguistics in a colonial world: a story of language, meaning, and power.* Oxford: Blackwell.

Featherstone, M. (2006). Genealogies of the global. *Theory, Culture & Society,* 23(2–3): 367–99.

Gardner, S. and Martin-Jones, M. (eds) (2012). *Multilingualism, Discourse and Ethnography.* New York: Routledge.

Heath, S. (1983). *Ways with words: language, life and work in communities and class-rooms.* Cambridge: Cambridge University Press.

Heller, M. (1999). *Linguistic minorities and modernity: a sociolinguistic ethnography.* London: Longman.

Heller, M. (2007). Bilingualism as ideology and practice. In M. Heller (ed.), *Bilingualism: a social approach* (pp. 1–22). Basingstoke: Palgrave Macmillan.

Jacquemet, M. (2005). Transidiomatic practices: language and power in the age of globalization. *Language & Communication,* 25: 257–77.

Kwa, C. (2002). Romantic and baroque conceptions of complex wholes in the sciences. In J. Law and A. Mol (eds), *Complexities: social studies of knowledge practices* (pp. 23–52). Durham, NC: Duke University Press.

Latour, B. (1990). Drawing things together. In M. Lynch and S. Woolgar (eds), *Representation in scientific practice* (pp. 19–68). Cambridge, Mass.: MIT Press.

Law, J. (2003). And if the global were small and non-coherent? Method, complexity and the Baroque, published by the Centre for Science Studies, Lancaster University, Lancaster LA1 4YN, UK, accessed July 2010 at http://www.comp.lancs.ac.uk/sociology/papers/Law-And-if-the-Global-Were-Small.pdf

Law, J. (2009). Actor network theory and material semiotics. In Bryan S. Turner (ed.), *The new Blackwell companion to social theory* (pp. 141–58). Oxford: Blackwell.

Lin, A. (1997). Hong Kong children's rights to a culturally compatible English education. *Hong Kong Journal of Applied Linguistics*, 2(2): 23–47.

Lo Bianco, J. (2010). The importance of language policies and multilingualism for cultural diversity. *International Social Science Journal*, 61: 37–67.

Makoni, S. and Pennycook A. (eds) (2007). *Disinventing and reconstituting languages*. Clevedon, UK: Multilingual Matters.

Martin-Jones, M. (2007). Bilingualism, education, and the regulation of access to language resources. In M. Heller (ed.), *Bilingualism: a social approach* (pp. 161–82). New York: Palgrave Macmillan.

Mesthrie, R. and Bhatt, R. M. (2008). *World Englishes: the study of new linguistic varieties*. Cambridge: Cambridge University Press.

Ong, A. (2007). Neoliberalism as a mobile technology. *Transactions of the Institute of British Geographers*, NS, 32: 3–8.

Prinsloo, M. and Baynham, M. (eds) (2013). *Literacy studies*, set of five vols. London: Sage.

Scribner, S. and Cole, M. (1981). *The psychology of literacy*. Cambridge, Mass.: Harvard University Press.

Street, B. (1984). *Literacy in theory and practice*. Cambridge: Cambridge University Press.

Street, B. (2004). The limits of the local – 'autonomous' or 'disembedding'? *International Journal of Learning*, 10: 2825–30.

Stroud, C. and Wee, L. (2012). *Style, identity and literacy: English in Singapore*. Bristol: Multilingual Matters.

Vertovec, S. (2007). Super-diversity and its implications. *Ethnic and Racial Studies*, 30(6): 1024–54.

Wallerstein, I. (1974). *The modern world system I: capitalist agriculture and the origins of the European world-economy in the sixteenth century*. New York: Academic Press.

Wallerstein, I. (1991). *Geopolitics and geoculture: essays on the changing world-system*. Cambridge: Cambridge University Press.

Widdowson, H. (2010).The theory of practice. In G. Cook and S. North (eds), *Applied linguistics in action: a reader* (pp. 7–18). London and Milton Keynes: Routledge and the Open University.

Wortham, S. (2006). *Learning identity: the joint emergence of social identification and academic learning*. New York: Cambridge University Press.

Wortham, S. (2012). Beyond macro and micro in the linguistic anthropology of education. *Anthropology and Education Quarterly*, 43(2): 128–37.

# Part I
# Studying Diversity in Education Settings

# 1

# Classroom Constructions of Language and Literacy Activity

*Constant Leung and Brian Street*

The need to improve achievement in literacy through school education has been a constant preoccupation in government policies across the globe. These concerns are exemplified by this British government policy statement: 'We will improve early numeracy and literacy, promoting systematic synthetic phonics and assessing reading at the age of six to make sure that all children are on track' (Department for Education, 2010: 43).

Similar concerns can readily be seen in various manifestations in (re)developing countries such as South Africa as well as countries such as the United States and others in the Global North. In terms of national policies we have seen that different national/regional administrations have adopted different 'fixes' at different times. For instance in the mid-1980s through to the 1990s a genre-based approach was adopted as a system-wide initiative in New South Wales, Australia (Veel, 2006). The UK governments from the early 1990s onwards have adopted a 'return to basics' approach which emphasises the traditional concerns of formal correctness and conventional usage at word, sentence and whole text levels, with a particular emphasis on the importance of teaching 'phonics' (DfEE, 1998; Department for Education, 2010). Perhaps we should add that 'language' and 'literacy' have been conceptualised entirely within a monolingual English perspective.

There continue to be critiques of this position by researchers experienced in the field and some of these connect closely with the approach we are taking here, emphasising a broader, more socially oriented perspective on the learning of literacy. For instance, Wyse (2011) argues that the National Literacy Strategy in England did originally provide scope for such wider pedagogy and content but it was government pressures that led to a narrower, less academically rooted, top-down approach. The Strategy seemed to move from description of selective features of literacy to pedagogic prescription which does not have much support in research. Indeed in another paper, Wyse and Goswami (2008) provide one of the strongest intellectual critiques of the National Literacy Strategy approach in general and of its adoption of 'synthetic phonics' in particular. Similarly, Myhill and her colleagues (2012), who have worked closely in the policy arena as researchers, critique the emphasis on 'policing grammar' that emerged as part of the 'top-down' approach: the concept of grammar has not been well theorised, they argue, and the denigration of many pupils' backgrounds as an explanation for their language 'deficit', may have contributed to the sense of alienation that is still felt. Goodwyn (2011: 6) observes that '[t]he literacy debate is far from over but we have learned a great deal what the debate should really focus upon and we are very clear that learning or literacy is not a "game"'. It is, then, from the perspective indicated by these critiques that we pursue research which likewise takes a different perspective than that to be found still in the current policy disposition in England. Similarly in the USA, the 'No Child Left Behind' policy, a major educational policy in the past decade that has spawned many subsequent initiatives, is strongly based on a perspective on teaching literacy in schools that emphasises setting high standards and establishing measurable goals, most of which are based on traditional literacy-as-skills views associated with static and monolingual norms (see further elaboration in a later section; Bloome et al., 2005).

In this chapter our primary purpose is not to evaluate the pedagogic efficacies of the various language and literacy teaching approaches, although our work does lead us to question the validity of the theoretical claims on which the USA and UK approaches cited above are based. More precisely, we wish to address a fundamental conceptual issue that is relevant to both educators and researchers: how is 'literacy' constructed and enacted by teachers and students in the classroom? Answering such a question obviously has considerable implications for both policy and pedagogy.

In order to address this question we will firstly provide a brief summary of the relevant theoretical and methodological issues in the fields of language and literacy studies; we will then introduce some classroom data that exemplify the issues raised in this chapter as they apply to researching and understanding the uses of language and the enactments of literacy activities in the classroom; finally, we will attempt to draw some conclusions both for research and practice. Although we draw on our work in London as a point of departure in this discussion, we believe that some of our observations and arguments will resonate with experiences elsewhere.

As indicated above in our references to national policy in the UK and USA, our account challenges the dominant approach in public education where the learning of language and literacy has often been construed from a monolingual perspective, where an assumption is made that students share a broadly similar language and cultural background, and that they share a common experiential base (taking age into account). This is an increasingly untenable assumption. Linguistic and ethnic diversity has been shown to be the norm in many parts of the world (see OECD, 2010). For instance, according to the 2011 UK census, 30 per cent of London's inhabitants (over 2 million people) were born outside the UK. In addition to the overseas-born residents, London has a large number of ethnic minority communities; 53.5 per cent of the London secondary school student population is classified as 'non-white' (Hamnet, 2011). Over 300 languages are spoken by school students in London (von Ahn et al., 2010), and 43 per cent (approx.) of London's school students speak English as an additional/second language (Department for Children Schools and Families, 2009). We can no longer assume London schools to be monolingual and monocultural institutions. While the English language is the medium of instruction and wider communication, it is unsafe to assume that teachers and students share a common language and cultural background, and that the diverse backgrounds do not impact on the way/s in which literacy activities are perceived and enacted (see next section for further elaboration). Similar arguments are being made by scholars working in other parts of the UK, such as Snell (2013) on pupil uses of dialectal varieties in classroom interaction in north-east England and indeed of the world, evident also in Creese et al. (2010) whose work on multilingualism addresses diversity within a variety of sociopolitical settings where the processes of language use create, reflect and challenge hierarchies and hegemonies.

There is also a tendency for curriculum discussions on literacy to focus on the 'language content' and 'standards' of literacy, as in the UK National Literacy Strategy and the USA 'No Child Left Behind' (now supplemented by a strategy known as 'Race To The Top'), while the account presented here challenges this dominant perspective. The teaching of literacy in schools in England in the past ten years or so, for example, has been prescribed in terms of a content that comprises vocabulary, sentence grammar, understanding and producing text in particular ways within English and/or literacy lessons. But literacy activities in school are an integral part of all curriculum areas, and it is important to recognise that literacy activities are mediated by spoken discourse and other forms of communication (see e.g. Lotherington and Ronda, 2012; Freitas and Castanheira, 2007). Reading and writing activities are as much a constituent part of science and history lessons as they are in English and literacy lessons. So 'content' has to be understood more broadly as comprising subject content meaning as enacted in classroom activities through language and other semiotic means. We draw, instead, upon a social practice perspective on literacy to address the complexity of such activities, taking account also of the language diversity issues signalled above. The term 'practice' is used in a particular sense in this discussion. Street (2000: 22) distinguishes 'literacy events' from 'literacy practices':

> The concept of literacy practices ... attempts to handle the events and the patterns of activity around literacy but to *link* them to something broader of a cultural and social kind. And part of that broadening involves attending to the fact that in a literacy event we have brought to it concepts, social models regarding what the nature of this practice is and that make it work and give it meaning. Those models we cannot get at simply by sitting on the wall with a video and watching what is happening: you can photograph literacy events but you cannot photograph literacy practices.

So one can observe a literacy event, but literacy practice can only be inferred from observed events. A further dimension of this approach is the recognition that literacy events and practices are inextricably linked with other modes of communication – visual, kinaesthetic and so on – in ways that are analysed in the research literature as multimodality (Kress, 2010; Kress and Street, 2006; Jewitt, 2006; Kress et al., 2005) – and in our accounts of classroom practice we will also pay attention to the frequent switching between modes, notably oral, written and visual, that form an integral part of contemporary communicative practices of teacher/student interaction. Elsewhere we have argued that

> Language (including English) can no longer be regarded as the primary means of communication; digital communication technology has put paid to that. In making use of and studying [the] new and unfolding communication practices, then, we need to conceptualise English differently, in conjunction with other semiotic resources and activities. (Leung and Street, 2014: xxviii)

Furthermore, we observe that language is but one facet of communication:

> ... it is no longer sufficient to be able to use English (indeed any named language) in the conventional sense of being able to understand and express meaning through words and sentences, when much of what we do in digitally mediated communication involves the use of a mixture of language, visual–audio and other semiotic resources, and technical know-how to navigate and exploit the technological facilities on computers and mobile devices. (Leung and Street, 2014: xxviii)

Given these complexities, there is a good case for asking the question: 'What is going on when teachers and students engage in talking, reading and writing?' In order to understand how such literacy is 'done' in school in contemporary conditions, one should ask the question: 'How is literacy construed and enacted by teachers and students across the curriculum?' As part of this orientation, we are interested in the ways in which language, in this case English, is used for communicative purposes (including reading and writing) in school contexts. For this reason the work of Hymes on the ethnography of speaking and communicative competence is directly relevant. In order to arrive at an empirical description of what takes place when people communicate with one another in any specific situation, Hymes (1972: 281) suggests that we should try to find out about the language (and other semiotic) resources being used, how these resources are being used and evaluated by participants, and more importantly from the point of view of descriptive adequacy for this discussion, we should ask questions such as '[w]hether (to what degree) something is in fact done, actually *performed*, and what it's doing entails' (original emphasis). We see a need, then, for combining classroom interactional discourse and literacy activities as linked concerns, a combination that is central in this discussion.

## Renewing theoretical frameworks for researching language and literacy

Whilst, as we have pointed out, many policy accounts still proffer grammar-based approaches to understanding, describing and teaching language, in the research field the limitations of this orientation were increasingly discussed as long ago as the 1960s and 1970s, and the merits of more real-life-oriented approaches received extensive attention. Halliday (1973, 1975; also Halliday et al., 1964) and Hymes

(1972, 1977, 1994) were among those whose work made a significant contribution to the shift from a grammar orientation. Whilst we draw upon this approach and certainly wish to move beyond the narrow prescriptive grammar of some policy positions, we also recognise that an understanding of the language and literacy practices of contemporary classrooms involves further development of these earlier social language positions. The work of Bloome and his colleagues (Bloome et al., 2008) and Green and her colleagues (2011) on classroom interaction has made a major contribution to this shift of focus, and our own accounts of classroom interactions in London classrooms build on this work, which resonates with the recent work of researchers who have attempted to bring together multilingualism, discourse and ethnography (e.g. Creese and Blackledge, 2010; Roberts, 2014). As Gardner and Martin-Jones (2012: 1) explain:

> Over the last two decades, sociolinguistic research on multilingualism has been transformed. Two broad processes of change have been at work: firstly, there has been a broad epistemological shift to a critical and ethnographic approach, one that has reflected and contributed to the wider turn, across the social sciences, towards critical and poststructuralist perspectives on social life. Secondly, over the last ten years or so, there has been an intense focus on the social, cultural and linguistic changes ushered in by globalisation, by transnational population flows, by the advent of new communication technologies, by the changes taking place in the political and economic landscape of different regions of the world. These changes have had major implications for the ways in which we conceptualise the relationship between language and society and the multilingual realities of the contemporary era. A new sociolinguistics of multilingualism is now being forged: one that takes account of the new communicative order and the particular cultural conditions of our times, while retaining a central concern with the processes involved in the construction of social difference and social inequality.

Both of these moves – towards an ethnographic perspective and to recognition of globalisation – represent the underpinning epistemology and methodology for the research we describe here. For instance, in keeping with the work of Hymes and others in the ethnography of communication, we recognise the importance of an 'emic' rather than an 'etic' perspective, focusing on the meanings of participants rather than simply imposing our own from outside. But at the same time, in keeping with Agar (1996), we are wary of overstating a dichotomy here. In the empirical accounts below, we try, then, to make links between the immediate data and the wider patterns of interest to readers of this volume. For instance, our own interest in the increasing numbers of ethnolinguistically diverse students participating in London classrooms requires us, as Gardner and Martin-Jones (2012) argue, to take account of the new patterns of language use emerging with globalisation and transnational flows. The shift that these authors signal regarding a critical and ethnographic approach has already been a significant part of the move to what is termed New Literacy Studies, which we explore below. The combination of sociolinguistic and ethnographic sensibilities (as described above) provides us, we believe, with a more supple capacity for analysing and making sense of the classroom data.

## Social literacies

The dominant policy-sponsored model in England is still of autonomous, skill-based, delivery. This view of literacy is exemplified by the earlier quote from a policy statement. Newspaper clippings from the last decade of press reports on literacy indicate a focus on 'falling standards', 'deficit', 'illiteracy', 'skills' or lack of them and very little influence from the more 'social' approaches discussed (for example, in the 'Get London Reading' campaign reported in *The Guardian* (2011)). The raising of expectations about 'literacy' and the preoccupation with 'falling standards' by current governments in countries such as the UK and the USA, and the media hype (even hysteria) about literacy may, however, create space for alternatives, as the dominant approach fails to 'deliver' (see also Freebody, 1998, 2007a, b on similar debates in Australia). A question for more socially oriented theorists and practitioners is: what do they have to offer with regard to practical applications and the mediating of theory into practice, to take account of the demands that will be made on education systems if the present round of interventions prove unsuccessful? Indeed, the lack of demonstrable improvements in 'literacy' attainment in schools in England has been accompanied by a de-emphasis of the literacy strategy in recent official policy discourse.

In a move away from the autonomous and singular perspective on literacy Gee (1990), Street (1984, 1993) and others have initiated an alternative approach in a series of papers and books, now generally known as the New Literacy Studies (NLS). For both research and teaching this approach treats language and literacy as social practices rather than technical skills to be learned in formal education. The research requires language and literacy to be studied as they occur naturally in social life, taking account of the context and their different meanings for different cultural groups. The approach requires curriculum designers, teachers and evaluators to take account of the variation in meanings and uses that students bring from their home backgrounds to formal learning contexts, such as the school and the classroom. NLS emphasises the importance of 'culturally sensitive teaching' (Villegas, 1991) in building upon students' own knowledge and skills (Castanheira, 2012; Heath, 1983; Heath and Mangiola, 1991).

These views on research and practice are based upon socially and experientially grounded ideas about the nature of language and literacy, of the kind we noted above. In turn the research conducted within this perspective has reinforced and developed these ideas (Collins, 1995). This perspective enables us to speak in terms of social literacies. This phrase, as explicated by Street (1995), refers to the nature of literacy as social practice and to the plurality of literacies that this enables us to observe. That literacy is a social practice is an insight both banal and profound: banal, in the sense that once we think about it, it is obvious that literacy is always practised in social contexts, and that would include even the school context, however 'artificial' it might be accused of being in its ways of teaching reading and writing. The school, like other contexts, has its own institutional values and behaviours into which its particular literacy practices are inserted. The notion is, in this sense, also profound in that it leads to quite new ways of understanding and defining what counts as literacy and has important implications for how we teach reading and writing. If literacy is a social practice, then it varies with social context including different school contexts and is not the same, uniform activity in each case, so that a uniform, 'standard' way of teaching 'literacy' in schools of the kind advocated by some national governments, fails to help learners negotiate the complex realities in which its use is actually embedded and given meaning.

We also drew upon the notion of 'situated participatory processes' (Green et al., 2011: 2) which refers to

> ... the ways of knowing, being and doing constructed in and through the actions of participants in a particular moment or across times and events in the classroom ... [this approach] enables us to focus more closely on *how* ... students have opportunities for developing a particular academic or social practice and how these opportunities are constituted in and through local and situated processes of inter-action among members.

We follow the teachers' and students' actions from this perspective, to identify and explore how spoken and written language, alongside other semiotic resources, is used to generate a particular set of opportunities for participating in classroom events and learning activities. Such a view can signal how the 'situated participatory processes' are enacted and made available to students in particular settings.

Drawing, then, on a social literacies perspective rather than the dominant 'skills' approach, we focus on these 'complex realities' of literacy practices in trying to reconceptualise the role of language and literacy varieties in schooling and their relationship to different modes of communication. Furthermore, we acknowledge that classroom interactions do not monolithically orient toward any simple notion of 'teaching' or 'learning'. As noted by Bloome et al. (2008) in their analysis of classroom interaction, language and other semiotic means are implicated in, among other things:

- the construction of 'relationships between individuals and political identities including students, teachers ...' (Bloome et al., 2008: 18);
- the construction and exercise of power relations; and
- the definition and creation of 'knowledge, including academic knowledge, disciplinary knowledge, pedagogic knowledge and everyday world knowledge' (Bloome et al., 2008: 18).

In keeping with the ethnographic perspective that informs much of our work, we will use concrete local examples in order to provide 'telling cases' of the larger conceptual issues discussed above. Drawing on Mitchell (1984), an anthropologist well aware of the critiques that can be levelled again such concrete case studies, we make the methodological point that such cases are not intended to be taken as 'representative' in terms of empirical typicality. Rather, they involve what Mitchell terms *analytical induction* rather than *enumerative induction*:

> What the anthropologist using a case study to support an argument does is to ask how general principles deriving from some theoretical orientation manifest themselves in some given set of particular circumstances. A good case study, therefore, enables the analyst to establish theoretically valid connections between events and phenomena which previously were ineluctable. From this point of view, the search for a 'typical' case for analytical exposition is likely to be less fruitful than a telling case. (Mitchell, 1984: 239)

The episodes we are presenting are part of the ordinary everyday flow of classroom activities in our data. We see these episodes as 'telling cases' of the issues regarding language and diversity that we have laid out above. The concrete and 'ordinary' character of the examples below precisely make the point that these larger themes can be found in local events and practices.

## Language and literacy in the classroom – accounts from London schools

The next stage of work in this area, then, is to move beyond theoretical critiques of the autonomous models and to provide concrete examples of what is going on in the classroom that can then be analysed from the broader perspective offered by a social-practices-oriented understanding of reading and writing in context. We turn now to some of the applications of these ideas to schooling, looking at some of the data we have collected in multilingual London schools. The data presented in this section are drawn from a research project focused on the uses of language and literacy in schools and universities in London.[1]

We focus on data from a biology lesson at the advanced subsidiary level (17-year-olds, penultimate school year before university) at West Town School in London (pseudonym). Its student population is ethnolinguistically very diverse, over 80 per cent of whom are classified as from minority language and community backgrounds. The school prides itself on being an 'inclusive' institution, that is, it is committed to equal entitlement and high expectations for all students, irrespective of their backgrounds. As a corollary of this, perhaps, despite the very high level of ethnolinguistic diversity in the school, in our data we have found little evidence of anyone in the school talking about this diversity explicitly in relation to curriculum and pedagogy; there is a kind of taken-for-granted assumption that all teachers and students alike are to participate in the life of the school without distinction.

Following Bloome et al. (2005, 2009), before we paid close attention to specific segments of the data, we first sought to discern the different activities in the focal classrooms. Through repeated viewing of the video recordings and asking of the question 'What's going on?', we inductively identified the following main and recursive 'activity phases' in the focal lessons: teacher-led classroom management; teacher-fronted talk on topic content; teacher-orchestrated, student-hands-on activities (including some initiation–response–evaluation exchanges between teacher and students); and student small group/individual seat work. In our inductive analysis of the meanings of the participants' utterances, we are informed by a principle drawn from conversation analysis: next-turn proof (see Hutchby and Wooffitt, 2008; Jenks, 2014). That is, where possible we try to make sense of an utterance by looking at how the interlocutors respond to it. Put differently, we seek the warrant for our understanding of an utterance by following other participants' reaction to it. In terms of presentation of the data we have deliberate adopted a 'narrativised' style because we would like to integrate contextual information and our observations with the 'flow' of the classroom interaction.

*Participants*:

| H | Hanna (teacher) |
|---|---|
| N | Nadifo (student) |
| Ss | students |
| Y | Yassir (student) |

*Transcription key*:

| (.) | pause of up to 1 second |
|---|---|
| (word) | unclear words |
| ? | utterance heard as a question (by researchers) |
| [ ] | noises and comments related to the utterance |

At the start of the episode of the biology lesson that we describe here, the teacher, Hanna (H, pseudonym), is orchestrating teacher-fronted talk involving some interaction with students on 'seeds' (about which the students must be able to answer questions in the examination). She opens this activity by saying: 'So we are going to look at seeds today and compare how seeds are used.' The classroom atmosphere is friendly and relaxed; there is some light-hearted bantering. The whiteboard at the front of the classroom displays the lesson topic 'Seeds' and related information. The teacher is moving around a group of students seated near the front of the classroom. She is leaning slightly towards the students in front of her.

> H: it's in your textbook if you want to have a look but it is too con-fusing for some people so maybe you want to leave it

One of the students, N, sitting near the teacher, responds:

> N: that's well horrible (.)are you calling me dumb now?

The teacher seems unconcerned by this challenge and simply states:

> H: if I was I would tell you to your face but I am not

To which the student replies, as the teacher is walking away from her:

> N: but you are implying it aren't you

The teacher reaffirms her previous answer and responds simply:

> H: no not at all ...

The teacher then moves away from this interpersonal exchange and proceeds to raise a question related to the content of the topic:

> H: why are seeds adapted?

One of the students, Y, attempts an answer:

> Y: if they aren't adapted they can't grow

But again the referential content of the topic under consideration – seeds and adaptation – is accompanied by an interpersonally oriented aside, as Yassir adds:

> Y: if you get that

The teacher seems to wish to ignore the possible meanings associated with this interjection and proceeds to address the question again:

> H: well what is the overall aim?

Yassir repeats the question:

> Y: overall aim

The teacher suggests another level of answer is expected:

> H: yeah but what have they got to get through before that happens?

At this point the students confer with one another, before they get back to the question. This time the teacher signals to Nadifo to join in:

H:   Nadifo what were you going to say?
N:   what did he say?

Nadifo appears to have misinterpreted the teacher's question; her response is a counter-question for clarification. Some of the other students chuckle at this apparent non sequitur. The teacher does not respond directly; instead she comments on Nadifo's disposition – being slow on the uptake:

H:   Nadifo what is wrong with you today?

Nadifo does not pick up on the teaher's ad hominem comment, but presses on with the point that she would like to clarify the teacher's intial question:

N:   but you asked me a question about what he said
H:   no I didn't (.) I asked you what you were going to say

Nadifo's response to the teacher's repetition of her initial question is a quip which the teacher chooses to ignore:

N:   you made me forget[low voice]
H:   you put your hand up and you were going to say something

At this point Nadifo remembers what she was going to say and apparently makes a move in the right direction for the teacher:

N:   I was going to say something about it being moved around

The teacher responds by saying:

H:   ooh, good lovely

And the teacher then proceeds to address another learning issue that recurs in other biology lessons that we have observed (not included in this data extract), the need for students to use specific technical terms, not just the students' own everyday ways of describing the processes under consideration.

H:   what is the posh name for things being moved around?

On other occasions the teacher uses terms such as *'science words'* to make this point ('posh name') and a good deal of the interaction seems to consist of such language substitution activities.

> Ss:   dispersion ... dispersal ...

Several students offer the term 'dispersion' and 'dispersal', the teacher builds on their responses:

> H:   good (.) dispersion or dispersal (.) either of those would be one of the three ways in which seeds are adapted (.) so dispersal if you don't know what that means Nadira has given us a lovely definition
> N:   it moves from place to place
> H:   yes so moves around (.) dispersal is one (.) that is one of the words they would use in the exams

Here the teacher also makes explicit why she is pursuing this issue of which word to use – there is a need to learn what the exams will require. We might say, then, that much of the teaching of biology in this lesson has consisted of attention to language, whether explicit meta markers of this kind for the science terms under consideration; or implicit, interpersonal social management moves to draw attention to what is going on amongst the students and teachers, what Green et al. (2011) might refer to as 'metadiscourse', or as teachers' attempts to extend this to 'inclusive practices', by means of which the teacher is attempting to 'include' the students in the social interactions of the classroom, beyond just teaching them 'academic' positions and likewise by the pupils addressing their personal relations with the teacher, beyond the academic focus of the lesson: in this case, these include comments by the teacher such as 'Nadira what is wrong with you today?' and by pupils such as 'Are you calling me dumb now?' or 'If you get that'.

It is clear that the literacy being engaged with here is deeply embedded in multifaceted classroom spoken discourse of a complex kind, not all of which is directly 'academic'. It is quite evident that all the participants involved in the interaction are aware that they are 'doing' a lesson – the right of the teacher to nominate next-turn speakers and the frequent reference to subject content all point to that collective awareness. But some of what goes on can be seen as light-hearted transgression, mock anger and ludic ad hominem attack. There is a sense that the tolerances of the established interpersonal relationship are both being put to a test and being reaffirmed at the same time. But the navigation is delicate and potentially perilous. The interspersing of interpersonal remarks with content-related talk is complex; it requires agile and skilful pragmatic interpretation by all involved, as the 'situated participatory processes' (Green et al., 2011) are being enacted. And as Bloome et al. have pointed out, participant relationships are being enacted, tested and reaffirmed in the process.

But there is also another level of communication that the students are expected to recognise and engage with, that of visual representations. A few moments later in the same lesson, as the teacher seeks to help the students deal with the question of 'the structure of seeds', she addresses the visual dimension with support materials:

> H:  so what we are going to look at now is the structure of seeds (.) i.e. so what seeds actually look like now (.) there are two pictures in your book (.) which is fine (.) but you have got to get used to other pictures (.) but if in the exam they don't give you that specific picture (.) and if you have never seen any other pictures (.) then you are going to be a bit lost okay

As with spoken language, the teacher suggests to the students that they may find all of this confusing, they may be 'a bit lost'. This time she does not get the person-oriented evaluative response we noted above, where Nadifo said 'Are you calling me dumb now?' But there is, in fact, another dilemma and another level of resistance, in this case over the teacher's request that a student pronounce the technical words she has indicated on the interactive whiteboard:

> H:  there are two main types of seeds that you will need to know about (.) and these words which you have probably never come across before (.) if you have please let me know [shows words on board] anyone?

A student, Mahmood (M), responds:

> M:  I'd rather not

We now have verbal interactions covering personal interaction and technical vocabulary as well as information transmission in another mode, visual representation on the interactive whiteboard. The teacher tries to keep on task with the pronunciation of the technical terms:

> H:  cotolyedon is the end bit.
> so mono and cotolyedon
> and di cotolyedon

After some further discussion of the meanings of these terms and their relationship to plants and leaves, the teacher offers another way of supporting the required account, writing on the board herself and again signalling the pictures:

> H:   so I will put some information up here and we will discuss it and see if it makes more sense (.) there's two pictures down there (.) you have got the one on the left is for mono and the one on the right is for di

She also refers them to another source, their textbooks:

> H:   again there are two seed pictures in your books that you can look at as well.

Again she acknowledges the difficulty of the task:

> H:   I have tried to write it as clearly as possible because if you look at it in the book (.) and the information that is around (.) it is very wordy and hard to understand
> N:   what's an endosperm?

Nadifo seems to have difficulty with the language text in the book. The teacher acknowledges this and tries to help the students learn how to 'read', or 'scan' them, as she addresses another key term raised by Nadifo:

> H:   let's try and find out what that is in your textbook (.) scan through the paragraph in front of you (.) what does endosperm mean?

Alongside this additional mode of working, the scanning of the document, there seems to be another level of critical interaction, as the teacher apparently scorns some of the students who are not making much effort with the books:

> H:   endosperm, that might involve some of you (.) opening your textbooks (.) getting your textbooks out of your bags

But she quickly reverts to the science lesson questioning:

> H:   what is an endosperm? have a quick scan through that paragraph or two (.) what does endosperm mean?

However, the interpersonal discourse remains high on her agenda and she attempts further irony to get their attention, again raising the question of how the discourse adopted can facilitate the 'situated participatory processes' mentioned above:

H: you do have a lesson it's Wednesday today (.) when do we ever believe what people say (.) so when there are rumours flying around about whether I am here or not (.) I may actually be here (.) what is the best thing to do?

X: ask

H: yeah ask or find out (.) cos obviously if I am not here you can't ask me (.) hands up who thought I wasn't here (.) so what is your excuse for not bringing your book

The lesson ends with attention to the original question:

H: so one more minute (.) try and fnd out in those two paragraphs (.) what does endosperm mean?

The interpersonal dimension in the discourse can also be found in other utterances during the lesson. For instance, at one point the teacher asks:

H: are there any questions? anything at all as we are going to move on (.) no questions at all (.) any questions Nadifo? your silence speaks no volumes at all (,) Mahmood, any questions? right wonderful.

Here the teacher's reference to Nadifo's apparent lack of overt response picks up on the ongoing nature of the interpersonal dimension in the classroom interaction. And the students' attention is drawn on other occasions to pictures and to the page layout. For instance, the teacher says:

H: explain how the seeds are spread around so this picture this one this one (.) discuss it (.) four bullet points (.) you should be able to explain (.) four bullet points

The students are asked to talk about the seed dispersal and to produce bullet points to represent what they have understood.

If we were only interested in the subject content of such a lesson, we might simply marginalise the interpersonally oriented discourse. But our conceptual frame indicates that precisely such data are important for our understanding of classoom discourse and that isolating the exam-oriented, curriculum-based elements misses much of what gives meaning to such contexts. Moreover, we also still need to take account of the different modes of interaction – spoken (in and about 'scientific' language); visual (pictures of seeds) and written (definitions written in the textbook, words on the interactive whiteboard; bullet points) (cf. Kress, 2010; Kress and Street, 2006). Eventually the students will have to produce their own writing, firstly as response to the class for the teacher to review and then in the exam itself, where the other communciative practices will be absent. Analysing the interpersonal and the multimodal dimensions of classroom interaction are, then, crucial for our understanding of what is going on.

## Extending conceptual and empirical framing

In terms of recognising the multimodal nature of the communication, we note for instance that the reading in this class includes collective work on the board, individual text work, feedback from other pupils, and feedback from the teacher. The literacy activities here assume group interaction with the written word and connection with spoken interaction. Working with a social literacies perspective, it would be possible to identify here many of the features evident outside of school – the links between oral and written and the growing role of visual modes. At the same time social-literacies-minded research would look for the social dimension of such literacy practices, notably in these cases the social and power relations of teacher and student signalled, for instance, by the uses of irony, implied crticism and other forms of person-oriented comments. Here literacy studies would need to link with the contemporary sensibilities in language studies signalled above by Gardner and Martin-Jones (2012), who would be looking for the effects of sociocultural and ethnolinguistic diversity and the advent of new communication technologies along with the notion of 'situated participatory processes' signalled by Green et al. (2011). The use of the pluralised notion of 'literacies', meaning a potential variety of literacy practices beyond those simply identified in the curriculum, to describe spoken and written language in use indicated above and their links to other modes of communication, is crucial if we are to avoid also the dangers of the narrow policy focus we outlined at the beginning. If these policy perspectives should be criticised for focusing on autonomous views of literacy, and on 'standard' language, including the 'assimilation' of students, second/additional language speakers, to a supposed dominant variety of English language and literacy practice, then we need to develop a clearer language of description for what is going on that can provide us with a sharper sense of the complexity and variety of actual practices on the ground.

It is still standardly assumed in policy discourse that 'literacy' is a skill or an ability that can be developed as a separate component in education, and in curriculum terms, it can be treated as a distinct area of pedagogy. However, the teacher–student interactions shown earlier strongly suggest that reading, for instance, can be tied to a number of professional, pedagogic and interpersonal concerns, particularly from the teacher's perspective. The teacher's estimation of the students' reading ability seems to have influenced her pedagogic approach – the textbook passages related to seeds may be judged to be too difficult for (at least some of) the students, without introductory talk and visuals. This observation in itself does not provide a new insight; teachers regularly devise and adjust their teaching actions and plans in accordance with their perceptions of their students' capacities and needs. But in this case the teacher's 'honesty' in disclosing her estimation of the students' ability is played out in a series of exchanges that involve understanding and enactment of shared locally established pragmatic meaning. The juxtaposing of mock insult and ludic playfulness with straight-faced content-related teacher–student talk is very much part of the support (some may say 'scaffold') with which the students get to do the reading.

The apparent interpersonal nature of some of the exchanges, seen in this light, is very much an integral part of the literacy event in this classroom. Our account here indicates that participating in literacy events in this classroom involves some knowledge and understanding of locally established and maintained sociocultural values and the associated pragmatics. It is these that can then be subject to pedagogic and assessment procedures that help students to learn the complexities of language and literacy practices they will need in the contemporary world and to demonstrate what they know. The policy implications of this subtler and more detailed account of what is going on in the classroom and the language of description needed to communicate it, may not yet be entirely clear to spell out – but it is evident that the traditional perspective will no longer do. In the light of these observations in relation to the data we discuss, and from the theoretical perspectives outlined, this chapter has attempted to contribute to the theme of this section of the book, concerned with how everyday, mundane diversity and heterogeneity of particular local contexts can remain elusive to practitioners and planners alike.

## Note

1. The data extracts shown here are drawn from the ESRC-funded research project 'Modelling for Diversity: Academic Language and Literacies in School and University' (RES-062-23-1666). This particular lesson took place on 18 March 2009.

## References

Agar, M. (1996). *The professional stranger*. London: Academic Press.

Bloome, D., Beierle, M., Grigorenko, M. and Goldman, S. (2009). Learning over time: uses of intercontextuality, collective memories, and classroom chronotopes in the construction of learning opportunities in a ninth-grade language arts classroom. *Language and Education, 23*(4): 313–34.

Bloome, D., Carter, S. P., Christian, B., Madrid, S., Otto, S., Shuart-Faris, N. and Smith, M. (eds) (2008). *Discourse analysis in classrooms*. New York: Teachers College Press.

Bloome, D., Carter, S. P., Christian, B. M., Otto, S. and Shuart-Faris, N. (2005). *Discourse analysis and the study of classroom language and literacy events: a microethnographic perspective*. Mahwah, NJ: Lawrence Erlbaum Associates, Publishers.

Burke, W. (2007). Moving beyond ACCE: an expanded framework for genetic test evaluation: a paper for the United Kingdom Genetic Testing Network. Cambridge: PHG Foundation.

Castanheira, Maria Lucia (2012). Indexical signs within local and global contexts: case studies of changes in literacy practices across generations of working class families in Brazil. In J. Kalman and B. Street (eds), *Literacy and numeracy in Latin America: local perspectives and beyond*. London: Routledge.

Collins, J. (1995). Literacy and literacies. *Annual Review of Anthropology, 24*: 75–93.

Creese, A. and Blackledge, A. (2010). Translanguaging in the bilingual classroom: a pedagogy for learning and teaching? *Modern Language Journal, 94*(1): 103–15.

Creese, A., Martin, P. and Hornberger, N. (eds) (2010). *Ecology of language*, vol. 9. New York: Springer.

Department for Children Schools and Families (2009). *Schools, pupils and their characteristics, January 2009*. London: DCSF.

Department for Education (2010). *The Importance of teaching: the Schools*. White Paper 2010. London: The Stationery Office.

Department for Education and Employment (DfEE) (1998). *The national literacy strategy framework for teaching*. Sudbury: DfEE Publications.

Freebody, P. (1998). Assessment as communal versus punitive practice: six new literacy crises (with replies by B. Street and C. Kell). Virtual Seminar series. Paper presented at the International Applied Linguistics Association (AILA) Special Commission on Literacy. www.education.uts.edu.au/AILA/VirtSem

Freebody, P. (2007a). *Australian Education Review: literacy education in school – research perspectives from the past, for the future*. Camberwell, Victoria: Australian Council for Educational Research.

Freebody, P. (2007b). *Literacy education in school: research perspectives from the past, for the future*. Melbourne: Australian Council for Educational Research.

Freitas, C. A. and Castanheira, M. L. (2007). Talked images: examining the contexualised nature of image use. *Pedagogies*, 2(3): 151–64.

Gardner, S. and Martin-Jones, M. (2012). *Multilingualism, discourse and ethnography*. London: Routledge.

Gee, James P. (1990). *Social linguistics and literacies: ideology in discourse*. Falmer Press: London and Philadelphia.

Goodwyn, A. (2011). Introduction: 'informed prescription' or 'deformed restriction'? In A. Goodwyn and C. Fuller (eds), *The great literacy debate: a critical response to the Literacy Strategy and the Framework for English* (pp. 1–7). Abingdon, Oxon: Routledge.

Green, J., Castanheira, M. and Yeager, B. (2011). Researching the opportunities for learning for students with learning difficulties in classrooms: an ethnographic perspective. In Claire Wyatt-Smith, John Elkins and Stephanie Gunn (org.), *Multiple perspectives on difficulties in learning literacy and numeracy* (pp. 49–90). New York: Springer.

Halliday, M. A. K. (1973). *Explorations in the functions of language*. London: Edward Arnold.

Halliday, M. A. K. (1975). *Learning how to mean: explorations in the development of language*. London: Edward Arnold.

Halliday, M. A. K., McIntosh, A. and Strevens, P. (1964). *The linguistic sciences and language teaching*. London: Longman.

Hamnet, C. (2011). Concentration or diffusion? The changing geography of ethnic minority pupils in English secondary schools, 1999–2009. *Urban Studies* (online version).

Heath, S. B. (1983). *Ways with words: language, life and work in communities and classrooms*. New York: Cambridge University Press.

Heath, S. B and Mangiola, L. (1991). *Children of promise: literate activity in linguistically and culturally diverse classrooms*. Washington, DC: AERA/NEA Center for Study of Writing and Literacy.

Hutchby, I. and Wooffitt, R. (2008). *Conversation analysis*, 2nd edn. London: Polity.

Hymes, D. (1972). On communicative competence. In J. B. Pride and J. Holmes (eds), *Sociolinguistics* (pp. 269–93). London: Penguin.

Hymes, D. (1977). *Foundations in sociolinguistics: an ethnographic approach*. London: Tavistock Publications.

Hymes, D. (1994). Toward ethnographies of communication. In J. Maybin (ed.), *Language and literacy in social practice* (pp. 11–22). Clevedon: Multilingual Matters, in association with the Open University.

Jenks, C. (2014). Conversation analysis. In C. Leung and B. Street (eds), *The Routledge companion to English studies* (pp. 274–86). Abingdon, Oxon: Routledge.

Jewitt, C. (2006). *Technology, literacy and learning: a multimodal approach*. London: Routledge.

Kress, G. (2010). *Multimodality: a social semiotic approach to contemporary communication*. London: Routledge.

Kress, G., Jewitt, C., Bourne, J., Franks, A., Hardcastle, J., Jones, K. and Read, E. (2005). *English in urban classrooms: a multimodal perspective on teaching and learning*. London: Routledge/Falmer.

Kress, G. and Street, B. (2006). Multi-modality and literacy practices. In K. Pahl and J. Rowsell (eds), *Travel notes from the New Literacy Studies: case studies of practice* (pp. vii–x). Clevedon: Multilingual Matters.

Leung, C. and Street, B. (eds) (2012). *English – a changing medium for education.* Bristol: Multilingual Matters.

Leung, C. and Street, B. (eds) (2014). *The Routledge companion to English studies.* Abingdon, Oxon: Routledge.

Lotherington, H. and Ronda, N. S. (2012). Multimodal literacies and assessment: uncharted challenges in the English classroom. In C. Leung and B. V. Street (eds), *English – a changing medium for education* (pp. 104–28). Bristol: Multilingual Matters.

Mitchell, J. (1984). Typicality and the case study. In R. F. Ellen (ed.), *Ethnographic research: a guide to general conduct* (pp. 238–41). New York: Academic Press.

Myhill, D. A., Jones, S. M., Lines, H. and Watson, A. (2012). Re-thinking grammar: the impact of embedded grammar teaching on students' writing and students' metalinguistic understanding. *Research Papers in Education,* 27(2): 139–66.

Organisation for Economic Co-operation and Development (2010). *PISA 2009 Assessment Framework: key competencies in reading, mathematics and science.* Paris: OECD.

Roberts, C. (2014). Interactional sociolinguistics. In C. Leung and B. Street (eds), *The Routledge companion to English studies* (pp. 195–214). Abingdon: Routledge.

Snell, J. (2013). Dialect, interaction and class positioning at school: from deficit to difference to repertoire. *Language and Education,* 27(2): 110–28.

Street, B. (1984). *Literacy in theory and practice.* Cambridge: Cambridge University Press.

Street, B. (1993). *Cross-cultural approaches to literacy.* Cambridge: Cambridge University Press.

Street, B. (1995). *Social literacies.* London: Longman.

Street, B. (2000). Literacy events and literacy practices. In M. Martin-Jones and K. Jones (eds), *Multilingual literacies: comparative perspectives on research and practice* (pp. 17–29). Amsterdam: John Benjamins.

*The Guardian* (2011). Greenslade Blog: standard launches campaign to overcome 'blight of illiteracy', accessed February 2012 from http://www.theguardian.com/media/greenslade/2011/jun/06/london-evening-standard-literacy

Veel, R. (2006). The Write it Right project: linguistic modeling of secondary school and the workplace. In R. Whittaker, M. O'Donnel and A. McCabe (eds), *Language and literacy: functional approaches* (pp. 66–92). London: Continuum.

Villegas, A. M. (1991). *Culturally responsive teaching.* Princeton: ETS.

von Ahn, M., Lupton, R., Greenwood, C. and Wiggins, D. (2010). *Languages, ethnicity and education in London.* London: Institute of Education.

Wyse, D. (2011). The public, the personal, and the teaching of English, language and literacy. In A. Goodwyn and C. Fuller (eds), *The great literacy debate: a critical response to the Literacy Strategy and the Framework for English.* London: Routledge.

Wyse, D. and Goswami, U. (2008). Synthetic phonics and the teaching of reading. *British Educational Research Journal,* 34(6): 691–710.

# 2
# What is Quechua Literacy for? Ideological Dilemmas in Intercultural Bilingual Education in the Peruvian Andes

*Virginia Zavala*

## Introduction

Discourses on diversity and education and, more specifically, on inter-cultural education are multiple and fragmented in various terrains: in the educational literature, in official policies and in the implementation of intercultural education in specific programmes and contexts. Differing terminology and varied conceptualisations reveal a field with complex struggles over meaning (May, 1999; May and Sleeter, 2010; Dietz, 2009). In Peru, over the past 30 years, diverse approaches to intercultural education have evolved. Distinctions could be made between political and technical discourses, between interculturalism for all and intercultural education only for indigenous peoples and between intercultural education as adaptation or as transformation (Aikman, 2012). Currently, the Peruvian government, non-governmental organisations (NGOs) and indigenous organisations all formulate their own definitions of intercultural bilingual education (IBE) and hence reveal different views of education in relation to society. In fact, various studies discuss the distinct ways in which different types of social actors conceive interculturality, intercultural bilingual education, and the purposes that IBE serves (Valdiviezo, 2009; Peschiera, 2010; Tubino and Zariquiey (MS), Aikman, 2012) and how this translates into a wide range of practices in the classroom. These differing parties struggle over the meaning of terms, especially in the case of Quechua literacy.

Numerous studies of literacy from a social practice perspective have uncovered the situated nature of literacy and the fact that it cannot be reduced to a technical skill (Street; 1984; Heath, 1983; Barton, 1994; Gee, 1996; Zavala et al., 2004). Differences between school and community literacy practices (Barton and Hamilton, 1998; Gee, 2004; Lankshear and Knobel, 2003) and even between those literacy practices utilised in different subject areas – such as English or maths – (Castanheira et al., 2001) have been discussed extensively and these studies have demonstrated the plurality of literacies. Following this line of study, and focusing specifically on reading and not writing, I will examine how two teachers from different IBE schools, which are considered to be 'successful' under different types of criteria, construct very different ways of reading in Quechua in relation to reading in Spanish. These case studies will show, once again, that there is not a single predetermined definition of reading, but that there are many that emerge from how people actually use written language to interact with each other and to act in the world where they live. How people engage in reading, how they interact with each other during a reading event, how they interpret a text, how they define what is and what is not reading, and how they connect reading to other events in their lives reflect and help to shape cultural ideologies (Street and Lefstein, 2010). Moreover, to be a reader entails knowledge of discursive practices (ways of talking about texts), semiotic systems (ways of communicating meaning through multiple sign systems) and cultural resources (prior knowledge and physical materials or tools). In addition, we will see that the variability of what counts as reading in Quechua results from the performance of diverse types of actions, which go from the micro-interactional level to the construction of discourses in the dimension of social structure. In fact, reading always becomes a social practice where representations, identities and social relationships are enacted, and also where different types of learning take place. After all, focusing on action without consideration of larger issues at work prevents literacy research from effecting change.

These distinct definitions of reading that will be analysed in specific interactions easily fit into a larger ideological dilemma (Billig et al., 1988) that began in the 1990s in Peruvian education. The concept of ideological dilemma makes reference to a tension that arises between two or more interpretative repertoires of the 'same' social object (Edwards and Potter, 2000). The interpretative repertoires constitute relatively coherent ways of talking about objects or events in the world, which are part of any community's common sense and provide a basis for shared social understanding (Edley, 2001). Within this framework, we could state that – in general terms – Peruvian education is dealing with supporting cultural homogeneity or diversity, although the option for cultural homogeneity is more widespread. Different types of actors, such as policy-makers, NGOs and the teachers themselves are differently influenced by these competing ideologies shaping Peruvian education and this has consequences in terms of different classroom outcomes.

On the one hand, Peruvian education has followed a neo-liberal trend of a technocratic discourse, aligned with a politically conservative ideology. The technocratic perspective promotes the instrumental value of education as if it were a purely technical and hence socially neutral process, bypassing social interests and values and imposing policy based on what the 'facts' (or standardised test scores) demand (Lemke, 1989). Co-opted by this technical logic and liberal agenda, and with the support of international organisations such as the World Bank, the Ministry of Education has started to prioritise standardised testing to measure student performance, but without truly understanding the results obtained or if they reveal actual student progress. Within a conservative free market ideology, educators no longer emphasise the learning process, but rather outcomes and accountability. Furthermore, the ultimate goal has become to educate successful businessmen and women who will be competitive and flexible enough to be functional in the labour market rather than to educate critical, ethical and political citizens, as happened in the 1970s in Peru with the influence of Paulo Freire and critical pedagogy (Oliart, 2011).

On the other hand, during the same period, Peruvian education discussions have incorporated the topic of intercultural education, influenced by the 'cultural turn' in development discourse (Degregori and Huber, 2007), criticisms of Eurocentrism, postcolonial theory and indigenous movements. Although government treatment of diversity has been superficial (or 'decorative') and more concerned with material aspects of culture, many NGOs and indigenous organisations have emphasised the importance of indigenous knowledge and have considered how to incorporate it into the schooling process. In general, and in contrast to more traditional views of IBE, some of these approaches no longer conceive of IBE as a transitional educational programme in which the use of Quechua serves only as a means to the acquisition of Spanish. Instead, they associate IBE with principles of interculturality, rights and citizenship, and view this type of education as a search for more democratic exercise of power. This conceptualisation implies a process of identity affirmation linked to the recovery of local cultural practices and a process of empowerment that promotes consciousness about discrimination and racism (Trapnell et al., 2008; Zavala, 2007). These proposals have generally criticised the homogenising project that underlies schooling practices, however they differ in the ways they conceptualise culture and intercultural education.

Some of these proposals not only misunderstand Quechua culture and language as indexing ancestral cultural practices (and not contemporary ones), but they also promote a type of ethnic separatism as a political action that reacts to centuries of oppression. Some of them emphasise a division between 'indigenous knowledge' and 'Western knowledge' with a view of culture and identity as static, bounded and discrete 'boxes' that are not part of fields of struggle (Rogoff and Angelillo, 2002). Moreover, they believe that Quechua becomes 'distorted' when used to communicate 'Western knowledge'. This dichotomic view does not correspond to the everyday cultural practices of people and communities and clearly does not consider change, contact, negotiation or cultural dynamism (Rengifo, 2005).

In terms of methodology, I follow an interactional ethnographic perspective (Castanheira et al., 2001) that is itself composed of diverse informing theories, such as cultural anthropology, interactional sociolinguistics, conversation analysis, discursive psychology and critical discourse analysis. Although I did not engage in doing ethnography in the full sense of this term, I stayed ten days in each school and used various ethnographic methods for data gathering. In the first place, I conducted interviews with the teacher of each case study, the school principals and the other teachers of both schools (eight interviews). In addition, I had informal conversations with the students, especially with the ones who attended the classroom that was mostly observed. Secondly, I collected documents such as schoolwork from students, class designs and projects from the teachers and official documentation from each school (curricular plans, institutional projects, reports, etc.) in order to obtain a more systemic appreciation of the dynamics of both institutions. Finally, I made observations inside (and outside) of all the classrooms in each school, although I focused on one teacher per institution.[1] For the case studies, I recorded audio and video classroom interactions in order to analyse reading practices at the micro level.

In what follows I will present two case studies of 'successful' IBE teachers from two different schools in the Cusco region, where 74 per cent of the population declares that Quechua is the language regularly used at home (Instituto Nacional de Estadística, 2001). However, the definition of success varies for each case according to the interpretative repertoires that each one enacts. According to the Peruvian Ministry of Education (the entity that recommended the gathering of data in the first school), Pumamarca constitutes a 'successful' IBE school because it achieved the highest scores in the Cusco region on the most recent national literacy test, on both Quechua and Spanish versions. However, according to some of the NGOs that have been working with IBE schools for more than two decades, the work of the NGO advising the school of Tikapampa – and the teacher of the third and fourth grade of Tikapampa specifically – represents what a good IBE should look like.[2]

In the southern Peruvian Andes where Quechua is spoken, IBE programmes have been mostly restricted to rural areas, although both rural and urban areas have Quechua speakers to a great extent.[3] In fact, the use of Quechua is not limited to rural peasant communities from the highlands, where people are immersed in a more traditional and 'indigenous' way of life. In the cities from the southern Andes, most people who are 50 years old and older speak Quechua (even from socio-economic elites who do not define themselves as indigenous), although the tendency is that the new generations born in the cities are being raised only in Spanish. Together with this phenomenon, we can also observe migration processes from rural to urban areas, where Quechua speakers move to the cities to attend high schools and then universities and more and more get to work in socially prestigious jobs, such as public servants or even mayors. The school of Tikapampa, for example, is situated on the edge of a small highway and only ten minutes from the closest city district. Most of the children go to the city for high school (and even for primary school) and, as they grow older, no longer live in the peasant community where their parents stay. Even though they have been socialised in Quechua when they were kids, they use mostly Spanish in the city. Quechua usually emerges when they go back to the rural community to visit their relatives. Although the school of Pumamarca is more distant from the nearest small city, the people living there constantly go to Cusco (and some of them even to Lima) in order to do commercial transactions, visit relatives or negotiate legal matters.

## Quechua literacy for 'understanding the text'

Pumamarca[4] primary school is situated 4000 metres above sea level in a peasant community where the students speak Quechua predominantly in domestic and communal life. As was just mentioned, on the most recent national literacy test, this school achieved the highest scores in the Cusco region. In contrast to the majority of rural schools, 100 per cent of fourth-grade students performed at the 'expected level' of reading comprehension on both Quechua and Spanish tests. The main factor that explains these results is testing pressure. Pumamarca teachers were obsessed with earning high scores on the test and made the students practise test-type exercises every day, even more so as test day approached, a phenomenon that has been observed as well in other contexts (De la Garza, 2008). In fact, the four teachers who worked in this multi-grade school mentioned that the goal of their work was to obtain 'achievements' from their students, which clearly referred to test performance. This statement was framed within what has been termed 'the ideology of achievement' (Mehan et al., 2010).[5]

The data in this school reveal the interpretative repertoire of aiming for cultural homogeneity. In what follows, I will focus on the second grade. The students in this grade were so familiar with the standardised test formats that they even longed for these types of exercises. Furthermore, the dynamics of working with the test-type exercises were so well established that students asked no questions about what to do or how to do it. This can be observed in the following excerpt, which constitutes an interaction mainly in Spanish, although the children include Quechua as well. Before the recording began, the teacher asked the children if they could guess what he had in his hand and, without having seen the material, the students immediately assumed that it was a test-type exercise.[6]

**Excerpt 1**[7]

   1. Students:   marca
                  multiple choice
   2. Teacher:   ah?
                  what?
   3. Students:   marca*na*
                  for choosing
   4. Teacher:   marcana, para marcar
                  for choosing, for choosing
   5.             de qué cosa está   ⎧ aquí?            ⎫
                  what's this        ⎪ about?           ⎪
   6. Boy:                           ⎨ síiiiiiiiiiiii, facilito ⎬
                                     ⎩ yeeeeeees, very easy ⎭
   7. Teacher:   de qué cosa estará?
                  what could this be about?
   8. Students:   (the kids whisper different things)
   9. Girl:      examen
                  test (in a soft voice)
  10. Boy:       <u>examen</u>
                  <u>test</u>

11. Teacher:    no es el examen, a ver
                it's not the exam, let's see

12.             voy a repartir          ⎧ ya?
                I'll pass them out,     ⎪ ok?

13. Students:                           ⎨ sí, sí, sí, sí,
                                        ⎪ yes, yes, yes, yes (hitting
                                        ⎩ their desks)

                (the teacher distributes the copies)

14. Girl:       facil*challa*
                very easy

15.             facil*challa*
                very easy

16. Students:   a, b, c
                a, b, c

17.             a, b, c
                a, b, c

18. Boy:        lee*spa* marca*na*
                for choosing after we read

19.             lee*spa* marca*na*
                for choosing after we read

20. Teacher:    ya
                ok

Two aspects of this excerpt catch my attention here. First of all, the children are very familiar with the literacy practices involved in the social practice of standardised literacy testing. They know in advance – and without being told – that the exercise includes multiple-choice questions that they will have to answer after reading the text ('for choosing', 'a, b, c', 'for choosing after we read', 'test'). Although the teacher seems to ask them repeatedly about the content of the text (the question before line 1, 'what is this about?' in line 5 and 'what could this be about?' in line 7), and even points out in line 11 that it is not an exam, the students continue to base their responses on the test-type format, as if this were the only aspect that mattered. The fact that the teacher asks the same type of question three times, shows that he is not satisfied with the students' answers in terms of the format of the exercise and is trying to obtain a repair (Schegloff et al., 1977; Sidnell, 2010) from them. After the third response from the students in lines 9 ('test') and 10 ('test'), the teacher rejects the answer in a more explicit way ('it's not the exam, let's see') and starts to distribute the copies of the exercise, although he no longer asks another question of the same type. The teacher does know that he is distributing a test-type exercise –and he accepts it in line 20 with an 'ok' – but it is the students who cannot get out of this frame during the interaction.

Second, it is worth observing the attitudes that the students display toward these types of exercises. Not only do they express excitement through the high volume of their voices, the repetition of 'yes' when accepting what the teacher proposes (lines 6 and 13), the production of simultaneous speech during the teacher's conversational turn (lines 6 and 13) and the slapping of their desks (line 13), but they also reveal this enthusiasm by declaring that the test will be easy and that they want to complete it (lines 6, 14 and 15). Throughout the interaction, students team up to comment on what the teacher is offering and they seem fully socialised into these types of practices.

As has been discussed in studies addressing other contexts, standardised testing usually has an important impact on school practices and dynamics, such as use of time, classroom activities chosen, materials selected, spatial organisation of the classroom, and even the way teachers and students perceive themselves and their work (Au, 2011; Cummins, 2007; Menken, 2010). Moreover, these studies have shown that students from rural schools who speak an indigenous language are more likely to receive instruction that focuses on test preparation in the form of rote memorisation and drills since they typically do not perform well on standardised tests (Cummins, 2007; Bunyi, 2001). This increased focus on testing occurs at the expense of other types of learning opportunities and other teaching methods that could more effectively meet the needs of this student population (Menken, 2010). In the case of the school of Pumamarca, this emphasis on test-type exercises clearly impoverished the curriculum: areas that were not covered in the tests (like social studies or science) received less attention, and reading in both Spanish and Quechua began to be associated only with the practices that the standardised literacy tests required.

In addition to the classroom changes mentioned above, the test-type practices affected the use of both languages. Since the second-grade test came only in Spanish, this language started to take priority over Quechua. At the same time, teachers introduced the practice of using Quechua as a means to learn content in Spanish due to the tests. In fact, the second-grade teacher at the school of Pumamarca knows that if he speaks in Quechua with his students they can complete more exercises in less time, since they will understand him better. As he stated: 'if I use the languages according to what IBE norms I will get zero for testing results' or 'if I only use Spanish to interact with my students, I will not get any results and it will not be the same'. As we will see in what follows, the teacher still encourages reading in Quechua, although it is not clear if he does so only as a means to obtaining good test results in Spanish. This clearly reveals a dilemma: teachers know that they have to teach Quechua literacy in order to follow an IBE official policy but they also know that they have to prioritise Spanish to comply with a national testing policy that mandates a literacy test in Spanish for second grade.

In the next excerpt, we can observe the reading practice that the teacher encourages when reading the text and before he starts to ask the multiple-choice questions:

**Excerpt 2**

| | | |
|---|---|---|
| 1. Teacher: | *punapis* | |
| | they say that in the highlands | |
| 2. Students: | *punapis huk* | |
| | they say that in the highlands a | |
| 3. Teacher: | *huk* | |
| | a | |
| 4. Students: | *atuqcha* | |
| | little fox | |
| | ( ) | |
| 5. Teacher: | ya, ya | |
| | ok, ok, | |
| 7. | *ñuqa primero ya?* | |
| | I'll go first, ok? | |
| 8. Students: | síiiiiiiiiii | |
| | yeeeeees (5.0) | |
| 9. Teacher: | ya, *ñuqa primero* | |
| | ok, I'll go first | |
| 10. | *punapis* | |
| | they say that in the highlands | |
| 11. Students: | *punapis* | |
| | they say that in the highlands | |
| 12. Teacher: | *huq* | |
| | a | |
| 13. Students: | *huq* | |
| | a | |
| 14. Teacher: | *atuqcha* | |
| | little fox | |
| 15. Students: | *atuqcha* | |
| | little fox | |

The teacher expects the students to keep repeating the words or phrases that he reads from the text. It is interesting to note that the students tend to move ahead and sometimes read more words than the ones read by the teacher ('they say that in the highlands' versus 'they say that in the highlands a little fox'). Nevertheless, the teacher is clear about how the adjacent repeated pairs (Sidnell, 2010) – such as 'punapis' (teacher) and then 'punapis' again (students) – must be organised in the interaction and how the students must respond in the repetition. In fact, when the students do not repeat exactly what he has said in the first part of the pair, he asks his students for a repair, which marks a 'possible disjunction with the immediately preceding talk' (Schegloff, 2000: 207). In lines 2 and 4, for example, the students skip ahead, adding 'one little fox' to the teacher's phrase. Here the teacher does not continue with what follows in the text. He first introduces the discourse marker 'ok, ok' (in line 5) to cut the flow of the interaction and then 'I'll go first, ok?' (in line 7) as a repair initiation to indicate that the students must repair the way they have been doing the dynamics. After the students formulate an acceptance ('yeeeeees' in line 8), the teacher waits several seconds while organising some pieces of paper from his desk and then confirms it, declaring again in line 9 how the interaction should work: 'Ok, I'll go first'. He then repeats the phrase 'they say that in the highlands' as the first part of an adjacency pair and waits for the students to say it again, but now after him. The phrase in line 11 ('punapis'), as an exact repetition of what the teacher has said in line 10, constitutes the repair itself (or correction) in relation to the 'trouble source' or 'the repairable' from lines 2–4. Nevertheless, although it seemed that the adjacency pairs would be re-established and the teacher would keep this initial reading pattern with the students following it, the latter subvert the rule one more time in line 15 and simultaneous speech is produced when they move ahead again with the reading.

In the following excerpt, the teacher starts with the questions of the test-type exercise.

**Excerpt 3**
1. Teacher: *pikunamanta?*
about whom?

(...)

2. Student: *atuqchamanta*
about the little fox

3. Teacher:      a ver, ñuqa, huk
                 let's see, I, number one
4. Students:     *huk*
                 number one
5. Teacher:      *atuqcha*
                 the little fox
6. Students:     *huk. atuqcha*
                 number one. The little fox
7. Teacher:      *huk atuqcha* oveja – oveja*man* – oveja*wan*
                 Number one. The little fox the sheep – to the sheep –
                 with the sheep
8. Students:     oveja*wan*
                 with the sheep
9. Teacher:      *ishkay*
                 number two
10. Students:    *ishkay*
                 number two
12. Teacher:     *pumacha*
                 the little puma
13. Students:    *pumacha*
                 the little puma
14. Teacher:     asno*chawan*
                 with the little donkey
15. Students:    asno*chawan*
                 with the little donkey
16. Teacher:     *kimsa*
                 number three
17. Students:    *kimsa*
                 number three
18. Teacher:     *puna atuqchamanta*
                 about the little fox in the highlands
19. Students:    *puna atuqchamanta*
                 about the little fox in the highlands
20. Teacher:     *mayqantaq chiqaq?*
                 which one is true?
21. Students:    tres
                 the third one
22. Teacher:     tres. *Puna::*
                 the third one. It's about the::
23. Students:    *puna atuqchamanta*
                 it's about the little fox of the highlands

24 Teacher:      *puna atuqchamanta*
                 it's about the little fox of the highlands

After the teacher asks the first question about the text (and the students repeat it in a section that does not appear in the excerpt), one of the students gives an answer right away according to the options presented in the multiple-choice format ('about the little fox', in line 2). Nevertheless, the teacher's use of the discourse marker 'let's see' shows misalignment with the student's response and marks a different path. He then pronounces 'I' to remind the students that their role is to repeat what he states first and then proceeds to read the answers of the multiple-choice question. The students keep repeating after him. At the end, in line 20, he asks 'which one is true?', as if the answers were intrinsically right or wrong. The text appears as an authority that cannot be deconstructed or questioned because what really counts is being able to state truths that hold regardless of context.

This is clearly a case of 'teaching to the test', where the teacher checks students' comprehension merely by using closed questions to seek brief information and to confirm that the students know the *true answers*. The teacher does not talk or provide information that goes beyond the test-type exercises. Moreover, his talk is more focused on managing the format of the exercise than on the academic content. When the students give the final answer in line 21 ('the third one'), he first stimulates them to give an explicit answer in line 22 and then confirms it in line 24, repeating exactly what the students had said. With this type of interaction pattern, he positions himself as the students' evaluator.

Quechua literacy has been affected by pedagogic practices such as these and by the ideology of achievement that underpins them. It is important to take into account that Quechua does not have a literacy tradition and that there is almost nothing that the children could read in Quechua outside of school. In this school, Quechua reading practices have been reduced to responding to the teacher's closed questions as a way of completing an exam; it does not have a purpose different from reading in Spanish. Through this way of reading in Quechua, the teacher and the students have constructed criteria and principles for appropriate and expected language use, ways of interaction and social action that are situated in the context of multiple-choice tests. The students have learnt how to be Quechua readers in this context and within these practices. And whenever students attempt to subvert the established norms by reading ahead of the teacher or answering the question without having read the multiple-choice options one by one in an ordered way, the teacher seems not to notice, since he is more concerned with how to make them follow the norms.

There is ample evidence that teaching practices based on high-stakes testing rarely result in increased learning among students, produce an impoverished curriculum that is restricted to the contents that are present in the textbooks and the tests, promote a wider use of teacher-centred pedagogies and develop reductive and impoverished cognitive abilities (Madaus and Clarke, 2001; Amrein and Berliner, 2002; Klein et al., 2000; Au, 2011). Current Quechua reading practices are definitely constraining the wide spectrum of abilities that students could develop in school and are positioning them as passive recipients of information who participate in the activities only to demonstrate knowledge on a test.

## Quechua literacy for 'chatting with the text'

The Tikapampa multi-grade primary school is also situated in the Cusco region, on the edge of a small highway at a lower altitude than Pumamarca. The children are bilingual and some of them speak in Spanish among themselves in some circumstances, although their parents speak Quechua as their dominant language. The school is being assessed by an NGO, which works with 25 other teachers of indigenous descent from other schools in the same area. These teachers have prepared an intercultural plan for the subject area of communication and language, and some of them are trying to implement it in their classrooms. The third- and fourth-grade teacher, whose practices I discuss here, is considered to be a very successful IBE teacher and the children's parents are very satisfied with his performance.

This teacher has an absolutely different approach towards reading, which reveals the interpretative repertoire of opting for cultural diversity. One big sign on one of the walls of his classroom states: 'Reading and writing from life for life'. He takes a critical stance and always emphasises that texts do not transmit truths, but rather people construct their meanings from different standpoints and ideologies. The posters or texts that he hangs on the walls of his classroom always include the source: 'the Internet', a specific book, 'the UMC' (the office of the Ministry of Education that constructs the standardised tests), the ONPE (the National Office of Electoral Processes) or the name of a member from the community who has contributed with a text about a certain topic. Moreover, whenever he works with his students, he always points out this constructed nature of texts: 'We always have to stay alert and ask ourselves who is saying this or where this information comes from.' In his classroom, knowledge does not come only from official books or canonical sources. The sources are varied and the children know that knowledge is heterogeneous.

During my stay at this school, the teacher designed a reading activity in Spanish about the topic of the Spanish conquest. The students studied different types of multimodal texts (Kress, 2003) that expressed varying versions of the same event. They started with a more traditional text from an official social studies textbook, called *The Encounter between Two Worlds*. For this first text, the teacher asked the students to go to the field outside the classroom to read it in pairs or by themselves at their own pace. Once they had finished, the teacher asked them questions about both the text and the graphics, making sure that they understood all the terms and could explain the sense of the reading in their own words. When they finished this phase of the activity, the students went to the computer lab and watched a video by Eduardo Galeano about the American conquest and then listened to a song by Víctor Heredia about the same topic. In contrast to the multiple-choice questioning practices of the second-grade teacher from the school of Pumamarca, this teacher started with open questions that allowed students to get a sense of the big picture and did not constrain their responses to overly specific and precise information. He asked questions such as: 'Let's see, what do we remember?'; 'What ideas could we share?'; 'Anything else we could add?'; 'Anything else that caught your attention?'; 'What have you listened to?'; 'What have you understood?'; 'What is this audio telling us?'; 'Why do you think he sang that song?' At the end of the event, the teacher provided a summary of the different versions about the Spanish conquest, which the children had read, heard and visualised, and questioned the representation of the conquest as an 'encounter' that the Ministry of Education constructs in the official textbook.

This event constituted an attempt to implement a perspective of critical literacy, which focuses on 'teaching and learning how texts work, understanding and re-mediating what texts attempt to do in the world and to people, and moving students toward active position-takings with texts to critique and reconstruct the social fields in which they live and work' (Luke, 2000). Even if we could question some of the teacher's strategies to apply this perspective, we must acknowledge that in this event the children were not demonstrating how good they were at reading in a testing situation but they were developing a different attitude toward texts and the social world. They were acting as text analysts and critics based on a rich corpus of multimodal texts. I will not analyse in detail the interactions that were developed in the context of this event since what I am really interested in is pointing out how this view of reading in Spanish contrasts with the one of reading in Quechua.

In fact, these literacy practices in Spanish differ from the ones the teacher develops in Quechua, since he argues that Spanish and Quechua literacy deserve a different strategy and treatment. According to him, 'one thing is to understand the text and another is to chat with the text'. He also argues that, while the category of 'understanding' belongs to the Spanish cultural matrix, 'chatting' with the text is a practice closer to the Quechua cultural matrix. As we will analyse in what follows, in this practice of 'chatting' neither questioning the text nor reducing it to a test-type format is allowed.

In his classroom, the teacher uses Quechua texts that he himself has recorded and transcribed from indigenous elders who have ample knowledge about certain topics. When reading these texts, the students have to 'tune in' to the *yachaq*,[8] or the person who has knowledge about some topic, and whose soul becomes present in the literacy event in order to share this knowledge. In the following excerpt, the teacher and students interact after reading two small texts about the role of the fox in Andean culture, texts produced by two elders from the community.

### Excerpt 4

1. Teacher: *imaninmi?*
   what does it say ? (addressing a girl)
2. Student: *sichus atuq ñawpaqta waqan chayqa nam kanqa ( )*
   it says that when the fox howls early it is going to be ( )
3. Teacher: *ajá?, imaynataq chayqa?*
   really?, how so?
4. Student: *chaynatam ninku* profesor
   that's what they say, teacher
5. Teacher: *riki, qamkuna uyarinkichischu chayta?*
   that's right. Do you have information about that? (asking everyone)
6. Students: *arí*
   yes
7. Teacher: a ver, *imaynata uyarinkichis?* (1.0)
8. *pim yapanman?* a ver
9. *arí nillankichismanriki?*
10. *imaynata qawanku tayta mamanchis?*
    let's see, how do you know? (1.0)
    who can add something?, let's see (whispers)

you said you could, didn't you? (mumbles)
how do our parents understand it?

11. Student: *munaychata qawarinku*
they find it very interesting

12. Teacher: *imaynatayá?*
well, how?

13. Students: *yachankuyá, ima tarpunankupaqpas*
14. *uyarinqa chuya waqayninta,*
15. *mana waqan chayqa mana tarpunkuchu*
you know, they plant every product according to that.
he is going to listen for its sharp howl,
if it doesn't howl then they don't plant.

16. Teacher: *arí, qawaychis, yachaykunaqa mana hukllachuriki*
17. *qawasqanchismanhina qawaychis:*
18. *Huk yachay kaypi kashanriki,*
19. *chay yachayqa yapakunmi,*
20. *chay yachayqa mana chayllachu kasqa.*
Yes, of course, look, knowledge isn't unique
according to what we are doing, look:
one notion is here, (draws a circle)
that notion is expanded with another notion (draws
another circle touching the first one)
that notion wasn't just that and nothing else (continues adding other circles around the first)

21. Student: *tikachahina tukukun*
it looks like a flower

22. Teacher: *tikachahina tukukun*
23. *kaq yapakun, yapakun, yapakun, yapakunriki*
24. *ñuqa apamurqaykichis, kay iskay runa*
*willawashanchisriki*
25. *huk kaypi*
26. *huk kaypipisriki*
it looks like a flower (keeps adding more, as if they
were flower petals)
again adding on, adding on, adding on, adding on
I brought you what these two people are telling us
(marks the middle circle with a cross)
here's one (points to the upper part of the
blackboard)
and another one here too (points to the lower part by
the other author)

At first, the teacher asks the open question of 'what does it say?' and a student responds in line 2 based on the content of the text. However, what is important for the teacher is not only to get information based on what the text states but based on what the children know from their lives and experiences ('Really, how so?' and 'Do you have information about that?'). He even asks them in line 10 about what their parents know ('how do our parents understand it?') using an inclusive 'our' (in *our* parents) that constructs a sense of community and a close relationship between the children and himself. This is not a typical practice in rural schools, where teachers usually consider that parents do not have anything to contribute to the knowledge imparted in the institution. The fact that parents even appear as the authors or sources of some of the texts hung on the classroom walls reconceptualises the hegemonic view of knowledge that dominates in school. The students understand that knowledge discussed in school could come from members of their community and that even the teacher could learn something from a *yachaq*. For them, knowledge does not come only from books:

**Excerpt 5**

Student:  profesor *maypitaq willarasunkiri?*
　　　　　teacher, where have you heard that knowledge? (about the
　　　　　poster hung on the wall)
Teacher:  ah, <u>*wasiypiyá,*</u> parla*rayku*
　　　　　oh, <u>in my house,</u> we have talked
Student:  *Florentinoqa?*
　　　　　and what about Florentino?
Teacher:  *wasinta rini. <u>Riqsinkichismiriki</u>*
　　　　　I go to his house. <u>You already know that</u>
Students:  <u>*arí*</u>
　　　　　<u>yes</u>
Teacher:  *payta tapurqani. Paymi chayta apamusqa.*
　　　　　I asked him about it. He is the bearer of that knowledge.

When the teacher explains the types of literacy practices that he develops in Quechua, he does it on the basis of the term *yapar*, which comes from Quechua 'yapay'[9] and means 'to add', 'to recreate' or 'to enrich what has been talked about'. He relates this to how knowledge works in rural areas: 'Andean knowledge is local and diverse and neither universal nor homogeneous.' He points out, for example, that knowledge about the fox is not the same in every Andean region: 'what is valid in this community is not for other places'. This is also what happens with how stories are told in some Andean communities. Mannheim (1999) has discussed this situated nature of storytelling: stories always emerge in conversations and are recreated through the telling. This is why we can find multiple versions of the same 'core' story, which is always adapted to different situations and the purposes of each interaction.

As happened with the reading event in Spanish, in the case of Quechua, the practice of *yapar* also dictates that texts are not fixed and do not contain unquestionable knowledge. According to the teacher, Quechua knowledge is diverse (and 'not unique' as he states in the above interaction) and is constantly enriched by community members: '*yapar* implies broadening knowledge and not limiting ourselves to our own visions'. The students learn that knowledge is constructed and that many people participate in this construction: not only 'canonically' literate people but also their parents, people from their community, and they themselves. The teacher picks up the metaphor of the flower proposed by one student at one point in the interaction in order to explain that knowledge is equivalent to flower petals: 'Again adding on, adding on, adding on, adding on.' Therefore, through their conversations with the teacher, students have the opportunity to understand that knowledge is social knowledge and that meaning is not contained within a text but can be negotiated in interactions. However, in contrast to the critical approach of the Spanish literacy event about the conquest, the teacher argues that *yapar* means 'adding with affection': '*yapar* is not done to offend someone or to criticise him'. Within a romanticising view of the Andean world, *yapar* means taking an opinion with respect and enriching it with more information, in order 'to see the topic in greater depth and solve the problem'. Therefore, it is not possible to address the texts in Quechua in the same way as the texts in Spanish. In Spanish you can analyse the text thoroughly, 'unpack' it and criticise it, while in Quechua you have to accept the text as it is and then add more information about it to enrich it.

Although we can suggest that, in general terms, in both Spanish and Quechua the teacher is adopting a critical approach towards the teaching of literacy, he is also establishing a division between the two languages, as well as between what can be read in each and how. The fact that Quechua literacy is only used to read about 'Quechua' topics and to reproduce 'Quechua' oral practices reveals – and at the same time constructs – a dominant interpretative repertoire that is shared among a sector of IBE promoters. In current ideological debates about Quechua (Blommaert, 1999), this language is conceived as an ancestral language that is important for interacting with the 'other' or with the 'real' peasant from the highlands (Zavala, 2014). Within this repertoire, Quechua indexes a static place that is resistant to change and modernity and that is situated in a different temporal order (Vich, 2010). This interpretative repertoire that anchors Quechua to the past or to the most distant rural communities prevents conceiving this language from a different standpoint and has very concrete political consequences for language policies.

As other studies in multilingual contexts have shown (Martin Jones and Jones, 2000), different languages, language varieties, and scripts add new dimensions to the diversity and complexity of the definition of literacy. In the case of Quechua, language ideologies about it – and the way Quechua indexes only traditional indigenous practices from peasant rural communities – have influenced some people's beliefs about the purposes of Quechua literacy in intercultural bilingual education. In this anchoring of Quechua to a utopian past, speakers remain confined in fixed identities and spaces, and other speakers who live within contexts of more cultural contact are ignored and conceived as illegitimate (Patrick, 2007: 127). Moreover, in the case under study, the representation that has been constructed about 'Andean' and 'Quechua' not only delegitimises what does not fit in this representation but also erases Andean practices and the use of Quechua in urban areas (Irvine and Gal, 2000). This could disempower many people who are a priori excluded from certain groups where they could fit as members under different criteria.

In the final section, I will develop an evaluation of the two case studies that have been analysed and I will offer some questions and reflections for future research about the phenomenon of Quechua literacy.

## Discussion: Quechua literacy, learning and empowerment

Current sociocultural theory has questioned the notion of learning as individual internalisation of knowledge and has proposed a new perspective on learning as increasing participation in communities of practice and as an integral aspect of social practice (Lave and Wenger, 1991). As such, learning implies not only a relation to specific activities but a relation to communities. It concerns the whole person acting in the world in the sense that 'it implies becoming a full participant, a member, a kind of person' (Lave and Wenger, 1991: 53). This view has emphasised that learning involves the construction of identities and that it is not possible for an individual to incorporate abilities from a certain community of practice without a change in identity. Therefore, community membership and identity definitively influence the opportunities for learning.

In the case studies that have been discussed in this chapter, we have seen that the attitudes that students develop toward texts, and the way they interact with them, construct them as different types of students and subjects. While Pumamarca students position themselves – and are positioned by the school and their teacher – as passive recipients of information who participate in the activities only to demonstrate knowledge on a test, in Tikapampa students are positioned as active researchers about stances of knowledge and as contributors to community knowledge. In the first case, the children act as schooled students who obey unquestionable reading rules, and in the second they negotiate textual meaning with their teacher and construct themselves as 'Quechua' community members who support and value the world where they have been socialised. Furthermore, while in the first case the teacher positions himself as the one who imparts and owns knowledge, in the second he challenges the students to value their funds of knowledge (González et al., 2005) and takes an interest in their cultural world. The identities and social relationships enacted are very different between the two cases and have differentiated consequences for the way people identify themselves and others, and are identified by others (Moje and Luke, 2009).

In addition, we know that the literate abilities that people acquire are related to the type of literacy practices that they develop (Scribner and Cole, 1981). Hence, what individual students have an opportunity to learn is supported, as well as constrained, by the opportunities for learning available in and through the discursive (oral and written) processes and practices that members develop across time and events. With this in mind, we can point out that the range of observed Quechua reading practices in Pumamarca constitutes a very narrow spectrum, which is framed within the social practice of the measurement of reading. In the case of Tikapampa, the children are acquiring other types of abilities that are more connected with critical skills and with knowing how to make links between what the text provides and their previous experiences and knowledge. In any case, what is important is to make clearer connections between the literacy events and practices that are developed in Quechua and the literacy abilities that the students would need to acquire in this language, although this is still an unresolved issue and a field of struggle. While some argue for 'full biliterate development' (Hornberger, 1989), others argue that the IBE schools should no longer promote a biliterate education because, even after several decades of implementation, it is not clear what the purposes of Quechua literacy should be.[10] Others – as we have discussed in this chapter – believe in a type of Quechua literacy in its own right and separate from Spanish literacy, mainly as a political option that reacts to historical oppression.

The cases under study raise important questions concerning the types of Quechua literacy practices that would empower Quechua students. How can we understand 'powerful biliteracy' or biliteracy that empowers the students? I concur with Street (1996), who suggests that 'for educationalists concerned with power, the question is not "how can a few gain access to existing power", nor "how can existing power structures be resisted", but rather how can power be transformed'. With this in mind, I will discuss this notion of 'powerful biliteracy' by starting to ask if the teacher from Pumamarca is empowering his students.

Some authors argue that measuring instruments such as standardised tests advantageously demand explicit, uniform and standard methods or goals for teaching that could reach a concrete record at all levels (Supovitz, 2009). In reality, in many rural schools, including those that supposedly administer an intercultural bilingual education programme, teachers have low expectations for their students and develop what Hornberger and Chick (2001) called 'safe practices' and 'safe talk'. These include very traditional practices of copying from the blackboard or from books, dictation during long periods of time, and reading aloud by repeating after the teacher, all with no understanding (Hornberger, 2003). At Pumamarca school, the teacher is very satisfied after obtaining good results from his students, and he has a clear goal that – he knows – is achievable: 'I know that I can achieve good results from my students, but I need more time.' In contrast to other cases where students are constructed as 'struggling', 'deviant' or 'deficient' readers (Moje and Luke, 2009), we could argue that at Pumamarca students are positioned as 'good readers' because the teacher believes that they are able to obtain good testing results. The students are clearly acting within this identity that is being offered by their teacher, rating their literacy abilities based on their test-taking skills.

Nevertheless, although the teacher from Pumamarca positions his students as 'good readers' and they show enthusiasm when they get involved in these types of practices, the children are somewhat subjugated to what the teacher rules and cannot develop abilities for interpreting, creating and being critical. These dominant practices of teaching methods based on skills for standardised testing, which have gained credibility and have even been legitimised as the only ones that measure intelligence and school achievement, have marginalised ways of speaking and knowing that are not valued inside of school contexts. The children from Pumamarca are being socialised with certain representations of reading, in which some ways of reading and using language are conceived as better than others and in which these other ways are the ones they bring from their cultural backgrounds. On the basis of this argument, we could state that this teacher is not empowering his students. Although the teacher offers the 'powerful weapon' of schooled literacy to the students, he does not question dominant representations that subordinate and exclude the students' language and cultural practices from the school domain.

Let us now ask if the teacher from Tikapampa is empowering his students. Hornberger and Skilton-Sylvester (2000) propose the need to counteract the traditional power weighting of the biliteracy continua by paying attention to and granting agency and voice to actors at the traditionally less powerful ends of the continua. The teacher from this school clearly does not constrain the official school context to schooled literacy practices and written texts in Spanish from the dominant culture, but pays attention to the traditionally less powerful ends of the continua of biliteracy by working with vernacular ways with words, promoting oral and written contexts for its use and introducing local and contextualised content.

Within a process model of power mentioned above, we can suggest that the teacher from Tikapampa is indeed contributing to the transformation of power, regardless of the test scores achieved by his students. He is challenging dominant representations and social relationships that have been historically reproduced in school, since the literacy practices he develops clearly try to unravel the hegemonic forces that construct certain epistemologies as absolute truths and dismiss others as deviant or incorrect. Moreover, acknowledging that how one reads and writes has an impact on the type of person one is recognised as being and on how one sees oneself, we can argue that this teacher is contributing to transforming how rural students have traditionally felt during the schooling process. In my conversations with the students, they manifested that they like their school because their teacher teaches them not to be ashamed of their culture. If education considers social justice as a central part of its agenda, with linguistically and culturally diverse learners the only ethically acceptable solution is to include the learner's voice and agency (Hornberger and Skilton-Sylvester, 2000).

The teacher from Tikapampa associates Quechua literacy with an 'essential' Quechua culture contained in rural peasant communities. This association is part of a 'strategic essentialism' (Bucholtz, 2003; Spivak, 1988) within an educational move from a sector of IBE promoters in a system that is constantly reinforcing the suppression and the silencing of difference.[11] This move promotes a political alliance and an oppositional identity that seek to redress power imbalances and counter negative ideologies toward the indigenous population. In addition, it constitutes an alternative way of approaching Quechua literacy after several decades of official measures for IBE schools, which have been nonsensical and assimilationist for its beneficiaries. Some would also argue that in the case of Quechua there are no 'real life' contexts where literacy is used outside of school and that it would be difficult to apply the notion of the 'social semiotic tool kit' that one would have to learn at school in order to develop as a citizen in today's society (Gee, 1996).

Nevertheless, in spite of the above issues, these reading practices restrict the possibilities of Quechua literacy in the long term. They reveal the construction of essentialised and frozen identities, in a context where indigenous people are functioning in a complex and intercultural world, employ different varieties of Spanish and Quechua, and display multiple identities in a variety of scenarios. If we take into account that Quechua culture is not only located in the rural and peasant world, but also in urban contexts, local and global scenarios, the young generation and the flow of cultural contacts, reading in Quechua could be developed with multimodal texts and within new practices in order to establish intercultural relationships with Spanish literacy and to start positioning Quechua as a language that is not restricted to the peasant world. If children believe that Quechua can only be spoken and written in relation to rural practices, they will replace it with Spanish as soon as they migrate to the cities.

Therefore, the option is not to construct a division between the languages (and cultures) and between the literacy practices associated with each of them, as if this were the only way of guaranteeing the maintenance of indigenous cultural identity and the non-assimilation to the dominant culture. The notion of the 'third space' (Gutiérrez, 2008) proposes a learning scenario that neither reproduces the dominant culture and language of the school nor those of the students from their backgrounds, but juxtaposes both types of practices. With this juxtaposition, the 'third space' generates new literacy practices built on the cultural and linguistic resources of the students' home and community contexts. This does not mean going back to the traditional practice of using the vernacular language and culture only as a means to learning the dominant language and culture. On the contrary, classroom literacy practices in the 'third space' can strengthen students' social identities and ties with their communities while they acquire school ways with words and academic literacies with a more critical stance regarding the power imbalances concerned. This is a possibility that Quechua literacy could pursue in order to counterbalance established dichotomies.

The case observed in Tikapampa radically differentiates literacy events and practices in Spanish and in Quechua and does not consider the connection and transfer of strategies across languages (Hornberger, 1989). It is important to ask what types of abilities the children should acquire through reading in Quechua and reading in Spanish, which abilities should be common to both and hence could be reinforced when reading in the two languages, and which should be different. Until today, intercultural bilingual education programmes have opted mostly for bringing 'authentic' texts from community domains into educational settings. But the teacher from Tikapampa has gone a bit further: he incorporates both the texts and the practices – or the ways of using them – from one context to another. However, although incorporating vernacular texts is important, the question is how to bring aspects of vernacular language practices or events into the classroom (and into reading events in *both* Spanish and Quechua) – such as collaborativeness, ways of interacting around texts or specific purposes of reading – and how to configure and combine them in a variety of ways (Ivanic, 2009). As Ivanic establishes: 'Reproducing some of the characteristics of the reading and writing in which the students engaged successfully in their everyday lives turned these practices into resources to enhance their success on their courses' (2009: 113).

In the official and dominant discourse, literacy with a capital L has consistently been presented as a key determinant of well-being, an important social entitlement, and a goal of human development (Maddox, 2008). Nevertheless, we know that literacy is always situated and that different types of literacy practices have distinct consequences for the individual and the community. As I have shown in this chapter, the purposes of Quechua literacy still constitute a field of struggle to be defined, together with a language policy that transcends the school site when deciding upon literacy in this language. This language policy will have to confront dominant interpretative repertoires that are still marginalising Quechua as an invisible language or – in the better case – as an ancestral language anchored in the rural world.

## Notes

1. I observed around 30 hours of class per school.
2. It is not clear if the 'successful' attribute refers to the whole school or to only one teacher. While the Ministry of Education refers to the whole school

as 'successful', the NGO makes reference to 'successful' IBE teachers. It is difficult to find IBE schools that work systemically in an IBE proposal and where all of the teachers apply it in a coherent way. In fact, there are many cases of schools where some teachers apply an IBE model and some other teachers do everything in Spanish.

3. This is because IBE has been assumed as a compensatory and remedial type of education for poor and rural children.

4. I am using pseudonyms for the names of the schools.

5. I would like to point out that the Peruvian Ministry of Education mandates a national literacy test in Spanish in the second grade throughout the entire country and a literacy test at the fourth-grade level in Spanish and in Quechua for bilingual schools. However, since the bilingual schools are not well registered, they sometimes have to apply the Spanish test in second grade, despite the fact that many of the students are acquiring Spanish as their second language. The teachers still feel very confused about the tests because they never know which type of test will be given in their school and at what time.

6. Transcription symbols:

| | |
|---|---|
| . | a stopping falling tone |
| , | continuing intonation |
| ? | rising inflection. It does not necessarily indicate a question |
| - | sharp cut-off of the prior word or sound |
| <u>under</u> | speaker emphasis |
| (.5) | time gap in tenths of a second |
| : | the speaker has stretched the preceding sound or letter. The more colons the greater the extent of the stretchings |
| { } | overlapping talk |
| ( ) | unclear fragment on the tape |
| (...) | talk that has not been transcribed |
| (comments) | description about aspects of context |

7. In the transcripts, Spanish contributions appear in regular font and Quechua contributions in italics, followed by the English translations. In the first excerpt, we can see that in the case of 'marcana', 'facilchalla' and 'leespa', the children are using a Spanish root (marca, facil and lee) with Quechua suffixes (na, cha, lla and spa).

8. The Quechua word 'yachaq' translates as 'the person who knows' or the wise person.

9. 'Yapay' is the infinite form of the Quechua verb and 'yapar' has the Spanish infinitive ending 'ar'.

10. There are some professionals working on IBE who have started to discuss this idea at some events and workshops. Aikman (1999) also considers this possibility in her book about intercultural education in the Peruvian Amazon.

11. Essentialism constitutes 'the position that the attributes and behavior of socially defined groups can be determined and explained by reference to cultural and/or biological characteristics believed to be inherent to the group' (Bucholtz, 2003). It rests on the assumption that groups can be clearly defined and that group members are alike. Strategic essentialism occurs when essentialising efforts are developed deliberately to create a political alliance through the construction of an oppositional common identity (Bucholtz, 2003). See Spivak (1988) for more discussion about the notion.

# References

Aikman, S. (1999). *Intercultural education and literacy. An ethnographic study of indigenous knowledge and learning in the Peruvian Amazon.* London: John Benjamins.

Aikman, S. (2012). Interrogating discourses of intercultural education: from indigenous community to global policy forum. *Compare,* 42 (2): 235–57.

Amrein, A. L. and Berliner, D. C. (2002). *An analysis of some unintended and negative consequences of high-stakes testing.* Tempe, Ariz.: Educational Policy Studies Laboratory, Arizona State University.

Au, W. (2011). Teaching under the new Taylorism: high-stakes testing and the standardization of the 21st century curriculum. *Journal of Curriculum Studies,* 43 (1): 25–45.

Barton, D. (1994). *Literacy: an introduction to the ecology of written language.* Oxford: Blackwell.

Barton, D. and Hamilton, M. (1998). *Local literacies. Reading and writing in one community.* London: Routledge.

Billig, M., Condor, S., Edwards, D., Gane, M., Middleton, D. and Radley, A. R. (1988). *Ideological dilemmas.* London: Sage.

Blommaert, J. (ed.) (1999). *Language ideological debates.* New York: Mouton de Gruyter.

Bucholtz, M. (2003). Sociolinguistic nostalgia and the authentication of identity. *Journal of Sociolinguistics,* 7 (3): 398–416.

Bunyi, G. (2001). Language and educational inequality in primary classrooms in Kenya. In M. Heller and M. Martin-Jones (eds), *Voices of authority: education and linguistic difference* (pp. 77–100). Westport, Conn.: Ablex.

Castanheira, M., Crawford, T., Dixon, C. and Green, J. (2001). Interactional ethnography: an approach to studying the social construction of literate practices. *Linguistics and Education,* 11 (4): 353–400.

Cummins, J. (2007). Pedagogies for the poor? Realigning reading instruction for low-income students with scientifically based reading research. *Educational Researcher,* 36 (9): 564–72.

De la Garza, Y. (2008). *Escritura y evaluación en un contexto bilingüe.* Mexico DF: Universidad Pedagógica Nacional.

Degregori, C. and Huber, L. (2007). Cultura, poder y desarrollo rural. In *Actas del Seminario SEPIA.*

Dietz, G. (2009). *Multiculturalism, interculturality and diversity in education: an anthropological approach.* Munster, Germany: Waxmann.

Edley, N. (2001). Analyzing masculinity: interpretative repertoires, ideological dilemmas and subject positions. In M. Wetherell, S. Taylor and S. Yates (eds), *Discourse as data. A guide for analysis.* London: Sage.

Edwards, D. and Potter, J. (2000). *Discursive psychology.* London: Sage.

Gee, J. (1996). *Social linguistics and literacies. Ideology in discourses.* London: Taylor & Francis.

Gee, J. (2004). *Situated language and learning. A critique of traditional schooling.* London: Routledge.

González, N., Moll, L. and Amanti, C. (eds) (2005). *Funds of knowledge. Theorizing practices in households, communities and classrooms.* New Jersey: Lawrence Erlbaum.

Gutiérrez, K. (2008). Developing a sociocritical literacy in the third space. *Reading Research Quarterly,* 43 (2): 148–64.

Heath, S. B. (1983). *Ways with words. Language, life and work in communities and classrooms.* Cambridge: Cambridge University Press.

Hornberger, N. (1989). Continua of biliteracy. *Review of Educational Research,* 59 (3): 271–96.

Hornberger, N. (2003). La enseñanza de y en quechua en el PEEB. In I. Jung and L. Enrique López (eds), *Abriendo la escuela. Lingüística aplicada a la enseñanza de lenguas.* Madrid: Proeib Andes, Invent and Morata.

Hornberger, N. and Chick, K. (2001). Co-constructing school safe time: safetalk practices in Peruvian and South African classrooms. In M. Heller and M. Martin-Jones (eds), *Voices of authority. Education and linguistic difference.* London: Ablex.

Hornberger, N. and Skilton-Sylvester, E. (2000). Revisiting the continua of biliteracy: international and critical perspectives. *Language and Education,* 14 (2): 96–122.

Instituto Nacional de Estadística, Peru (2001). *Encuesta Nacional de Hogares* (ENAHO).

Irvine, J. and Gal, S. (2000). Language ideology and linguistic differentiation. In P. Kroskrity (ed.), *Regimes of language. Ideologies, polities and identities* (pp. 35–84). Santa Fe, NM: School of American Research Press.

Ivanic, R. (2009). Bringing literacy studies into research on learning across the curriculum. In M. Baynham and M. Prinsloo (eds), *The future of literacy studies.* New York: Palgrave Macmillan.

Klein, S., Hamilton, L., McCaffrey, D. and Stecher, B. (2000). What do tests scores in Texas tell us? *Education Policy Analysis Archives,* 8 (49).

Kress, G. (2003). *Literacy in the new media age.* New York: Routledge.

Lankshear, C. and Knobel, M. (2003). *New literacies: changing knowledge and classroom learning.* Philadelphia: Open University Press.

Lave, J. and Wenger, E. (1991). *Situated learning. Legitimate peripheral participation.* Cambridge: Cambridge University Press.

Lemke, J. (1989). Semantics and social values. *Word,* 40 (1–2): 37–50.

Luke, A. (2000). Critical literacy in Australia. *Journal of Adolescent and Adult Literacy,* 43.

Madaus, G. F. and Clarke, M. (2001). The adverse impact of high-stakes testing on minority students: evidence from one hundred years of test data. In G. Orfield and M. L. Kornhaber (eds), *Raising standards or raising barriers? Inequality and high-stakes testing in public education* (pp. 85–106). New York: Century Foundation Press.

Maddox, B. (2008). What good is literacy? Insights and implications of the capabilities approach. *Journal of Human Development,* 9 (2).

Mannheim, B. (1999). Hacia una mitografía andina. In J. C. Godenzzi (ed.), *Tradición andina y amazónica. Método de análisis e interpretación de textos* (pp. 47–79). Cusco: Centro de Estudios Regionales Andinos 'Bartolomé de las Casas'.

Martin-Jones, M. and Jones, K. (eds) (2000). *Multilingual literacies. Reading and writing different worlds.* Philadelphia: John Benjamins.

May, S. (1999). *Critical multiculturalism: rethinking multicultural and antiracist education.* London: Routledge.

May, S. and Sleeter, C. (2010). Introduction. Critical multiculturalism: theory and praxis. In S. May and C. Sleeter (eds), *Critical multiculturalism: theory and praxis* (pp. 1–18). London: Routledge.

Mehan, H., Khalil, N. and Morales, C. (2010). Entre dos espacios: los retos de atravesar los espacios culturales y geográficos entre el hogar y la escuela. In G. P. Bonilla and C. Pérez Fragoso (eds), *Discursos e identidades en contextos de cambio educativo* (pp. 37–66). Mexico DF: Benemérita Universidad Autónoma de Puebla and Plaza y Valdés.

Menken, K. (2010). NCLB and English language learners: challenges and consequences. *Theory into Practice*, 49: 121–8.

Moje, E. B. and Luke, A. (2009). Literacy and identity: examining the metaphors in history and contemporary research. *Reading Research Quarterly*, 44 (4): 415–37.

Oliart, P. (2011). Discursos, tecnologías y prácticas de una reforma importada. *Políticas educativas y la cultura del sistema escolar en el Perú*. Lima: IEP and TAREA.

Patrick, D. (2007). Language endangerment, language rights and indigeneity. In M. Heller (ed.), *Bilingualism: a social approach*. New York: Palgrave Macmillan.

Peschiera, R. (2010). Un análisis sobre la interpretación de los diferentes actores en torno a la educación intercultural y bilingüe y sus políticas. *Revista Peruana de Investigación Educativa*, 1 (2): 27–58.

Rengifo, G. (2005). Explorando caminos para la incorporación del saber local en la escuela. In *Saber local en la comunidad y la escuela*. Lima: PRATEC.

Rogoff, B. and Angelillo, C. (2002). Investigating the coordinated functioning of multifaceted cultural practices in human development. *Human Development*, 45: 211–25.

Schegloff, E. (2000). When 'others' initiate repair. *Applied Linguistics*, 21: 205–43.

Schegloff, E., Jefferson, G. and Sacks, H. (1977). The preference for self-correction in the organization of repair in conversation. *Language*, 53: 361–82.

Scribner, S. and Cole, M. (1981). *The psychology of literacy*. Cambridge: Harvard University Press.

Sidnell, J. (2010). *Conversation analysis. An introduction*. Oxford: Wiley-Blackwell.

Spivak, G. C. (1988). Subaltern studies: deconstructing historiography. In R. Guha and G. C. Spivak (eds), *Selected subaltern studies* (pp. 3-32). London: Oxford University Press..

Street, B. (1984). *Literacy in theory and practice*. New York: Cambridge University Press.

Street, B. (1996). Literacy and power? *Open Letter*, 6 (2): 7–16. Sydney, Australia: UTS.

Street, B. and Lefstein, A. (2010). *Literacy. An advanced resource book*. New York: Routledge.

Supovitz, J. (2009). Can high stakes testing leverage educational improvement? Prospects from the last decade of testing and accountability reform. *Journal of Educational Change*, 10: 211–27.

Trapnell, L., Calderón, A. and Flores, R. (2008). *Interculturalidad, conocimiento y poder*. Lima: Instituto del Bien Común, Ford Foundation, Oxfam América.

Tubino, F. and Zariquiey, R. (MS). Las prácticas discursivas sobre la interculturalidad en el Perú de hoy. Propuesta de lineamientos para su tratamiento en el sistema educativo peruano.

Valdiviezo, L. (2009). Bilingual intercultural education in indigenous schools: an ethnography of teacher interpretations of government policy. *International Journal of Bilingual Education and Bilingualism*, 12 (1): 61–79.

Vich, V. (2010). El discurso sobre la sierra del Perú: la fantasía del atraso. In J. Ortega (ed.), *Nuevos hispanismos interdisciplinarios y transatlánticos*. Mexico DF: Iberoamericana-Vervuert.

Zavala, V. (2007). *Avances y desafíos de la Educación Intercultural Bilingüe en Bolivia, Ecuador y Perú*. Lima: CARE and IBIS.

Zavala, V. (2014). An ancestral language to speak with the 'Other': closing down ideological spaces of a language policy in the Peruvian Andes. *Language Policy*, 13(1): 1–20.

Zavala V., Niño-Murcia, M. and Ames, P. (eds) (2004). *Escritura y sociedad. Nuevas perspectivas teóricas y etnográficas*. Lima: Red para el Desarrollo de las Ciencias Sociales en el Perú.

# 3

# Growth of Communicative Competence in a Dynamic African Context: Challenges for Developmental Assessment

*Robert Serpell*

## Introduction

Communicative competence is a cardinal feature of the human species (Gumperz and Hymes, 1964). Over the life course of the organism it represents a key developmental achievement. The infant (one who does not speak) is expected in all societies to grow into a person who can communicate with others. Normally this is done primarily through the medium of a language – a formal code for representing ideas. The child's capacity to communicate using language is from the outset embedded in social relations (Halliday, 1975; Bruner, 1983); it is foundational to most the higher-level processes of cognition (Vygotsky, 1978); and in the modern world of standardised educational measurement, early indicators of linguistic competence are highly predictive of success at later stages of formal education (Snow, 1994). As a result, the assessment of children's competence to communicate with language is a widely valued application of psychology, responding to felt needs of parents, teachers and educational planners in most contemporary societies. I shall argue in this chapter that getting it right has significant implications for the design of mainstream educational curricula geared to the promotion of progressive social change in a multilingual African society. I shall also seek to show that, in order to get it right, we need to think outside the boxes that currently dominate professional discourse about the design of curricula and instruction.

The naturally occurring languages of human societies vary in many respects, including their lexicon, their grammar and their phonology. In many social configurations, such as a nation state or a local community, several languages coexist as resources for communication.

This phenomenon, sometimes termed linguistic diversity, is variously regarded as a positive feature or a problematic one. From one perspective, the coexistence of multiple languages in a society is culturally enriching (UNESCO, 2012). Moreover, for an individual to be fluent in several languages is increasingly recognised by psychology as an empowering resource for his or her cognitive functioning (Mohanty and Perregaux, 1997; Bialystok et al., 2009). Yet the phenomenon of individual bilingualism has often been construed as problematic. The key premise of this view seems to be that learning how to represent the world twice over must logically be more difficult than learning to do so just once. However, a pragmatic theoretical perspective on language highlights the fact that competence in any language includes knowing how to match different parts of the speaker's stock of representational resources to the social context, and in this respect appropriate use of two languages is merely a special case of the selection of what Halliday terms *register* (Gregory, 1967), or of what Bakhtin termed *heteroglossia* (Bailey, 2007). In this chapter, I shall argue that monolingual bias not only tends to over-problematise individual multilingualism, but also to distort its interpretation in the context of assessment. I shall also suggest that professional assessment is vulnerable to such distortion partly as a consequence of cultural hegemony.

The growth of a child's communicative competence is monitored by her family, peer group and school in different ways arising from the task demands of various activity settings. Peer-group play is typically unselfconscious about matters of linguistic form, focusing primarily on mutual intelligibility. Adult family members who consider themselves responsible for the child's socialisation are especially attentive to the child's adherence to norms of politeness. Both of those types of criterion may also be applied by teachers, but in addition teachers often stipulate a more restrictive set of norms, some of which may arise from functional demands of the school curriculum (Scheleppegrell, 2001; LeVine et al., 2012), while others reflect a more political agenda.

Children in Zambia and many other countries in the SADC region grow up in a sociolinguistic setting where most adults are competent in three or more language varieties, where the varieties have a strong core of grammatical and lexical commonalities, and where the borders between varieties are porous. The communicative socialisation they receive in such a speech community is likely to influence their performance on measures of verbal cognition and literacy. Yet this is often overlooked in the design of formal assessment procedures. This chapter examines two case studies of research on developmental assessment of children's communicative competence in Zambia, each of which raises issues of hegemonic bias that threatens to generate damaging misapplications to educational decision-making.

In Zambia, it is common to hear the number of languages indigenous to Zambia cited in public discourse as 73. But that figure was generated by a colonial era survey of tribes (Brelsford, 1956, 1965). Kashoki and Mann (1978) analysed the core vocabulary among various subsets of the 80 indigenous, Bantu speech varieties claimed as a mother tongue by respondents to the 1969 national census of population. Their quantitative cluster analysis of commonalities generated 14 groupings. If all the varieties within each grouping are considered as dialects of a single language,[1] then in 1969 only 10 languages were cited as their mother tongue by more than 1 per cent of the nation's population (Kashoki and Mann, 1978: Table 1.1, 19–21).[2] Seven of those clusters are represented by one of the official languages adopted for basic education, and two particular varieties from within two of the clusters are also widely recognised as lingua francas: Town Nyanja and Town Bemba (Kashoki, 1972; Spitulnik, 1998). As Felix Banda (2012) has observed, the popular theme that Zambia has an overwhelming diversity of languages reflects an outsider's perspective and overlooks an equally remarkable homogeneity: all ten of the indigenous languages share a great deal of commonality in phonology, morphology and grammar. As a result of those commonalities, many Zambians who migrate from one part of the country to another testify that they were able to 'pick up' some competence in the local language in a matter of weeks even if they had little or no prior exposure to it. This rapid acquisition of a second or third language is regarded as normal in Zambian society. Adults resident in urban areas (nearly 50 per cent of the population) typically claim fluency in three or more languages (one of which is English), and those in rural areas in two or more (Mytton, 1974).

As in many postcolonial states (Fishman, 1967), the language of the former colonial administration, English, is generally used in Zambian society for many of the *diglossic* social functions classified as H(igh) by Ferguson (1959), while most of the L(ow) social functions are performed in one of the indigenous languages, which thus come to represent the domain of 'hearth and home'. The association of English with urbanisation and 'modernisation' of lifestyles endows it with great prestige in the public domain, but solidarity with ethnic kin remains an important dimension of social intercourse that is represented by the use of indigenous languages, hereafter referred to as Zambian languages. Moreover, a further dimension of social significance is represented by the urban lingua francas that transcend ethnic boundaries without the connotations of formality that often constrain the use of English. I have discussed elsewhere how this 'superposition' of English over the Zambian languages influences the growth of communicative competence in different discourse domains among young children with different mother tongues in the capital city of Lusaka (Serpell, 1980).

Code-switching and mixing are very widespread in Zambia, as well as lexical adoption of English into the Bantu languages. Underwood et al. (2003, 2007) conducted a nationwide survey of reading attitudes, practices and proficiencies among literate adults in Zambia. A selection of the self-reported language use they elicited from a nationwide sample of 2000+ adults is presented in Table 3.1. It is apparent that the context and topic of conversation influenced respondents' perception of their choice between English and a Zambian language to a greater degree than the identity of their interlocutor. According to speakers' self-descriptions, talk at home (79 per cent) and about family matters (80 per cent) was overwhelmingly conducted in Zambian languages alone, whereas English was quite widely used in conversations at work (31 per cent on its own and 32 per cent mixed with a Zambian language).

The same survey also revealed a bias towards English literacy: while oral conversations about child health were predominantly conducted in Zambian languages (55 per cent), most respondents expressed a preference for reading about child health in English (60 per cent alone and

*Table 3.1*  Percentage of self-reported language use by Zambian adults nationwide in 2002

|  | Zambian language L1 and/or other | English only | Zambian language and English |
|---|---|---|---|
| **Talk with:** <br> parents–siblings– children | 87–78–82 | 1–2–4 | 4–15–14 |
| **Talk at:** <br> home–church–work | 79–60–35 | 1–14–31 | 13–26–32 |
| **Talk about:** <br> family matters– political issues– child health | 80–72–55 | 3–26–18 | 11–1–25 |
| **Prefer to read about:** <br> child health | 29 | 60 | 10 |

*Source*: Underwood et al. (2003).

10 per cent in combination with a Zambian language). The authors assessed the reading competence of their respondents for comprehension of health materials written at fourth- and eighth-grade levels in whichever they preferred among the seven officially recognised Zambian languages and also in English. They found that respondents who had completed seven or less years of formal schooling scored significantly higher when the test was in a Zambian language than when it was in English. Respondents with at least an eighth-grade education scored equally well or better on English-language compared with Zambian-language tests. Many University of Zambia students report that they can only read simple texts in a Zambian language and would find it difficult to understand academic texts of the kind they are required to read for their studies if these were presented in their mother tongue or any other Zambian language.[3] Because of the social prestige and economic leverage it imparts, many Zambian parents construe the acquisition of English language competence as a priority educational goal for their children.

## Design of a standardised test of preschool child development

Marfo (2011: 141) has envisioned 'an African child development field grounded in local contexts but simultaneously open to knowledge systems from other cultures'. The Western cultural practice of developmental assessment, formalised in the twentieth century with particular emphasis on cognitive competencies, is a conspicuous example of an exogenous understanding that may be of value in African societies as they seek to adapt the institution of schooling to their own sociocultural and politico-economic contexts. At its best, the practice is potentially helpful for clinical diagnosis and for educational guidance. However, because of its approach to measurement, it relies critically on standardisation, and is potentially harmful if misapplied (Serpell and Haynes, 2004).

One of the most conspicuous pitfalls is the use of a formal test designed in a Northern/Western hemisphere, More industrialised country (NoWeMic) such as the UK, the Netherlands or the USA, to assess the functioning of a rural African child by comparing his or her individual scores with those of a NoWeMic standardisation sample. Doing so can lead to spurious designation of the child in question as cognitively incompetent or developmentally delayed, when in fact the task on which she or he has been assessed is one that is completely alien to the child's regular effective environment and hence of little or no relevance to her current adaptation or to her potential to adapt to challenges she is likely to encounter in her future environment. Cross-cultural comparisons of quantitative indices of psychological functioning can only be meaningfully interpreted if the measures on which they are based are functionally equivalent (Van de Vijver and Poortinga, 1997). As the project discussed in this section illustrates, establishing functional equivalence is a very complex undertaking.

The Zambian Early Childhood Development Project (ZECDP) was launched in 2009 in collaboration between the University of Zambia and Harvard University, with support from the Zambian Ministry of Education, the Examinations Council of Zambia and UNICEF. The broad motivating goal of the project was 'to determine the effect of early childhood environment, health and education on children's development before and throughout their schooling careers' (Fink et al., 2012: 3). A key objective of the study was to establish a valid criterion by which to evaluate the impact of interventions such as malaria prevention and early childhood education. The project's first output was a Zambian Child Assessment Test (ZamCAT) 'designed to provide a broad, multiple-domain based assessment of children of pre-school age in the Zambian context' (Fink et al., 2012: 3). More specifically, the authors set out to develop a tool that

- yields internationally comparable multi-domain measures of child development
- is sensitive to local culture and linguistic differences and
- can be adapted to other developing countries.

One of the resources used for this purpose was the Peabody Picture Vocabulary Test (PPVT), a widely used American test of language development (Dunn and Dunn, 1997). In this test the child is presented with a series of spoken stimulus words in order of increasing difficulty, and for each stimulus the child is asked to choose among four pictures, one of which is an illustration of the spoken word. A child's score is the number of words whose meanings she identifies correctly in this way. This test had previously been used with Lusaka schoolchildren by Matafwali (2010), who found PPVT scores to be a significant predictor of literacy outcomes at the end of Grade 2. In its original form, the test is culturally biased in several ways against the performance capabilities of many African children, especially those from families with limited formal education, living in underserved rural or urban neighbourhoods.

For instance, it relies on an unfamiliar face-to-face discourse format with adults (Harkness and Super, 1977), on an unfamiliar mode of pictorial representation (Serpell and Deregowski, 1980), on unfamiliar cultural artefacts and practices represented in some of the pictures, and on the unfamiliar linguistic medium of English. It was therefore adapted and pilot-tested before inclusion as a component of the ZamCAT.

In addition to obviously inappropriate items, such as pictures of ocean liners and children in Halloween costumes, a combination of intuitive appraisal informed by previous research on pictorial perception by Zambian children and systematic pilot testing was used to eliminate pictures from the test that six-year-olds in Lusaka found difficult to interpret. On the language dimension, the English stimulus words were translated into each of the seven Zambian languages designated by the Ministry of Education as a medium of instruction in the early grades of public schools. However, during pilot pretesting of the instrument, in several languages, locally recruited assessors reported that a child in that province would typically use a different word to describe the target picture.

In the case of ciNyanja,[4] a major challenge arose because of dialectal variations. In the capital city of Lusaka, the ciNyanja spoken as a lingua franca differs from the official standard version (based on ciCewa spoken in the Eastern Province) in being heavily influenced by ciNsenga and by English. So a child whose lexicon includes an appropriate word for the concept in only one of these dialects would not necessarily know the meaning of the stimulus word on that item if the test were presented in the other dialect.

The authors addressed this challenge as follows:

> We asked native speakers of each language to review the translations, keeping in mind differences in local dialects as well as the level of language a six-year-old would speak and understand. ... It is important to stress here that the original PPVT instrument was heavily adapted for the ZamCAT instrument. The PPVT has a list of age-normed and difficulty-ordered vocabulary words that correspond to sets of four pictures in the stimulus book. However, as described above, given the context-inappropriateness of some pictures and words, we were unable to use all items as suggested. To develop new items, we selected pages where all four picture tiles were appropriate, then chose a word represented by one of those tiles. While these adaptations were clearly necessary in order to obtain culturally-appropriate pictures of equal difficulty, the adaptations mean that

the PPVT scores of children assessed with the ZamCAT tool cannot be directly compared to scores based on the original PPVT module. (Fink et al., 2012: 8–9)

Nor indeed is it clear whether the vocabulary tested in each of the different Zambian language versions is of equivalent difficulty.

Looking ahead to the application of this carefully refined instrument, it is clear that one hazardous assumption is likely to remain: restricting the stimulus words to one dialectal variant based on superficial categorisation of a child's 'first language (L1)' or 'home language'. If the outcome of assessment (such as a test score, or a profile of strengths and needs) is to be a valid representation of a child's communicative competence, the formal process must be sensitive to the various real world contexts in which a child has been exposed to language. If the contexts of family life, children's play and formal learning activities at school have each rendered a different speech variety familiar to the child, then the procedures of assessment and the criteria for evaluating the child's performance will need to be correspondingly adjusted. In other words, if the purpose of assessment is to gauge the level of a child's communicative competence, rather than recording performance indicators of whether the child understands word X or says X in response to a picture, it would be more useful to pose the competence questions 'Can she understand X?' and 'Can she say X in an appropriate context?' Furthermore, if assessment is to provide a valid guide to instruction, it needs, in addition to contextual sensitivity, to gauge the ease with which a learner can adapt to the demands of a learning task. Thus, a process of dynamic assessment (Grigorenko and Sternberg, 1998) should address the questions 'Can she learn to understand X?' (and, if so, 'How fast?') and 'Can she learn to say X? (and, if so, 'How well?').

One set of constraints will be the range of linguistic variation across which such learning is required. Transfer of learning from one speech variety to another will typically be easier in cases where commonalities exist in grammar, phonology and/or vocabulary (for example, within a language family such as the Bantu languages). The notion of a dialect invokes this phenomenon by positing that learning a new dialect of a language one already knows is easier than learning a new language. However, in Zambia and elsewhere in the Bantu language region, it is often unclear how to draw the boundaries between cognate speech varieties. Myers-Scotton (1993) has explained this problem for the various indigenous languages of Kenya and Zimbabwe, Banda (2009) for the Bantu languages of South Africa, and Kashoki and Mann (1978) for the

Bantu languages of Zambia. The implications for educational policy will be considered below.

## Choice of linguistic medium for initial literacy instruction

Zambia's national policy on the medium of instruction for basic education underwent a major change in the late 1990s, due to what has been described as 'a quiet revolution' (Tambulukani et al., 2001). Shortly after independence, in the 1960s a policy of immersion in English from the first grade was launched, based on a complex mixture of political and administrative considerations (Mwanakatwe, 1968; McAdam, 1978). That English Medium Scheme replaced the earlier, colonial policy of introducing basic literacy to children in the lower grades through one of the local indigenous languages (Ohannessian, 1978). By the mid-1970s, it had become apparent that the English immersion policy was giving rise on the one hand to precocious mastery of English by a minority of the learners enrolled in government primary schools, and on the other to a rising number of learners failing to achieve basic literacy (Serpell, 1978). The matter received close attention in the context of a national debate on educational reforms. Yet, despite strong advocacy from many local intellectuals (e.g. Kapwepwe, 1970) for a return to the practice of teaching initial literacy in the medium of a familiar, indigenous Zambian language, it was not until 1996 that the cardinal value of that principle was officially recognised.

The Ministry of Education (1996: 40–1) declared that 'all pupils will be given an opportunity to learn initial basic skills of reading and writing in a local language', but also that 'English will remain as the official medium of instruction'. This ambiguous new policy was implemented gradually between 1998 and 2004, using pilot studies to refine and justify the curriculum, followed by large-scale production of learning materials and teacher training. The ambivalence reflected in the policy generated practical operational challenges. For instance,

> it was agreed that the teaching of English be delayed for some time. However, there was no absolute agreement on how long that delay should be. Many participants favoured the introduction of oral English no later than the third term of Grade 1, while others thought it should wait until Grade 2. (Sampa, 2005: 32)

Theorists who advocate such a 'transitional model' generally contend that a strong foundation of initial literacy in a familiar language needs to be established before introducing learners to reading a second language (Cummins, 2001; Heugh, 2000). There is growing evidence that in the conditions prevailing in most Zambian public schools more than one year is needed to establish such a foundation for more than a minority of children (e.g. Jere-Folotiya et al., 2014).

## Demographic linguistic profiles of geographical zones

Another significant challenge arose in deciding which of the various Zambian speech varieties should be offered in each school. A policy of zoning was adopted, based on the practices of the colonial and post-independence English Medium Scheme eras. The national population census data presented in Table 3.2 show that in some districts, a single speech variety was reported as the 'predominant language of communication' by an overwhelming majority of the local population, for example Chewa in the Katete and Chadiza districts of Eastern Province and Lozi in the Mongu District of Western Province. In other districts, however, the most widely cited speech variety accounts for only half or less of the resident population: for example, Chewa was reported as a predominant language of communication by only 33.9 per cent of residents in Chipata District of Eastern Province and Nyanja by only 50.6 per cent of residents in the capital city of Lusaka. Note that in Lusaka, 7.5 per cent of respondents reported their predominant language of communication as English, and 21.9 per cent as one of the other major indigenous Bantu languages (Bemba, Tonga or Lozi), whereas none of these languages were widely reported as their predominant language of communication by respondents in Chipata District. Thus the diversity of speech varieties used in Chipata is locally understood as mainly a matter of variation in dialect rather than language.

Nevertheless the zoning policy adopted for designating a given language as the official medium of initial literacy instruction specified Lozi for Mongu District and Nyanja both for Lusaka and for all the districts of Eastern Province. Note that in two districts of Eastern Province a clear majority of respondents to the 2000 census reported as their predominant language of communication a speech variety that has not been adopted as an official medium of initial literacy instruction anywhere in the country: 77.3 per cent of respondents in Petauke District (and 89.3 per cent of those in the less populous adjacent district of Nyimba) reported Nsenga; and 76.4 per cent of those in Lundazi District reported Tumbuka (while 78.6 per cent of those in the less

Table 3.2 Percentage of respondents in various parts of Zambia citing each variety as their predominant language of communication (2000 census)

| | Chipata District EP | Zambia | Zambia | Western Province (WP) | Mongu District WP | Lusaka Urban District | Chipata District EP‡ | Katete District EP | Lundazi District EP | Petauke District EP | Eastern Province* (EP) |
|---|---|---|---|---|---|---|---|---|---|---|---|
| (N) | 277,548 | 7,383,105 | 9,337,425† | 663,842 | 143,373 | 993,404 | 317,682‡ | 166,202 | 204,414 | 207,629 | 1,306,173§ |
| | 1990 | 1990 | 2000 | 2000 | 2000 | 2000 | 2000 | 2000 | 2000 | 2000 | 2000 |
| Nyanja group of languages | 93.8 | 20.1 | 20.6 | 0.4 | 0.5 | 57.8 | 90.6 | 94.4 | 12.7 | 94.8 | 70.6¶ |
| Chewa | 33.5 | 5.7 | 4.9 | | | 2.1 | 33.9 | 90.8 | 9.1 | 15.9 | 33.8 |
| Nyanja | 24.2 | 7.8 | 10.7 | | | 50.6 | 31.0 | 0.4 | 1.9 | 1.0 | 9.6 |
| Kunda | 7.9 | – | – | | | – | 0.3 | 1.0 | 0.2 | 0.2 | 2.6 |
| Ngoni | 23.2 | 1.7 | 1.2 | | | 0.5 | 21.3 | 0.8 | 0.5 | 0.4 | 6.6 |
| Nsenga | 5.0 | 4.3 | 3.4 | | | 4.6 | 4.1 | 1.4 | 1.0 | 77.3 | 20.6 |
| Tumbuka | 2.0 | 2.9 | 2.5 | – | – | 1.0 | 1.8 | 0.2 | 76.4 | 0.2 | 14.8 |
| Senga | 0.3 | 0.7 | 0.6 | – | – | – | 0.2 | 0.0 | 0.5 | 0.0 | 4.6 |
| English | 0.7 | 1.1 | 1.7 | 0.3 | 0.4 | 7.5 | 0.5 | 0.1 | 0.1 | 0.1 | 0.2 |
| Other: Bemba, Tonga, Lozi, etc | 0.7 | | | | | | 4.8 | 4.8 | 5.1 | 4.2 | 5.0 |
| Bemba group | | 29.7 | 35.0 | 0.4 | 0.5 | 17.3 | | | | | |
| Tonga group | | 11.0 | 12.8 | 0.3 | 0.4 | 3.0 | | | | | |
| Lozi group | | 6.4 | 5.7 | 60.0 | 84.6 | 1.6 | | | | | |

*The four other, less heavily populated districts of Eastern Province in 2000 reported clearly dominant percentages of the following speech varieties as their 'predominant language of communication': Chadiza (pop. 73,034, 89.5% Chewa); Chama (pop. 63,691, 78.6% Chewa); Maambwe (pop. 41,434, 62.6% Kunda); Nyimba (pop. 60,862, 89.3% Nsenga). Senga is a closely cognate variety to Tumbuka, and Kunda is a closely cognate variety to Chewa.

†Zambia's population continued to grow over the next decade at an average annual rate of 2.8%, reaching a total of 13,046,508 in 2010.

‡In the 2000 census report, unlike earlier census reports, the authors make it clear that language data were calculated excluding children aged less than 2 years.

§The population of Eastern Province grew steadily over the preceding four decades: 509,515 in 1969; 650,902 in 1980; 916,845 in 1990.

¶The percentage of Eastern Province respondents reporting each of the languages within the Nyanja group was very similar in 1990 to that in 2000.

populous adjacent district of Chama reported Senga, a speech variety close to Tumbuka). (Tumbuka and Nsenga are two of the three languages representing clusters identified in the Kashoki and Mann (1978) taxonomy as spoken by more than 1 per cent of the national population which have not received recognition as an official language designated as a medium of instruction in the public schools. The third is Mambwe, a language reported as mother tongue by 8.5 per cent of the residents of Northern Province in the 2000 census.)

The demographic profile of Chipata District presented in Table 3.2 shows that roughly equal proportions of residents reported each of three different speech varieties as their predominant language of communication: Chewa (33.9 per cent), Nyanja (31 per cent) and Ngoni (21.3 per cent). But simply relying on such frequencies could be misleading, since Chewa and Nyanja are generally regarded as very closely related variants of the same language, such that the two names are used almost interchangeably, whereas Ngoni is much closer to Nsenga. Note also that the proportion of Chipata residents reporting Nyanja as their predominant language of communication rose from 24.2 per cent in 1990 to 31 per cent in 2000. This is unlikely to be a consequence of migration. It almost certainly reflects a growing tendency for Chewa speakers outside the core rural areas of Chewa settlement (Katete and Chadiza) to cite as their predominant language of communication Nyanja, which is the more widely accepted name of their language across the nation, especially in urban areas (see the columns for Zambia and Lusaka Urban in Table 3.2).

## Use of a language other than the mother tongue

In the 1969 census, respondents were asked to state for each member of a household 'the first language spoken as a child' (CSO, 1973: 53). The limitations of this question for eliciting an account of a person's language competence were noted in the Zambia Language Survey conducted in 1970–71 (Mytton, 1974; Ohannessian and Kashoki, 1978). As a result, in the next national population census in 1980 (CSO, no date) respondents were asked to state three language characteristics for each member of the household:

- 'first language spoken as a child'
- 'first language of communication', and
- 'second language of communication'.

In the 1990 and 2000 censuses (CSO, 1995: 2003), essentially the same three characteristics were recorded, but relabelled:

- ethnic group (Zambian tribe); ethnicity
- predominant language of communication; predominant language
- second language of communication; second language

The authors of the 1980 census analytical report cited a number of factors that influence 'the mix of languages that are used in specific areas', including 'the spread of a particular language, level of educational attainment, language composition of the migrant population and presumably inter-marriages', which they interpreted as 'ripples of undercurrents of prevailing social and economic forces ... eroding the language barriers' (CSO, no date: 13).

From these and other data (Mytton 1974; CSO, 1995: Descriptive Tables, Vol. 10) we can confidently infer that in the 1970s and 1990s Nyanja was the predominant lingua franca of both the capital city of Lusaka and the Eastern Province, and according to popular consensus that has remained the case up to the present day (2012).

## The question of mutual intelligibility

Several methods were used by Kashoki and his colleagues to assess the degree of similarity among these language varieties in use in Zambia's Eastern Province. The first method was 'shared basic vocabulary' assessed by eliciting from long-term, adult residents of the area the terms for a list of about 95 items including parts of the body, family relationships, basic human actions, counting, physical and geographical objects, etc. This showed only about 50 per cent correspondence between Nyanja (Cewa) and each of the following widespread language varieties in Eastern Province: Nsenga (54–61 per cent), Kunda (52 per cent), Tumbuka (49 per cent), Senga (53 per cent).[5]

Table 3.3 illustrates some commonalities and differences among Nyanja (Cewa), Nsenga (the version spoken by the Ngoni of Chief Mpezeni's area in Chipata District), Tumbuka and Kunda. In this non-random sample of four nouns, two adjectives, two verbs and two adverbs, the degree of diversity across the five language varieties could be rated as high for three of the terms, as low or non-existent for three others, and as intermediary for the other four. But how should we arrive at an average level of commonality across the full vocabulary of these varieties, and how different are their grammars?

*Table 3.3* Some core vocabulary* items in four speech varieties widely spoken in Chipata District, Eastern Province, Zambia

| English | Nyanja (Chewa) cluster J | Nsenga cluster I | Tumbuka cluster L | Kunda cluster A |
|---------|--------------------------|------------------|-------------------|-----------------|
| Child | -ana | -ana | -ana | -ana |
| Tree | -tengo | -(mu)ti | -kuni | -ti |
| Water | -adzi | -anzi | -aji | -inzi |
| Buy | -gula | -gula | -gula | -sita |
| New | -tsopano | -lomba | -leelo | -bwangu |
| Where? | kuti | kuni | ngkhu | kwani |

*Source*: *Zambia Language Survey 1970* (Kashoki and Mann, 1978).

A second approach adopted by Kashoki (1978b) was to ask informants without prior exposure to one another's language varieties to listen to tape-recorded passages of speech in a given variety and assess the degree to which they understood the passage as a whole. The participants were Grade 9 high school pupils aged 13–20, and their understanding of each passage was tested in English. By these criteria, the mutual intelligibility of Nyanja and Bemba was rated as low, with mother-tongue speakers of Bemba obtaining an average listening score of 42 per cent on the Nyanja test, and mother-tongue speakers of Nyanja obtaining an average of 25 per cent on the Bemba test (rated to two linguistic indices: degree of correspondence in basic vocabulary, and degree of correspondence of combined root and grammatical morphemes).

As Kashoki noted, this experimental test was an extreme case among the range of conditions prevalent in Zambian society. Great care was taken to recruit individuals without prior exposure to other language varieties. This would be more difficult to achieve in modern-day Zambia, because of the ever-increasing mobility of people from one region of the country to another. On the other hand, there is considerable anecdotal evidence that the variety of ciNyanja adopted as standard in the instructional texts developed by language experts at the Ministry of Education's National Curriculum Development Centre is difficult to understand for fluent speakers of Lusaka Nyanja. One Lusaka schoolchild in the 1990s, for instance, testified to Williams (1998: 71): 'when we are told to write, we are given different things, things that are spoken by other people, and not the Nyanja we speak'.

## Compatibility between a child's first language and the medium of instruction at school

Tambulukani and Bus (2012) set out to examine the influence on early literacy acquisition of varying degrees of compatibility between a pupil's first language and the medium of instruction at school. The study was conducted in 2006–7 among eight-year-olds enrolled in Grade 2 at four government schools in the capital city of Lusaka, in rural and urban areas of Chipata District, Eastern Province and in rural areas of Mongu District, Western Province. In order to establish comparison groups with varying degrees of familiarity with the language used as a medium of literacy instruction, each child was assigned a score based on her or his expressive vocabulary in response to a set of pictures (a mirror image of the procedure used in the Peabody Picture Vocabulary Test). This 'familiar language test' was described as follows:

> The child was asked to name objects and actions on a picture depicting common objects – like water, people, and dress – and actions – like swimming and buying.... Children were asked to name what they saw on the illustration in a Zambian language. The researcher noted how many words were named in the Zambian language used for teaching, that is, Nyanja in Lusaka and Chipata, and Lozi in Mongu, and how many words in another Zambian language that is common in the district, that is, town Nyanja in Lusaka and Chipata, and Mbunda in Mongu. To make scoring easier the researcher disposed of two lists of often named words, one in the language of teaching and one in the other local Zambian language... As an indicator of children's familiarity with the language of instruction we calculated the percentage of responses in the language of instruction. (Tambulukani and Bus, 2012: 147)

A child's response with a given word, A, to the question 'What is this?' posed about a picture may be a reasonable index of the most familiar term in the child's lexicon for designating the object depicted. But it is silent about how easily the child would understand an alternative word, B, in the presence of that picture, let alone in other communicative contexts. Consider, for instance the pairs of English words (A) 'river' (B) 'stream', (A) 'dish' (B) 'bowl', (A) 'kids' (B) 'children', (A) 'nice' (B) 'lovely'. An English-speaking child who uses word A in each of these pairs is surely quite likely to understand that word B has a similar meaning. The same may well apply to many children growing up in Lusaka calling a river (A) 'kamana' and hearing a teacher call it (B) 'mtsinje', or being used to express the concept 'happy' with the word (A) 'temwa' and hearing a teacher say (B) 'kondwa' (another ciCewa/ciNyanja pair on the study's score sheet). Likewise, in Chipata, many children who have learned to greet someone in their home environment with the expression (A) 'muli tyani ?' would have little or no difficulty recognising the meaning of (B) 'muli bwanji?'

As evidence of the validity of their index of 'familiarity', the authors report that children whose teachers identified them as L1 speakers of the language of instruction scored significantly higher on average (90.75 per cent) on the test than children identified as L2 speakers (30.18 per cent). The average familiarity scores of children in the schools sampled in Mongu ranged from 90 to 100 per cent, in the Chipata schools from 14 to 55 per cent, and in the Lusaka schools from 6 to 9 per cent. And it is to these differences in average familiarity with the medium of instruction that the authors attribute the significant variations they found in average reading competency scores in Grade 2. But note that this elicitation of the child's language preference was done in a school testing context. So it may simply index the child's comfort with the language of instruction at school, rather than truly representing the child's home language or her language of play.

Table 3.4 presents a sample of the 20 items listed by Tambulukani and Bus (2012: Table 1, 148) for the test of familiarity used in Mongu. The authors remark that 'from the 20 listed words only makonde [bananas] is the same word in Lozi and Mbunda, all other words differ. A similar list was available for Nyanja and Town Nyanja.' Table 3.4(b) presents a sample of items from the latter list,[6] where it is apparent that at least the first three items are actually very similar across the two speech varieties.

The relation between linguistic similarity and mutual intelligibility is complex. What matters for a child's growth in communicative competence is not only structural similarity of the target variety to the one the child uses most often at home, but also exposure in the contexts of play and other everyday interactions with people outside the family, and the frequency and quality of opportunities to learn the variety, at school or in other structured contexts.

The interplay among these factors is likely to be quite different across particular sociolinguistic settings. In many Lusaka schools, for instance, Grade 1 children are likely to be exposed to a much wider range of variation in the speech they hear than in Chipata schools. Simply coding the percentage of children whose families claim to speak ciCewa as L1 obscures the fact that 90 per cent or more of the

*Table 3.4* Terms produced by children in response to pictures on the Familiar Language Test (Tambulukani and Bus, 2012)

(a) Silozi score sheet *(5 of the 20 items)* used in Mongu

| Lozi | Mbunda | English |
| --- | --- | --- |
| batu | banu | people |
| banana | banike | children |
| mezi | mema | water |
| nuka | ndonga | river |
| makonde | makonde | bananas |

(b) Cinyanja score sheet *(5 of the 20 items)* used in Lusaka and Chipata

| Cicewa | Cinyanja | English |
| --- | --- | --- |
| anthu | wanthu | people |
| ana | wana | children |
| madzi | manzi | water |
| mtsinje | kamana | river |
| nthoci | vikonde | bananas |

non-L1-Chewa-speaking families in Chipata speak as L1 a variety that falls within the 'Nyanja language group', whereas in a Lusaka school the non-L1-Chewa-speaking families typically include speakers of Bemba, Tonga and Lozi – varieties that are far less mutually intelligible with Nyanja than most of the other speech varieties prevalent in Chipata.

The situation in Mongu, the third district sampled by Tambulukani and Bus (2012), was quite different from Chipata. Mbunda, which was classified by Kashoki and Mann (1978) in Group E together with Luvale, Lucazi and Cokwe, was reported in the 2000 census as ethnic group (mother tongue) by 13.8 per cent of those in Mongu District, and as predominant language of communication by 6.0 per cent.[7] Thus less than half of the Mongu residents who identified as Mbunda by tribe reported the Mbunda language as their predominant language of communication. According to Kashoki and Mann's (1978) criterion, Lozi and Mbunda shared only 15 per cent of core vocabulary, whereas Cewa shared between 52 and 61 per cent of core vocabulary with the various language varieties widely spoken in Chipata: Ngoni, Nsenga, Kunda, Senga and Tumbuka. On the other hand, claims to bilingual fluency are very high among the Mbunda residents of Mongu District, a sociolinguistic phenomenon acknowledged by Tambulukani and Bus as follows: 'In four schools in Mongu, pupils were familiar with Lozi – the language of instruction: They preferred Lozi to Mbunda when they named details in a picture and teachers classified them as Lozi users' (Tambulukani and Bus, 2012: 155).

Tambulukani and Bus (2012: 156) concluded that their

> findings contradict the assumption that Zambian children easily switch from a vernacular language to the official local Zambian language that is used for instruction. Even though there is some overlap between pupils' vocabularies and the language of instruction in most Chipata schools, children experience serious problems with reading as the low scores of Chipata pupils on the reading tests indicate....

According to their interpretation, 'despite the language medium policy, most Zambian children are not instructed in their most familiar language' (p. 158). But this conclusion ignores the complexity both of what constitutes a language as distinct from a dialect and of how to assess a child's familiarity with a given speech variety. If we include the possibility that Nyanja and Chewa are two dialects of the same language, as affirmed by the authors of the Zambia Language Survey (Ohannessian and Kashoki, 1978) and of four successive national censuses of population (CSO, no date, 1995, 2003), then most of the children they studied in Chipata schools were, in fact, receiving instruction 'in their most familiar language', albeit in a dialect of that language that differed in varying degrees from the dialect prevalent in their homes. Moreover, if the authors' assessment of familiarity had probed the children's competence across a wider range of communicative contexts and included a more dynamic focus on how easily the children could adapt to the medium of instruction, they might well have concluded that it was an appropriate one for the majority of learners enrolled in Chipata schools.

## Discussion and conclusions

The research questions initially posed by each of the two studies of young Zambian children's communicative competence reviewed above would be easily applicable to the situation of an immigrant minority group in a predominantly monolingual, highly literate, industrialised society with a language that is very distinct from that of the (host) majority. But, as I have shown, the sociolinguistic conditions of Zambian society are very different. Consequently two specific methodological hazards arose: superficial categorisation (for example, this child is an L1 speaker of language X), and assuming equivalence (for example, a given linguistic diversity index has the same meaning across contexts). A young child growing up in Zambia in this period of history is likely to encounter multiple strands of language before entering formal school or early childhood care and educational services. The forms in which those strands of language are presented will seldom be explicitly labelled as an utterance in a particular language or dialect. Indeed, the following reminiscence by a multilingual African university graduate may well represent the norm for many younger children attending school in urban areas: 'The various languages we brought from our homes became like one language which we used to communicate in the classroom, but also took home with us and spoke with our siblings' (Mwanza Nakawala Maumbi, personal communication, November 2012).

Banda and Bellonjengele (2010: 107) have described 'socially transforming multilingual discourses which draw on rural and urban indigenous Zambian languages, (Zambian) English and mixed codes', and argued that 'current accounts of English use in Africa fail to account for Africans' experiences and the realities around the use of language' (p. 109). They highlight 'the creative agency that goes into the construction of multilingual discourses in late modern Africa' (p. 109), and warn that the application in so-called 'peripheral' speech communities of norms of language and discourse derived from monolingual speech communities 'at the centre' can lead to a situation where 'what should be seen as examples of multilingual competencies is then seen as monolingual [English] incompetence' (p. 118).

Even the functional analysis of code-switching may inadvertently tend to legitimise the ideological presumptions that monolingualism is normal and that a standard form of each language is essential. To posit a need to explain why an individual alternates between two or more speech varieties implies that those varieties exist in the speaker's repertoire as distinct elements. But for some members of multilingual speech communities, multilingual talk may represent 'one code in its own right' (Meeuwis and Blommaert, 1998). In Zambia, this appears to be the case for both Town Nyanja and Town Bemba, also known as iciKopabeluti, the 'language of the Copperbelt'. In such contexts, 'the insistence on two distinct languages as the frame of reference for this form of speech is not helpful in terms of interpreting it'

(Bailey, 2007: 265). By focusing the assessment of competence on one speech variety at a time, the methods used by Fink et al. (2012) and by Tambulukani and Bus (2012) generated puzzles that do not match the social practices of contemporary Zambian speech communities; for example,

- How many of the pupils in this classroom are receiving instruction in their mother tongue?
- Is it fair to regard the ciCewa of the school curriculum as a familiar language for Chipata-resident children of Ngoni families?

If communicative competence is the psychological function that education seeks to promote, and competence in this community requires flexible integration of several codes, assessment methods should be designed to capture that integrated pattern of discourse.

Teachers trained in a conventional, monoglossic tradition may perceive this approach to assessment as incompatible with their instructional objectives. But if initial literacy is to be taught effectively to children enrolled in multilingual, multidialectal classrooms, it seems essential to respect their prevailing patterns of communication. Reflecting on the challenge this poses for pedagogy, Kramsch (2012) has proposed a search for new criteria of authenticity for the multilingual speaker, to replace the traditional reliance of applied linguistics on the authority of the monolingual native speaker. She distinguishes two broad approaches to this task: a modernist approach that seeks to 'empower learners to adopt more satisfactory identities as members of inclusive speech communities' (Kramsch, 2012: 118), and a postmodernist one that treats all the languages of a given multilingual speech repertoire 'as available semiotic resources, not as structural rules or self-enclosed systems' (Kramsch, 2012: 122), paying explicit attention to registers, genres and indexicality, and bringing back translation into the resources for instruction.

Such changes of perspective on communicative competence will require extensive debate before they gain acceptance in the mainstream of educational practice. But they deserve attention, not only because they afford a theoretical way of addressing multilingual patterns of discourse, but also because celebrating the multilingual character of contemporary Zambian speech communities is likely to support the achievement of a broader goal for progressive educational policy: unification of separated ethnocultural groups around the superordinate goal of peaceful national coexistence.

# Notes

1. In everyday discourse a dialect is often conceived as one of several cognate varieties of speech, all subordinate to a single superordinate language. But this overlooks the historical and political processes through which one particular variety becomes the superordinate standard (Haugen, 1966). In this chapter therefore the term 'dialect' is used to connote a popular perception, rather than a technical one,
2. Later census reports have slightly varied these groupings, so that, for instance, Nsenga and Kunda have been counted as dialectal varieties of the 'Nyanja group' (labelled J), rather than the Group I and Group A respectively of Kashoki and Mann's taxonomy (see Kashoki and Mann, 1978: 57, Table 2.4, and p. 60, Diagram 2.2).
3. Serpell (unpublished data, 1996).
4. Following the recommendations of Banda et al. (2008), I have adopted the orthographic convention of capitalizing the initial letter of the root of Bantu language names, preceded by the appropriate prefix. However, when citing other published documents I have adhered to the spelling convention preferred by the cited authors.
5. Whereas the correspondence between two varieties of Nsenga (Petauke and Mpezeni) was 91 per cent, that between Tumbuka and Senga was 73 per cent, and Kunda corresponded 77 per cent with Nsenga and 63 per cent with Senga.
6. I am grateful to Mr Geoffrey Tambulukani for making this list available to me for analysis.
7. Whereas less than 1 per cent of respondents in Mongu District cited Luvale, Lucazi or Cokwe as their predominant language.

# References

Bailey, B. (2007). Heteroglossia and boundaries. In M. Heller (ed.), *Bilingualism: a social approach* (pp. 257–74). Basingstoke, UK: Palgrave Macmillan.

Banda, F. (2009). Critical perspectives on language planning and policy in Africa: accounting for the notion of multilingualism. *Stellenbosch Papers in Linguistics PLUS*, 38: 1–11.

Banda, F. (2012). Towards postcolonial orthographic design: speaking and writing across linguistic, ethnic and national boundaries in Southern Africa'. In M. N. Maumbi and R. Serpell (eds), *Consultative workshop on harmonisation of orthographies for Zambian languages*. Lusaka: University of Zambia, CAPOLSA.

Banda, F. and Bellononjengele, O. (2010). Style, repertoire and identities in Zambian multilingual discourse. *Journal of Multicultural Discourses*, 5(2): 107–19.

Banda, F., Mtenje, A., Miti L., Chanda, V., Kamwendo, G., Ngunga, A., Liphola, M., Manuel, C., Sitoe, B., Simango, S. and Nkolola, M. W. (2008). *A unified standard orthography for southcentral African languages (Malawi, Mozambique and Zambia)*, 2nd rev. edn. Cape Town, South Africa: Centre for Advanced Studies of African Society (Monograph Series No. 229).

Bialystok, E., Craik, F. I. M., Green, D. W. and Gollan, T. H. (2009). Bilingual minds. *Psychological Science in the Public Interest*, 10(3): 89–129.

Brelsford, W. V. (1956). *The tribes of Northern Rhodesia*. Lusaka: Government Printer.

Brelsford, W. V. (1965). *The tribes of Zambia*. Lusaka: Government Printer.

Bruner, J. S. (1983). *Child's talk: learning to use language*. Oxford: Oxford University Press.

CSO (Central Statistical Office) (1973). *Census of population and housing 1969: final report*, Vol. I *Total Zambia*. Lusaka: Government Printer.

CSO (Central Statistical Office) (no date). *Zambia 1980 census of population and housing – analytical report*, Vol. II. Lusaka: Government Printer.

CSO (Central Statistical Office) (1995). *Census of population, housing and agriculture 1990*.

CSO (Central Statistical Office) (2003). *Zambia 2000 census of population and housing, Zambia analytical report*, Vol. 10. Lusaka: Government Printer.

CSO (Central Statistical Office) (2012). 2010 *Census of population and housing preliminary report*. Lusaka: Government Printer.

Cummins, J. (2001). Bilingual children's mother tongue: why is it important for education? *SPROG FORUM*, 19: 15–20.

Dunn, L. M. and Dunn, L. M. (1997). *Peabody Picture Vocabulary Test III*. Circle Pines, Minn.: American Guidance Service.

Ferguson, C. A. (1959). Diglossia. *Word*, 15: 325–40.

Fink, G. (2010). Pilot evidence from the Zambian Child Development Test. Poster presented at the 21st Biennial International Congress of the International Society for the Study of Behavioural Development (ISSBD). Lusaka, Zambia: 18–22 July 2010.

Fink, G., Matafwali, B., Moucheraud, C. and Zuilkowski, S. S. (2012). *The Zambian Early Childhood Development Project – 2010 assessment final report*. (retrieved November 2012 from http://developingchild.harvard.edu/activities/global_initiative/zambian_project/)

Fishman, J. A. (1967). Bilingualism with and without diglossia; diglossia with and without bilingualism. *Journal of Social Issues*, 23: 29–38.

Gregory, M. (1967). Aspects of varieties differentiation. *Journal of Linguistics*, 3: 177–98.

Grigorenko, E. L. and Sternberg, R. J. (1998). Dynamic testing. *Psychological Bulletin*, 124: 75–111.

Gumperz, J. J and Hymes, D. (eds) (1964). The ethnography of communication. *American Anthropologist*, 66 (6): part 02.

Halliday M. A. K. (1975). *Learning how to mean*. London: Edward Arnold.

Harkess, S. and Super, C. (1977). Why African children are so hard to test. *Annals of the New York Academy of Sciences*, 285: 326–31.

Haugen, E. (1966). Language, dialect, nation. *American Anthropologist*, 68(4): 922–35.

Heugh, K. (2000). The case against bilingual and multilingual education in South Africa. PRAESA Occasional Papers 6. Cape Town: University of Cape Town.

Jere-Folotiya, J., Chansa-Kabali, T., Munachaka, J., Sampa, F., Yalukanda, C., Westerholm, J., Serpell, R. and Lyytinen, H. (2014). The effect of using a mobile literacy game to improve literacy levels of grade one learners in Zambian schools. *Educational Technology Research and Development*, 62: 417–32.

Kapwepwe, S. (1970). Closing address by his Honour the Vice President, the Hon. Simon Kapwepwe, in *Report on First National Education Conference* [held at Evelyn Hone College of Further Education, Lusaka, 30 Sept. – 2 Oct. 1969]. Lusaka Ministry of Education.

Kashoki, M. E. (1972). Town Bemba: a sketch of its main characteristics. *African Social Research*, 13: 161–86.

Kashoki, M. E. (1978a). The language situation in Zambia. In S. I. Ohannessian and M. E. Kashoki (eds), *Language in Zambia* (pp. 9–46). London: International African Institute.

Kashoki, M. E. (1978b). Between-language communication in Zambia. In S. I. Ohannessian and M. E. Kashoki (eds) *Language in Zambia* (pp. 123–43). London: International African Institute.

Kashoki, M. E. and Mann, M. (1978). A general sketch of the Bantu languages of Zambia. In S. I. Ohannessian and M. E. Kashoki (eds) *Language in Zambia* (pp. 47–100). London: International African Institute.

Kramsch, C. (2012). Authenticity and legitimacy in multilingual SLA. *Critical Multilingualism Studies*, 1 (1): 107–128.

LeVine, R. A., LeVine, S., Schnell-Anzola, B., Rowe, M. and Dexter, E. (2012). *Literacy and mothering: how women's schooling changes the lives of the world's children.* New York, USA: Oxford University Press.

McAdam, B. (1978). The New Zambia Primary Course. In S. I. Ohannessian and M. E. Kashoki (eds) *Language in Zambia* (pp. 329–53). London: International African Institute.

Marfo, K. (2011). Envisioning an African child development field. *Child Development Perspectives*, 5 (2): 140–7.

Matafwali, B. (2010). The relationship between oral language and early literacy development: case of Zambian languages and English. Lusaka, Zambia: University of Zambia unpublished PhD dissertation.

Meeuwis, M. and Blommaert, J. (1998). A monolectal view of code-switching: layered code-switching among Zairians in Belgium. In P. Auer (ed.), *Code-switching in conversation: language, interaction and identity* (pp. 76–98). London and New York: Routledge.

Ministry of Education (1996). *Educating Our Future.* Lusaka: Government Printer.

Mohanty, A. K. and Perregaux, C. (1997). Language acquisition and bilingualism. In J. W. Berry, P. R. Dasen and T. M. Saraswathi (eds) *Handbook of Cross-Cultural Psychology* (2nd edn), Volume 2 (pp. 217–53). Boston, Mass.: Allyn & Bacon.

Mwanakatwe, J. M. (1968). *The growth of education in Zambia since Independence.* Lusaka: Oxford University Press.

Myers-Scotton, C. (1993). *Social motivations for codeswitching: evidence from Africa.* Oxford: Oxford University Press.

Mytton, G. (1974). *Listening, looking and learning: report on a national mass media audience survey in Zambia (1970–73).* Lusaka: University of Zambia Institute for African Studies.

Ohannessian, S. (1978). Historical background. In S. Ohannessian and M. E. Kashoki (eds), *Language in Zambia* (pp. 271–85). London: International African Institute.

Ohannessian, S. and Kashoki, M. E. (eds) (1978). *Language in Zambia.* London: International African Institute.

Sampa, F. K. (2005). *Zambia's Primary Reading Program (PRP): improving access and quality education in basic schools.* ADEA: African Experiences – Country Case Studies, No. 4 (ISBN No. 92-9178-055-3). Paris: Association for Development of Education in Africa (ADEA), Paris, 2005 (retrieved August 2012 from http://www.adeanet.org/pubadea/publications/pdf/04_zambia_en.pdf )

Schleppegrell, M. J. (2001). Linguistic features of the language of schooling. *Linguistics and Education*, 12(4): 431–59.

Serpell, R. (1978). Some developments in Zambia since 1971. In S. Ohannessian and M. E. Kashoki (eds), *Language in Zambia* (pp. 424–47). London: International African Institute.

Serpell, R. (1980). Linguistic flexibility in urban Zambian children. *Annals of the New York Academy of Sciences,* 345 (Studies in Child Language and Multilingualism, edited by V. Teller and S. J. White): 97–119.

Serpell, R. and Deregowski, J. B. (1980). The skill of pictorial perception: an interpretation of crosscultural evidence. *International Journal of Psychology*, 15: 145–80.

Serpell, R. and Haynes, B. (2004). The cultural practice of intelligence testing: problems of international export. In R. J. Sternberg and E. Grigorenko (eds), *Culture and competence: contexts of life success* (pp. 163–85). Washington, DC: American Psychological Association.

Snow, C. E. (1994). Enhancing literacy development: programs and research perspectives. In D. Dickinson (ed.), *Bridges to literacy: children, families and schools* (pp. 267–72). Cambridge, Mass.: Blackwell.

Spitulnik, D. (1998). The language of the city: Town Bemba as urban hybridity. *Journal of Linguistic Anthropology*, 8 (1): 30–59.

Tambulukani, G. and Bus, A. G. (2012). Linguistic diversity: a contributory factor to reading problems in Zambian schools. *Applied Linguistics*, 33 (2): 141–60.

Tambulukani, G., Sama, F., Musuku, R. and Linehan, S. (2001). Reading in Zambia – a quiet revolution through the Primary Reading Program. In S. Manaka (ed.), *Proceedings of the 1st Pan-African Conference on Reading for All* (pp. 70–88). International Reading Association.

Underwood, C., Serlemitsos, E. T., Nkhata, G. and Macwang'i, M. (2003). *Language uses and reading comprehension among literate Zambians: findings from a 2002 survey.* Lusaka: Central Board of Health/USAID/ZIHP and Boston: Center for International Health, School of Public Health, Boston University (limited circulation report).

Underwood, C., Serlemitsos, E. T. and Macwang'i M. (2007). Health communication in multilingual contexts: a study of reading preferences, practices and proficiencies among literate adults in Zambia. *Journal of Health Communication*, 12 (4): 317–37.

UNESCO (2012). UNESCO promotes linguistic diversity and multilingualism. (retrieved November 2012 from http://www.unesco.org/new/en/culture/themes/cultural-diversity/languages-and-multilingualism/)

Van de Vijver, F. J. R. and Poortinga, Y. H. (1997). Towards an integrated analysis of bias in cross-cultural assessment. *European Journal of Psychological Assessment*, 13: 29–37.

Vygotsky, L. S. (1978). *Mind in society: the development of higher psychological processes* (edited by M. Cole, V. John-Steiner, S. Scribner and E. Souberman). Cambridge: Harvard University Press.

Williams, E. (1998). Investigating bilingual literacy. Evidence from Malawi and Zambia. *Education Research Paper*, 24: 1–130 (retrieved 10 June 2014 from http://r4d.dfid.gov.uk/pdf/outputs/misc_education/paper24.pdf)

# 4
# Moving between *Ekasi*[1] and the Suburbs: the Mobility of Linguistic Resources in a South African De(re)segregated School

*Carolyn McKinney*

## Introduction

Recent analyses of youth culture, and of popular culture more broadly, emphasise mobility – of people across global spaces and of global cultural flows. Yet for most youth, physical movement across national boundaries is relatively restricted. In South Africa, there are of course large internal flows of people between urban and rural areas, and significant for the focus of this chapter, a number of youth who travel between their homes in the townships on city peripheries, or inner-city areas, and the previously 'White' suburbs in pursuit of quality schooling (Fataar, 2009; Soudien, 2004). Historically 'White', now desegregated suburban schools in South African cities are important spaces for the production of an expanding 'Black' middle class (Soudien, 2004) as well as for scrutiny of a society in transition. This chapter examines the discursive practices of girls attending a suburban school in the urban metropolis of Johannesburg, South Africa, where 'Black' learners have replaced 'White' learners, i.e. a resegregated school (Orfield, 2004). It is informed by the view that exploration of complex everyday language practices offers us insights into changing cultural practices as well as into the different kinds of identity work performed by the girls.

We have come some way since Roger Hewitt's (2003) indictment of the treatment of the language/identity relationship in sociolinguistics. A central contribution of Hewitt's, and following this Rampton's work (1995, 2006), has been to show empirically the 'instability' of ethnicity 'and its impure language' (Hewitt, 2003: 197). An acknowledgement of the complex and often tenuous threads between language, 'race'[2]/ethnicity and class underlies my analysis of the language practices of the girls who are moving back and forth between the more working-class and 'Black' environments of the townships where they live and the middle-class previously 'White' suburb where they go to school. In this chapter, I focus on how the girls draw on the range of language resources in their repertoires (Blommaert and Backus, 2011) and in particular on what happens to these resources as they travel to and are deployed in the school context. Drawing on the notion of *polycentricity* (Blommaert, 2010), I pose the micro-question of what centres are visible in the girls' interactions and what different centres they are orienting to. At the more macro-level, I ask the question of what these data on girls' heteroglossic language practices in a multilingual African post-colonial context might add to our understanding of recent discussions around the complexity of 'mixed' or hybrid language practices as captured in notions such as polylanguaging (Jorgensøn, 2008).

The analysis in this chapter is informed by a number of recent developments in sociolinguistic research and theory: the interrogation of the ideology of languages as stable, bounded entities (Blommaert, 1996; Makoni, 2003; Makoni and Pennycook, 2006; Jorgensøn, 2008; Blommaert and Rampton, 2011); the challenges in describing mixed language practices in multilingual environments (Creese and Blackledge, 2010; Jorgensøn, 2008; Otsuji and Pennycook, 2010); and the complexity of relationships between language and identity (Hewitt, 2003; Cameron, 1997; Rampton, 2006). I move on now to a brief discussion of each of these insights.

## Ideologies of language

There have been a number of comprehensive discussions of the ideology of languages as discrete, stable, bounded entities (e.g. Blommaert, 2006; Heller, 2007; Makoni and Pennycook, 2006), an ideology as much sustained by linguistic research as held in popular views on language (Blommaert, 2006). Analytically I find myself inevitably, albeit uncomfortably, falling into the trap of sustaining this ideology: the urge to categorise and code as part of a sense-making process means that it is hard to resist the identification of languages used in interaction, especially since it can be relatively straightforward to identify prototypical examples of the use of named languages. However, such naming may or may not resonate with the language users or 'languagers' and it is clear that it becomes much harder to do when faced with the evidence of language use at the boundaries. The recognition that languages are not distinct bounded systems also has important repercussions for our understanding of what it means to 'know' a language (Jorgensøn, 2008; Blommaert and Backus, 2011). As Jorgensøn argues,

> Since we can not determine with certainty where one language ends and the other one begins, it follows that we can not always be sure to be able to count languages. We can not determine exactly which languages an individual knows, and consequently we can not tell how many languages this person knows. We can, however, observe that there is a wide spectrum of variation available to any individual, and we can also observe that this spectrum is different from person to person. (2008: 165)

Accounting for this 'wide spectrum of variation' has led to a proliferation of terms in recent studies of hybrid language practices in multilingual urban settings (Creese and Blackledge, 2010; Jorgensøn, 2008; Jorgensøn et al., 2011; Otsuji and Pennycook, 2010) as indexed by the recent thematic session at the Sociolinguistic Symposium 19 titled 'Prefixing lingualism: Trans, poly, metro or zero?' (in Hüning and Reich, 2012). While there is no consensus on defining code-switching, broad definitions such as that offered by McCormick (2001: 447) would draw more agreement than most: 'the term "code-switching" refers to the juxtaposition of elements from two (or more) languages or dialects'. But even a broad definition such as this inevitably makes use of the notion of discrete, bounded languages. Garcia attempts to overcome this problem in her definition of the term 'translanguaging' as: 'the act performed by bilinguals of accessing different linguistic features or various modes of what are *described as autonomous languages*' (2009: 141, my emphasis). While distancing herself from the notion of autonomous languages, Garcia's definition is still necessarily informed by it. How might we redefine bilingualism without counting language resources? Jorgensøn and others have used the term 'polylanguaging' to refer to 'the use of resources associated with different "languages" even when the speaker knows very little of these' (Jorgensøn et al., 2011: 27), which is reminiscent of, but apparently broader than, Rampton's notion of crossing: 'the use of language varieties associated with social or ethnic groups that the speaker does not normally "belong" to' involving speakers in moving 'across ethnic (or social) boundaries' (1995: 507). And Otsuji and Pennycook (2010) introduce the term 'metrolingualism' to describe language practices that are 'a product of modern and often urban interaction, describing the ways in which people of different and mixed backgrounds use, play with and negotiate identities through language' (p. 240). All of these terms are useful in foregrounding aspects of hybridity and identity work in current urban language practices. However, when deployed analytically they do not completely escape the relationship (however uneasy) with the ideology of discrete or autonomous languages.

## Language, ethnicity and identity

Our understanding of the complexity of the relationship between language and identity has benefited from the increasing interest in documenting urban language practices and in understanding the ways in which such practices index processes of social change as well as the conviviality of everyday life (Blommaert and Rampton, 2011). That people draw on the full range of their linguistic repertoires to perform different 'acts of identity' (Le Page and Tabouret Keller, 1985 in Mesthrie and Tabouret Keller, 2001) has been acknowledged for some time. However, rather than revealing pre-existing identities, there is now a body of research that focuses on how different kinds of identities are constructed and performed through interaction (Cameron, 1997; Rampton, 2006). It is also acknowledged that people often espouse identifications with fixed notions of languages despite their own hybrid language practices (McKinney, 2007; Nongogo, 2007). In South Africa with its apartheid history of 'ethnicity [imposed] from above' (Pieterse, 1992 in Zegeye, 2001: 3) and of the use of discrete named languages as a divide and rule strategy for 'Black' people, language practices are a particularly 'sensitive index of social changes, and what is more, of changes still in the process of growth' (Voloshinov, 1986: 19).

That English is a language of aspiration among young people in South Africa is widely recognised and reported in sociolinguistic research (De Klerk, 2000a, b; Kamwangamalu, 2003; Kapp, 2004; Rudwick, 2004). However, young people's orientations to different *varieties* of English is relatively unexplored, as are the changing language practices of 'Black' youth attending previously 'White' schools. Recent research in this area (McKinney, 2007, 2013; Mesthrie, 2010) points to the prestige attached to the ethnolinguistic repertoires (Benor, 2010) of 'White' speakers of English. Previously I have argued that the historical racial labelling of varieties of English in South Africa (ethnolects) such as 'White' South African English (WSAE), coloured English, South African Indian English and 'Black' South African English (BSAE) (e.g. Lass, 2002; Mesthrie, 2004; van Rooy, 2004) contributes, albeit unwittingly, to the essentialist (re)construction of 'race' as such labels construct the false impression that all people of the same 'race' speak English in the same way. We are caught here by the dilemma of how to describe variation in language use that developed during the time of apartheid racial segregation without essentialising 'race' or indeed ignoring other salient features of variation aside from 'race'. Mesthrie's (2010) research on the deracialisation of the GOOSE vowel in South African English which shows 'Black' middle-class females who attend/ed previously 'White' schools adapting to the norm of fronting the GOOSE vowel, a 'prestige White middle-class norm' (p. 3), provides a welcome contribution to our understanding of changing language/'race' relationships. In a context of upward social mobility where both aspirants and members of the 'Black' African middle class have moved from township schooling to private and previously 'White' schools in the suburbs, Mesthrie (2010: 13) has proposed the term *crossing over* 'as the most appropriate sociolinguistic term for the habitual use (i.e. appropriation) of an accent that is not traditionally associated with people of one's presumed ethnicity'. Mesthrie argues that crossing over differs from crossing (Rampton, 1995) in that it is not a (playful) stylistic or strategic choice but rather 'reflects the vernacular usage of the individual, and is therefore a crucial ingredient in issues pertaining to social, cultural and identity change' (Mesthrie, 2010: 13). However, both crossing and crossing over rely on the notion of identifiable ethnic boundaries.

Despite practices such as 'crossing' and 'crossing over' that destabilise the notion of racialised varieties, my research data show that *assumptions* about speakers' language use are still strongly racialised and the prestige attached to 'White' ethnolinguistic repertoires remains (see McKinney, 2007; Mesthrie, 2010). Significantly, such prestige contributes to constituting the ongoing normativity of whiteness, and 'othering' (at times stigmatisation) of blackness in desegregated suburban schools (McKinney, 2010, 2011, 2013). I move now to sketch the particular context of the school which was the research site for this chapter, as well as to outline the methodological approach.

## The research site and methodology

Data on girls' language practices and discourses were collected over two school terms at a school situated to the north-east of central Johannesburg which accommodates about 750 learners. While previously a 'White' English medium of instruction school catering for predominantly Jewish girls, the school now accommodates 'Black' girls who live mainly in townships and the inner city, and most of whom are from working-class backgrounds, with less than half paying the annual school fees which were R5500[3] at the time of data collection (2005). Learners are predominantly 'Black' African with about 25 Indian and 'coloured' learners and about two or three 'White' learners in the school, thus fitting the description of a resegregated school (Orfield, 2004). My focus was on two classes of Grade 10 girls (15–16 years old). Most of these learners (57/69) reported linguistic repertoires of between three and seven named languages. Learners typically had either a Sotho or Nguni[4] language as their home language with English as an additional language. The school began desegregating in 1991 and remains English medium. In 1991, its enrolment was down to 385 learners. To a great extent, opening its doors to 'Black' learners has ensured the survival of the school, situated in an area in which the population is ageing and which accommodates another highly elite, private girls' school. Changes in the 'racial' demographic in staffing were less dramatic: at the time of fieldwork, the principal, a 'White' woman, had been at the school for more than 30 years, while the more recently appointed deputy head was an Indian woman. The teaching staff were majority 'White' women (22/34) with a few 'White' men, while 'Black' staff (3 'Black' African, 6 Indian and 3 'coloured' teachers) made up the minority.

The girls' use of English presented a somewhat mixed picture, with almost all of the girls in the top streamed class (10X) habitually using an ethnolinguistic repertoire associated with 'White' South African Englishes in the classroom and in group interviews – in Mesthrie's terms having 'crossed over' – with a wider range of Englishes in the lower streamed class (10Y) and more variation in the use of phonological features associated with the repertoires of 'White' and 'Black' Englishes.

The research design drew on traditions of school ethnography from sociology of education (Hey, 1997; Youdell, 2003, 2004), and particularly ethnography of communication (Duff, 2002; Rampton, 1995, 2006).[5] Data collection tools included observation (captured in field notes and through selected video recording), group interviews with self-selected learners (captured in audio recordings), limited recording of naturally occurring talk captured by individual learners wearing a digital recorder and the completion of learner surveys and language network diagrams. In this chapter I focus on a few telling moments of language use from different sites of the school, including inside the formal classroom, outside on the school grounds, and in interview discussion. Data come from the two classes I followed on different days of the week over two terms, one of which was streamed as the top achieving academic class and the other as the significantly lower achieving, second from the bottom class (there were five Grade 10 classes of around 36 learners).

## Data analysis: the mobility of linguistic resources in Girls' School

The first two data extracts presented below provide insight into the girls' orientations to English and are discussed as context for the girls' language practices. Both are taken from interviews, extract 1 from a group interview with girls in the top streamed class (10X) and extract 2 from a discussion with the lower streamed class (10Y). Extract 1 is a response to my question about what the girls felt distinguished their school from schools in the township.

> ### Extract 1 – 'township English'
> You know I think it's the level of English. Their [township schools'] English is not that brilliant, it's not that high, but then here it's different. From when you listen to a township person like speaking English and then a person from [Girls' school] you can hear. (Group interview 4, 10X, 30 May 2005, p. 10)

Significant for our understanding of young people's awareness of the differently valued Englishes around them is the notion that the school itself produces or provides access to a prestige variety of English. While a generalisation of how young people in township schools use English, the girls are pointing to the fact that the variety of English typically accessible in township schools operates at a lower scale level (Blommaert, 2010) than their own. This is related to the fact that schools in the township offer English as an additional language while suburban schools such as their own follow the English home language curriculum and all school subjects are typically taught through the medium of English by highly proficient speakers of the language.

In a discussion about language use with girls in the lower streamed class, I specifically asked about learners' awareness of English used around them. Again there is an indication of what counts as prestige English and stigmatised English.

> ### Extract 2 – 'smooth perfect English'
> CM: (...) do you think that people speak English in different ways, or does everybody sound the same?

Thandi: I think people speak in different ways because of their backgrounds and where they come from and how they are taught to speak. Like, if let's say she's brought up by people, let's say White people and I'm brought up by Blacks who can't speak English, I'm going to speak that broken English and she's going to speak that smooth perfect English. So ... And your primary school ... the people who taught you at primary school, it depends on how they taught you. (Girls' school, 10Y whole class discussion, 16 May 2005, p. 5)
CM = Carolyn McKinney

Here 'White' people's English is depicted as 'that smooth perfect English', clearly illustrating the value attached to it and signalling the fluency of first language speakers. But in reference to being brought up by 'Black' people, the speaker is careful to qualify this with 'Blacks who can't speak English' as those who would produce 'broken English'. The learner does not thus imply that all 'Black' people speak English in this way. Taken together, the two extracts allude to the intersections of language practices and 'race' in ascribing prestige to the ethnolinguistic repertoire of whiteness.[6]

Moving now to interactional data, we can see the ways in which discourses on English as expressed above shape the girls' language practices. On several occasions I heard learners 'policing' each other's accents (i.e. the system of 'speech sounds' and 'their combinatorial possibilities', Simpson, 2001: 293) in a manner which identified phonological features of 'Black' varieties of English as incorrect. One brief example from field notes taken in a lesson with a group of girls from the lower streamed class illustrates this. One girl, Ayanda, is giving an oral presentation standing at the front of the class:

Extract 3 – policing accents
Ayanda: when I talk about fesh, feshion ['e'- 'ten', BSAE] (several girls laugh) oh fæshion ['fæsh'- 'hat', WSAE], Senton city [e - ten, BSAE]
Some girls: Senton, Senton
Teacher: Shh, be quiet
(T and T, 28 Feb. 2005) (**bold** = International phonetic alphabet, **IPA**)

In this example, several girls react to a peer's pronunciation of the words 'fashion' and 'Sandton' using phonological features associated with 'Black' Englishes. In the first instance, Ayanda's use of the phonological feature 'e' in the word 'fashion' generates laughter from several girls. She immediately shifts her pronunciation – oh fæshion – which

I interpret as Ayanda 'correcting' her pronunciation according to the expectations of her peers once their laughter has alerted her to her 'mistake'.

Ayanda's shift indexes her knowledge of the phonological features typical of the repertoires of both 'White' Englishes and 'Black' Englishes, however her initial pronunciation of the word 'feshion' indicates that she may be more comfortable with the phonology of 'Black' Englishes than that associated with ethnolinguistic repertoires of whiteness – using Mesthrie's term (2010), she has not (yet) 'crossed over' entirely. This interpretation is supported by the fact that shortly after repeating the word feshion as fæshion, Ayanda produces the form Senton, again generating censure from her peers, this time marked through their repetition of her perceived incorrect pronunciation. On this occasion the teacher reprimands the girls for interrupting Ayanda's presentation and possibly for their undermining of her. Ayanda is juggling different demands here, which may lead to her orienting to an inappropriate 'centre': delivering a competent oral presentation that demonstrates her knowledge of the topic (this was not an English lesson but a lesson in travel and tourism); communicating in the official language of the classroom, English, which is not her first language, and maintaining insider status with her peers in the class. Ironically it is Ayanda's peers who demand the use of phonological features categorised as 'White' South African English, not her teacher (herself an Afrikaans L1 speaker which influences her own accent in English) and thus it is her orientation to the 'centre' of her peer group that motivates the presenter to 'correct' her pronunciation of 'feshion' as 'fæshion'. While fluency in English is generally a highly valued resource, the labelling of learners who live in townships and attend suburban schools as coconuts (see McKinney, 2007; Rudwick, 2008), as well as research on the perspectives of township-schooled youth on peers' attending suburban schools' use of English, suggests that when orienting to the 'centre' of township-schooled youth, it would be the use of phonological features associated with the ethnolinguistic repertoires of whiteness that would be ridiculed.

In contrast to extract 3, extract 4 from field notes taken in the top streamed English class illustrates an unusual moment where codes other than ethnolinguistic repertoires of whiteness are deliberately adopted in the classroom. One learner, Zweli, was giving an oral presentation on George Orwell's *Animal Farm* again standing at the front of the class, and mistakenly replaced the word 'apples' with 'animals'. Her peer Catherine quickly corrected her by providing the word 'apples' using phonological features associated with 'White' Englishes. This was the exchange that followed:

**Extract 4 – playful switching**
Zweli: Oh, sorry 'apples'
Catherine:[laughing] *Hayi* too late (No tʊ -lɑ̄yĭt) / ʊ not fronted and not lengthened)

Zweli's self-correction here is met with laughter and a playful admonishment from her peer. My first analysis of Catherine's reply described it as a code-switch into Zulu (*Hayi* – no) followed by a switch back into a different variety of English – 'too late' pronounced using phonological features associated with 'Black' Englishes in tʊ -lɑ̄yĭt, with the shortened, back GOOSE vowel in 'too'. I have subsequently grappled with whether the phrase tʊ -lɑ̄yĭt here does indeed count as a switch to English or whether the entire reply might be better described as a switch to an urbanised vernacular Zulu (Makoni et al., 2007), especially given that Catherine's (and the majority of the other girls in the class) usual use of English in this setting draws on the phonological norms of 'White' South African Englishes and thus relative fronting of the GOOSE vowel in 'too' (Mesthrie, 2010). However, whether a switch to Zulu and 'Black' South African English or to urban Zulu alone, Catherine is clearly moving away from the linguistic norms expected both by the English teacher and her peers in this top streamed English lesson. I suggest in switching to features of a linguistic repertoire that is commonly only used in informal spaces at the school (at break times, in the corridor), Catherine softens her earlier move of taking up a teacher voice, or positioning herself as more powerful, to correct Zweli. Thus in this incident Catherine is simultaneously indicating her power to show Zweli up in front of the class by taking on the teacher's voice, as well as showing some solidarity with Zweli through the use of Zulu and possibly a different variety of English. Furthermore, language choice here enables her to distance her censure from that which would be produced by the English teacher (in English and using the ethnolinguistic repertoires of 'White' Englishes). Catherine's switch is significantly different from that of Ayanda in the previous extract 3, in that there is no doubt that it is a strategic shift rather than a result of incomplete mastery of the ethnolinguistic repertoire of 'White' Englishes. Catherine could be described as having 'crossed over' in her habitual use of English in the formal school context such that it is her playful use of another language/variety of English that becomes marked as 'crossing' as it is unexpected in the

English-only domain of the English class where norms are framed by whiteness (see McKinney, 2011). Despite habitually using phonological features associated with 'White' South African Englishes, Catherine shows that her linguistic repertoire includes competence in a different variety of English, as well as of Zulu.

Extracts 3 and 4 show how the use of phonological features associated with 'Black' South African Englishes, a generally stigmatised variety, shifts in the possible meanings indexed through momentary language practices in two different classroom contexts. In extract 3, Ayanda's use of 'feshion' and 'Senton' is perceived as not orienting appropriately to the prestige variety of English valued at the girls' school, thus the centre of the formal school domain, and which sets its learners apart from those who are schooled in the township (cf. extract 1). While in extract 4, deviation from this norm is valued, orienting to the centre of the 'underlife' (Gutierrez et al., 1995, after Goffman, 1961) of the classroom. As Jorgensøn points out: 'It is part of the social negotiations for which language is used that meanings and values may always be changed' (Jorgensøn, 2008: 167).

On a different occasion I observed the lower streamed class playing circle games outside on the field while they waited for their teacher to arrive with sports equipment. The games involved the girls dancing in a large circle while choral singing (with call and response as well as rhythmic repetitions) in a range of languages. Such games are very common in the playgrounds of primary schools in Soweto (Harrop-Allin, 2011a, b) and have been described as 'epitomis[ing] young urban township culture' (Harrop-Allin, 2011a: 2). In an interview with two girls from this class after school later that same day, I asked them to explain how the games worked. In the extract below, Grace is explaining to me (with some help from her friend who had described the previous game) how the game 'dulakadu' (**dʊlɘkaːdʊ**[7]) works.

**Extract 5.1**
CM: ok. Do you wanna do the other one? [do you want to explain the other circle game/song]
Grace: the second one is eh, is basically ...
Friend: ... has lots of things
Grace: ja. Ok.
Friend: (inaudible)
CM: yes
Grace: it's called 'Dulakadu' (**d ʊlɘkaːdʊ**)
CM: 'Dulakadu' (**d ʊlɘkaːdʊ**)

Grace: ja. What we do is we form a big circle and everybody sings and the person who is in the centre of that circle has to, you know, eh, dance.

CM: aha

Grace: ... everybody around the circle is gonna do, they gonna do what she's doing, the one in the circle.

CM: so, they have to copy the one in the centre?

Grace: ja

CM: the style?

Grace: ja. Then she is gonna go back and then the person she picks has to go in ...

CM: ok.

Grace: ... again and so on.

CM: ok. So, you keep picking different people to come in?

Grace: ja, ja

Friend: ... (inaudible) lots of things

Grace: lots

CM: and the, the, does, does 'Dulakadu' [dʊlɪka:dʊ] mean something or is it just like eh, 'du: ɘka:dʊ'? [du:lɪka:dʊ (u: fronted)] oh! Oh!

F: so, we do whatever they are doing.

CM: oh! Man! Do like I do [du: laik ai du:]

Grace: is it?

CM: ja

Grace: oh my gosh! I didn't know. I thought ...

Friend: ... do like I do [du: laik ai du:], do like I do [du: laik ai du:].

Grace: I don't, I don't know. Wow! I just only find out ... (laughs)

CM: how does the, how does the song go?

Friend: do like I do, ah, and then she says 'do like I do' and then the people say 'I do, I do'

Grace: oh! 'do like I do' (laughs)

Friend: 'do like I do', 'I do, I do'. And she does whatever and everyone does it.

In general, the circle games index the value of African languages in youth culture in the school, as also pointed to by the code-switch to Zulu in extract 4. In keeping with the previous game described which was characterised as using Zulu by the girls, I had named the game described above as 'dulakado' in my field notes and had assumed that it was a made-up word drawing on the phonological features of either Zulu or Sotho. Clearly the language of this song was not recognisable as English either to me or Grace (though her friend does seem aware of this). Arguably it is the linguistic ideology of the interviewer (myself) that transforms the term 'dulakado' into the recognisable English phrase 'do like I do' both for Grace and myself. It is my fronting of the GOOSE vowel when I repeat the beginning of the phrase 'du'/**dʊ** as **du:**, a phonological feature associated with ethnolinguistic repertoires of 'White' South African Englishes, together with the context of Grace's explanation, that they 'do' what the person in the centre of the circle does that makes the word become recognisable as the English word 'do' to me. I then convince Grace that this is the English phrase 'do like I do':

> CM: oh! Man! Do like I do [du: laik ai du:]
> Grace: is it?
> CM: ja [yes]

I have deliberated over describing Grace's use of the term 'dulakadu' in the interview, considering whether it should be named as English, and further whether it is as an example of polylanguaging (rather than codeswitching which implies some awareness of one's practice in switching across 'languages'). While Jorgensøn et al. gloss polylanguaging as 'the use of resources associated with different "languages" even when the speaker knows very little of these' (Jorgensøn et al., 2011: 27), they do not discuss whether the speaker is aware that the features used are associated with a particular named language. In a more elaborated explanation of the polylingual norm, Jorgensøn (2008) implies knowledge of language sources:

> Language users employ whatever linguistic features are at their disposal to achieve their communicative aims as best they can, regardless of how well they know the involved languages; this entails that the language users may know and use the fact that some of the features are perceived by some speakers as not belonging together. (Jorgensøn, 2008: 163)

In deciding how to describe Grace's initial use of the phrase 'dʊlika:dʊ', it is useful to consider Blommaert and Backus's discussion of language competence where they point out that 'we often learn bits of language(s) without being aware of it' (Blommaert and Backus, 2011: 15). We might describe Grace's use of the phrase 'dʊlika:dʊ' as unacknowledged *use* of bits of language, but she does not seem to display the 'recognising competence' which Blommaert and Backus (2011: 17) name as a fourth basic level of linguistic competence. It is questionable then whether this is a 'learned' bit of language; rather it seems to be a 'bit' of language that is appropriately deployed in a ritualistic way.

## Conclusion: polycentricity, hybrid language practices and language boundaries

At the beginning of this chapter I outlined two questions, firstly concerning what centres are visible in the girls' interactions and what different centres they are orienting to, and secondly what these data on girls' language practices in a multilingual African postcolonial context might add to recent discussions around the complexity of hybrid language practices. In answering these questions, I have largely drawn on data extracts which have troubled me in some way – in relation to identifying 'bits of language' as features of particular named languages or in my influence as researcher on the data produced. Thus along with other researchers whose data have stretched their available languages of description (e.g. Jorgensøn, 2008; Otsuji and Pennycook, 2010), I have been challenged in the process of identifying and describing the 'linguistic repertoires' (Blommaert and Backus, 2011) that the girls are drawing on in particular moments.

Though inhabiting an overwhelmingly English space where the prestige variety is that associated with the ethnolinguistic repertoire of whiteness and where languages other than English are not valued in official domains (see Makoe and McKinney, 2011), it is clear from their language practices that the girls are orienting to multiple centres in different moments. Orientation to teachers and peers who privilege 'White' South African English repertoires is visible in formal oral presentations, but so too is orientation to peers who are familiar with the ethnolinguistic repertoires of 'Black' South African Englishes and Nguni and Sotho languages. Unsurprisingly, what we see is the girls positioning each other in different moments both as members of a relatively elite state suburban school who are expected to produce a particular kind of English, and as peers in broader social networks that cross over their suburban schooling context and that of the townships where they live and which include others who are township schooled. Most of the participants in this study have not 'crossed over' fully in the sense that the majority of solidly middle-class 'Black' African youth in Mesthrie's (2010) study had.

In a discussion of nexus analysis, Scollon and Scollon pose the question 'Under what conditions and for whom is it meaningful to construct a boundary?' (Scollon and Scollon, 2007: 608). The process of analysis can be described as one of constructing and imposing boundaries; for example, my recontextualising the term 'dulakadu' as the English phrase 'do like I do' in interview discussion, redraws a boundary for Grace, constructing a boundary that did not exist for the language user herself prior to the interview discussion. Similarly, my decision to describe 'tʊ -lāyɪ̆t' as English drawing on phonological features of 'Black' South African Englishes rather than as continued use of urban-ised vernacular Zulu again indexes a dispute about the construction of boundaries. Perhaps like the Afrikaans words '*ja*' or '*trek*' that have made their way into South African English, it is both Zulu and English. As the language/bits of language travel and are recontextualised, they are transformed. Boundaries are not only recreated in different contexts but are increasingly difficult to impose in urban mixed language practices. Despite the range of attempts to move beyond the code-switching assumption of two or more clearly identifiable languages that the user can draw on as well as the ideology of autono-mous, boundaried languages, it seems difficult to let go of the desire to identify named languages and of how these language resources/bits of language travel with the girls as they move between their homes *ekasi* and their suburban school.

## Notes

1. 'Kasi' is a popular term for township, and is derived from *lokasie*, Afrikaans for 'location' which was an apartheid term for townships (*ekasi* – 'in the town-ship' or 'the township').
2. While I continue to use the apartheid (and post-apartheid, ironically, as used by Statistics South Africa and the Employment Equity Act) 'race' categories of 'White', 'Black', 'Indian' and 'coloured' in this chapter, I signal my anti-essentialist understanding of 'race' as a social construct by using quotation marks for the term. I further draw attention to my discomfort with the use of 'race' descriptors by placing them in quotation marks, e.g 'Black' and 'White'. For discussions of the term 'coloured' (under apartheid denoting one who was not 'White', 'Black' or 'Indian') see Erasmus (2001).
3. The school fees were R5500 (about USD550) per learner per annum and only 50 per cent of learners paid full or partial fees. Relatively low school fees for a sub-urban school were further cited as one of the reasons learners chose the school.
4. The Sotho language group includes three mutually intelligible languages, Tswana, Sotho and Pedi, while the Nguni language group includes the mutu-ally intelligible languages of Zulu, Xhosa, Swati and Ndebele. All of these are official languages in South Africa.
5. Data presented in this chapter are drawn from a larger research project explor-ing language, identity and processes of inclusion and exclusion in four deseg-regated suburban schools in Johannesburg.

6. Thandi's qualification also seems to echo that of de Klerk and Gough (2002) who in their discussion of 'Black' South African English (see also Makoni, 1999) signal the difficulty in conflating English produced by 'Black' learners of English who are not yet proficient with the phonological features and varieties of highly proficient speakers including many politicians and television and radio presenters.
7. Note: International phonetic alphabet (IPA) transcription bolded in extracts 5.1 and 5.2.

# References

Benor, Susan (2010). Ethnolinguistic repertoire: shifting the focus in language and ethnicity. *Journal of Sociolinguistics*, 14(2): 159–83.

Blommaert, J. (1996). Language planning as a discourse on language and society: the linguistic ideology of a scholarly tradition. *Language Problems and Language Planning*, 20 (3): 199–222.

Blommaert, J. (2006). Language ideology. In Keith Brown (editor-in-chief), *Encyclopedia of language and linguistics*, 2nd edn (Vol. 6, pp. 510–22). Oxford: Elsevier.

Blommaert, J. (2010). *The sociolinguistics of globalisation*. Cambridge: Cambridge University Press.

Blommaert, J. and Backus, A. (2011). Repertoires revisited: 'knowing language' in superdiversity. Working Papers in Urban Language and Literacies (WPULL) Paper 67. [http://www.kcl.ac.uk/innovation/groups/ldc/publications/working papers/67.pdf accessed 30 August 2012]

Blommaert, J. and Rampton, B. (2011). Language and superdiversity. *Diversities*, 13(2): 1–22. (Theme Issue: Language and Superdiversities.)

Cameron, Deborah (1997). Performing gender identity: young men's talk and the construction of heterosexual masculinity. In Sally Johnson and Ulrike Meinhof (eds), *Language and masculinity* (pp. 47–64). Oxford: Blackwell.

Creese, A. and Blackledge, A. (2010). Translanguaging in the bilingual classroom: a pedagogy for learning and teaching? *Modern Language Journal*, 94: 103–15.

De Klerk, V. (2000a). To be Xhosa or not to be Xhosa … that is the question. *Journal of Multilingual and Multicultural Development*, 21 (3): 198–215.

De Klerk, V. (2000b). Language shift in Grahamstown: a case study of selected Xhosa-speakers. *International Journal of the Sociology of Language*, 146: 87–110.

De Klerk, V. and Gough, D. (2002). Black South African English. In R. Mesthrie (ed.), *Language in South Africa*. Cambridge: Cambridge University Press.

Duff, P. (2002). The discursive co-construction of knowledge, identity, and difference: an ethnography of communication in the high school mainstream. *Applied Linguistics*, 28 (3): 289–322.

Erasmus, Z. (2001). *Coloured by history, shaped by place: perspectives on coloured identities in the Cape*. Cape Town: Kwela Books; London: Global.

Fataar, A. 2009. Schooling subjectivities across the post-apartheid city. *Africa Education Review*, 6(1): 1–18.

Garcia, Ofelia (2009). *Bilingual education in the 21st century*. Malden, Mass. and Oxford: Wiley-Blackwell.

Goffman, E. (1961). *Asylums: essays on the social situation of mental patients and other inmates*. New York: Anchor.

Gutierrez, K., Rymes, B. and Larson, J. (1995). Script, counterscript and underlife in the classroom. *Harvard Educational Review*, 65(3): 445–71.

Harrop-Allin, Sarah (2011a). The implications of South African children's multimodal musical games for music education. Paper presented at the Leading Music Education Conference, University of Western Ontario, London, Ontario, 28 May–1 June.

Harrop-Allin, S. (2011b). Playing with Barbie: exploring South African township children's musical games as resources for pedagogy. In Lucy Green (ed.), *Learning, teaching and musical identity: voices across cultures* (pp. 156–69). Bloomington, Ill.: University of Illinois Press.

Heller, M. (ed.) (2007). *Bilingualism: a social approach*. Basingstoke: Palgrave Macmillan.

Hewitt, R. (2003). Language, youth and the destabilisation of ethnicity. In B. Rampton and R. Harris (eds), *The language, race and ethnicity reader* (pp. 188–98). London: Routledge.

Hey, V. (1996). *The company she keeps: an ethnography of girls' friendships*, Buckingham: Open University Press.

Hüning, Matthias and Reich, Ulli (eds) (2012). *Language and the city*. Sociolinguistics Symposium 19, Berlin, 21–24 August. Abstracts (p. 57).

Jorgensøn, J. N. (2008). Polylingual languaging around and among children and adolescents. *International Journal of Multilingualism*, 5 (3): 161–76.

Jorgensøn, J. N., Karrebæk, M. S., Madsen, L. M. and Møller, J. S. (2011). Polylanguaging in superdiversity. *Diversities*, 13(2): 23–38. (Theme Issue: Language and Superdiversities.)

Kamwangamalu, N. (2003). Globalisation of English, and language maintenance and shift in South Africa. *International Journal of the Sociology of Language*, 164: 65–81.

Kapp, R. (2004). 'Reading on the line': an analysis of literacy practices in ESL classes in a South African township school. *Language and Education*, 18(3): 246–63.

Lass, Roger (2002). South African English. In R. Mesthrie (ed.), *Language in South Africa* (pp. 104–26). Cambridge: Cambridge University Press.

McKinney, Carolyn (2007). 'If I speak English, does it make me less black anyway?' 'Race' and English in South African desegregated schools. *English Academy Review*, 24(2): 6–24.

McKinney, Carolyn (2010). Schooling in black and white: assimilationist discourse and subversive identity performances in a desegregated South African girls' school. *Race Ethnicity and Education*, 13(2): 191–207.

McKinney, Carolyn (2011). Asymmetrical relations of knowing: pedagogy, discourse and identity in a de(re)segregated school. *Journal of Education*, 51: 29–51.

McKinney, C. (2013). Orientations to English in post-apartheid schooling. *English Today*, 29(1): 22–27.

McCormick, Kay (2001). Code-switching: overview. In R. Mesthrie (ed.), *Concise encyclopedia of sociolinguistics* (pp. 447–54). Oxford: Elsevier.

Makoe, P. and McKinney, C. (2011). Linguistic ideologies as a barrier to policy implementation in South African desegregated schools. Paper presented at the 16th World Congress of Applied Linguistics (AILA), Beijing, 23–28 August.

Makoni, S. (1999). Book review, 'Vivian De Klerk, Editor: *Focus on South Africa*. Amsterdam and Philadelphia: Benjamins, 1996. Varieties of English around the World, 1997. 325 pp.' *International Journal of the Sociology of Language*, 136: 135–40.

Makoni, Sinfree (2003). From misinvention to disinvention of language: multilingualism and the South African Constitution. In Sinfree Makoni et al. (eds), *Black linguistics, language, society, and politics in Africa and the Americas* (pp. 132–53). Clevedon: Multilingual Matters Press.

Makoni, S., Brutt-Griffler, J. and Mashiri, P. (2007). The use of 'indigenous' and urban vernaculars in Zimbabwe. *Language in Society*, 36: 25–49.

Makoni, S. and Pennycook, A. (2006). Disinventing and reconstituting languages. In S. Makoni and A. Pennycook (eds), *Disinventing and reconstituting languages* (pp. 1–41). Clevedon, Avon: Multilingual Matters.

Mesthrie, Rajend (2004). Indian South African English: phonology. In Edgar Schneider, Kate Burridge, Bernd Kortmann, Rajend Mesthrie and Clive Upton (eds), *A handbook of varieties of English*. Vol. 1 *Phonology* (pp. 953–63). Berlin, Germany: Mouton de Gruyter.

Mesthrie, Rajend (2010). Socio-phonetics and social change: deracialisation of the GOOSE vowel in South African English. *Journal of Sociolinguistics*, 14(1): 3–33.

Mesthrie, R. and Tabouret-Keller, A. (2001). Identity and language. In R. Mesthrie (ed.), *Concise encyclopedia of sociolinguistics* (pp. 165–9). Oxford: Elsevier.

Nongogo, Nomakhalipha (2007). *Mina NgumZulu Phaqa* language and identity in a private desegregated high school in South Africa. *English Academy Review*, 24(2): 42–54.

Orfield, G. (2004). The American experience: desegregation, integration, resegregation. In M. Nkomo, C. McKinney and L. Chisholm (eds), *Reflections on school integration: colloquium proceedings* (pp. 95-124). Cape Town: HSRC Press.

Otsuiji, E. and Pennycook, A. (2010). Metrolingualism: fixity, fluidity and language in flux. *International Journal of Multilingualism*, 7(3): 240–54.

Rampton, B. (1995). *Crossing: language and ethnicity among adolescents*. London: Longman.

Rampton, B. (2006). *Language in late modernity: interaction in an urban school*. Cambridge: Cambridge University Press.

Rudwick, S. (2004). 'Zulu, we need [it] for our culture': Umlazi adolescents in the post-apartheid state. *Southern African Linguistics and Applied Language Studies*, 22 (3 and 4): 159–72.

Scollon, Ron and Scollon, Suzie (2007). Nexus analysis: refocusing ethnography on action. *Journal of Sociolinguistics*, 11(5): 608–25.

Simpson, J. M. Y. (2001). Accent. In Raj Mesthrie (ed.), *Concise encyclopedia of sociolinguistics* (pp. 293–7). Amsterdam: Elsevier.

Soudien, Crain (2004). 'Constituting the class': an analysis of the process of 'integration' in South African schools. In Linda Chisholm (ed.), *Changing class: education and social change in post-apartheid South Africa* (pp. 89–114). Cape Town: HSRC Publishers.

Van Rooy, Bertus (2004). Black South African English. In Edgar Schneider, Kate Burridge, Bernd Kortmann, Rajend Mesthrie and Clive Upton (eds), *A handbook of varieties of English*, Vol. 1 *Phonology* (pp. 943–63). Berlin, Germany: Mouton de Gruyter.

Voloshinov, V. N. (1986). *Marxism and the philosophy of language* (trans. L. Matejka and I. R. Titunik). Cambridge, Mass.: Harvard University Press.

Youdell, D. (2003). Identity traps or how black students fail: the interactions between biographical, subcultural and learner identities. *British Journal of Sociology of Education*, 24(1): 3–2.

Youdell, D. (2004). Wounds and reinscriptions: schools, sexualities and performative subjects. *Discourse: Studies in the Cultural Politics of Education*, 25 (4): 477–93.

Zegeye, A. (ed.) (2001). General introduction. *Social identities in the New South Africa: after apartheid* – Vol. 1. Cape Town and Maroelana: Kwela Books and SA History Online.

# 5
## Shades, Voice and Mobility: Remote Communities Resist and Reclaim Linguistic and Educational Practices in Ethiopia

*Kathleen Heugh*

### Introduction

Remote communities in Africa are variously positioned as without voice and in need of external aid from agents of the centre, or they are assumed to exhibit recalcitrant behaviour resistant to change and modernity (Carr-Hill and Peart, 2005). An alternative view of communities that exist on the peripheries in the global South is offered here through a discussion of ethnographic data collected during a country-wide study of language medium education from a range of stakeholders including: education officials, teachers, students and community representatives in Somali, Afar and eastern Oromiya Regions in Ethiopia. It will be argued that community participation in education is collaborative rather than recalcitrant. In addition, community views of language and identity indicate that such communities do not need to be spoken for, rather they are indicative of political agency, claims of citizenship knitted into 'language ideologies' (e.g. Jaffe, 1999), and rejection of 'language regimes' (Kroskrity, 2000, following Laitin, 1993) within the linguistic ecology of a difficult-to-reach part of Ethiopia.

In order to illustrate the argument in this chapter, the discussion that follows draws from a larger body of ethnographic data collected during a study of medium of instruction in the Ethiopian primary school system (Heugh et al., 2007). Ethnographic data collection which samples an entire country such as Ethiopia requires the researcher to embark on a journey which is multidimensional. It is at once spatial, in that the terrain includes sparsely populated distanced settings and limited routes for overland travel; temporal, in that it takes time, patience and persistence to find hard-to-reach communities; and inner, in that it necessitates discarding of layers of preconceived notions cultivated in the global North. The latter include views which percolate amongst education authorities, within government offices of the capital city and among development agencies which resource education and research. Such a journey has methodological and theoretical implications for ethnographic research. As far as was possible, the journey of this researcher included an attempt to unhear the cacophony of noise of the centre and to try to find distant communities' views of language, education and citizenship.

The discussion includes accounts of interviews and discussions with a cross-section of stakeholders and what these reveal of cooperation and resistance amongst communities, local, regional and federal education authorities. An understanding of 'linguistic citizenship' (Stroud, 2001), where people exercise strong views about language choice accompanied by expressions of compliance with, or resistance to, administrative regimes, was used as a filter to analyse data collected from interviews with community representatives. The chapter concludes, suggesting that linguistic citizenship offers a methodological lens with theoretical implications for ethnographic research. It permits respondents' views to emerge in ways which offer a counter-discourse to the dominant language (and educational) regimes of the centre.

## Contextual background

Ethiopia with a population of 74 million people (Population Census Commission, PCC, 2008), 85 per cent of whom are engaged in agricultural or pastoral enterprise, is one of the poorest countries in the world. Most people live in rural or remote settings, and between 12 and 14 million people are pastoralists (PACT Ethiopia, 2008: 5–6). Most pastoralist (nomadic) communities traverse desert-like regions which are geographically remote and distanced from domestic and international centres of political and economic power. Despite federal and international frameworks of commitment to school retention and gender equality since 1990, girls, especially in the eastern Oromiya, Afar and Somali Regions are confronted with abduction, early marriage and forced migration. Cross-border raids from neighbouring Somalia, Yemen and Saudi Arabia (via Djibouti) discourage girls' retention in the school system, especially if school sites are some distance from mobile villages or pastoral routes. From the perspective of agents of the global North, one might understand if researchers were to slip into the mainstream narratives which position such communities as without voice or agency, discriminatory towards girls and resistant to formal education.

Access to schools by communities on the fringes is vexed and transient at best, even after a rapid expansion of the system since a change in government in the early 1990s. There is a long history (150 years) of resistance to use of one Ethiopian language, Amharic, as the language of governance and education across much of the country. Approximately 73 per cent of the population in regions further from Addis Ababa (the capital city) and the Amhara Region have at one time or another engaged in various political struggles of resistance against a vertically imposed language regime (exclusive use of Amharic for governance, education and the formal economy) intended for political domination until the early 1990s.

The consequence of this resistance led to very low school enrolment, particularly amongst communities who use one of the 80 Ethiopian languages other than Amharic. Political change in the early 1990s was followed by the *Education and Training Policy* (MoE, 1994) based on a principle of ethnolinguistic self-determination within eleven administrative (including two city-state) regions. This policy replaces the earlier use of Amharic, with the use of regional or local languages as mediums of instruction through primary schooling. English, spoken by 0.3 per cent of the population (CSA, 2007), is used for the few who proceed to secondary education and beyond. Historical circumstances and earlier resistance to formal education in Amharic have meant that enrolment in Ethiopia has lagged behind that in other sub-Saharan countries, which, in turn, is very low in relation to international statistics.

Low participation, retention and throughput to secondary school during the 1990s and the first decade of the twenty-first century have continued subsequent to international frameworks and agreement on universal primary education and gender equality. Attached to these agreements are development agencies with aid packages and educational consultants offering 'assistance' in the form of ready-made education curricula, programmes, learning materials, assessments, evaluations and other resources. Most have been designed for European and North American clienteles, which the agencies are willing to translocate or resell to communities of the South. Resources such as these have a certain cachet in postcolonial African contexts. They promise the symbolic and material capital which lead towards a globalised world of rich rewards and flight from poverty. Yet, this promise is usually a mirage and the gap between those with access and those without, widens (Coleman, 2011).

Such interventions are not new in Africa. Successive generations of expertise from without were introduced as offering access to modernity and Western or Northern epistemologies, scripts and texts. Yet after 200 years, not much has changed for poor people on the margins of society (Bamgbose, 2000; Ouane, 2003). Nor is it likely to via education systems borrowed or laid down from the North (Coleman, 2011). Most countries in Africa have experienced successive layers of exogenous systems cast over complex endogenous practices. Instead of finding liberty or access to what is promised in the North, African communities have found themselves increasingly impoverished and simultaneously often distanced from access to endogenous literary and educational traditions, especially where these coexist with Islamic rather than Christian faith (e.g. O. Alidou, 2005).

Ethiopia has had a different trajectory. First, the longest literary tradition in Africa emerged from this country by the second century CE. Modern Amharic text uses Ethiopic script that followed *Ge'ez* in early sacred texts of the Ethiopic Coptic Church. Coptic Christianity is the dominant faith of Ethiopia, particularly in the western regions, and it has been a significant conveyancer of scholarship for centuries. A second literary tradition also related to sacred texts, in Arabic, has been part of the faith-based, literary and educational ecology, particularly in eastern Ethiopia (Somali, Afar and eastern Oromiya Regions) from the seventh century onwards. Attendance in Qur'anic schools in these parts (Carr-Hill and Peart, 2005; PACT, 2008), even by nomadic children, has been a feature of social cohesion. Just as the resurgence of Islam over the last 50 years has increased participation in Qur'anic schools across much of North and West Africa, the pattern of attendance in what may be understood as alternative or non-formal education continues amongst Muslim communities that are mobile in neighbouring Somalia as well as in the Somali, Afar and Oromiya Regions of Ethiopia. The second major difference between Ethiopia and other African countries is that it never succumbed to colonisation, although it did experience a short Italian occupation during the Second World War. The Ethiopic and Islamic faith-based literary traditions and absence of colonial interference have meant that internal systems and ecologies did not articulate with Western traditions until the second half of the twentieth century.

Western histories and literature, meanwhile, continue to position people of Africa as without literacy and education. If one understands literacy as that delivered through the Latin script, education as that based on Western epistemology, and schools that look like those in Europe and North America, one might argue thus. There is alternative evidence of a long history of scholarship; multi-age teaching and learning groups; portable classrooms under trees or temporary shelters; and literary traditions in Africa. However, this has been marginalised and rendered invisible during the colonial period, most forcibly under French colonial administration in many West African countries (H. Alidou, 2004; O. Alidou, 2005; Heugh, 2011a). Having been rendered invisible does not mean that local practices have ceased nor does this mean that they have remained static and impervious to socio-economic or political changes evident in the mainstream. Nevertheless, a positioning of African communities as 'without literacy' is accompanied by one in which African communities are cast as, on the one hand, 'orate', yet, simultaneously as 'without voice' or agency (see also Carr-Hill and Peart, 2005; O. Alidou, 2005; Brocklesby et al., 2009). The inherent contradiction within this view and the ahistorical understanding of horizontal layers of literary, faith, educational and economic practices of the continent lie at the heart of misguided, inappropriate and fundamentally flawed responses to poverty, famine and contemporary education.

The Western perspective of Africa has been persuasive and enduring despite evidence which challenges such a view. In part this may be ascribed to an enduring 'Orientalist' perception of Islam within Europe, dating back to the Crusades of the eleventh century, and also to a failure to recognise the significance of scholarship and literary practices which accompanied the spread of Islam from the Horn of Africa across the North and into West Africa from the seventh century onwards (e.g. Foucault, 1977; Said, 1979; O. Alidou, 2005). Inattention to productive discourses within intricate ecologies of mobility and horizontal systems, especially when this coincides with Islam, has permitted a recasting of African communities as lacking and thus requiring of international literacy, education, modernity and Christianity or secularism. Communities on the geographic margins are further cast as presenting an increased degree of need or difficulty for those whose purpose it is to intervene.

> Nomadic populations are generally included under the category of disadvantaged and hard-to-reach groups and represent a particular challenge for development in general and education.... [T]he rate of primary school enrolment of children for nomadic communities is significantly below the national average.... [T]heir low participation rates ... contribute to denying them the chance to effectively participate in planning and development activities ... (Kabbaj and Matsuura 2005: 5–6)

Postcolonial African governments have purchased such views and remedies, and thus become tied into long-term debt. Despite Ethiopia's escape from colonisation, these discourses crossed political boundaries and are evident even where remote communities live at significant distances from the country's administrative centre, Addis Ababa. Western systems and epistemologies have brought about rapid alterations to the political, educational and economic ecology of the country over the last twenty years, escalating more recently. Challenges to a misrepresentation of communities on the margins, nevertheless, demonstrate that pastoralists, for example, have articulate voice and stance in relation to education and citizenship (Krätli, 2001; Carr-Hill and Peart, 2005; PACT Ethiopia, 2008; Brocklesby et al., 2009). Just as earlier Western-oriented educational systems in other parts of Africa passed over indigenous knowledge (IK) systems and practices, changes in Ethiopia have not articulated productively with existing networks of Qur'anic schools in the eastern regions. In neighbouring Somalia, which has terrain and conditions similar to the Somali and Afar Regions of Ethiopia, it is estimated that 85 per cent of pastoralists are within 0.5 km of such a school, whereas only 28 per cent live within this distance of formal primary schools, and none in reach of secondary schools (Maxey, 2004 in PACT, 2008: 27). The proximity to Qur'anic schools is often facilitated by their portability and thus their architecture matches that of the communities whose needs they serve. Addis Ababa, the country's capital, is located in the Coptic Christian western side of the country and the proximal distance between this centre of power and the West is closer on a philosophical level, and less threatening to those fearful of or discriminatory towards the Islamic dominant eastern side of the country. It is easier to address educational needs as understood through the lens of the international priorities and Addis Ababa. The needs of eastern regions some four to five days' hard driving along poor gravel roads across sparsely populated arid lands and prone to civil conflict, cross-border raids and kidnapping of development agency personnel, make the east difficult to assess. Practices on the margins, particularly where these might include non-formal education, Arabic script and Islamic texts are thus not well understood.

This discussion now turns towards evidence of clearly formulated views on literacy, language and educational practices illustrated in the alternative or unconventional literature referred to above. Officials and communities in the east believe that the federal government underserves these regions with inadequate resources and infrastructure, and particularly in regard to allocation of funds. An undercurrent suggests discrimination occurs along lines of faith and language. First, the views of education officials in Jijiga, the capital of the Somali Region, are contrasted with data from education officials and a remote community in Afar. These data illustrate that although remote communities may be cast as without voice or uncooperative, they in fact exhibit both voice and agency that resonate with local, regional, national and even international educational concerns. There is a difference, however, between education officials and the communities they serve. Whereas officials appear more careful and compliant with regard to the regulations laid down by federal government and its administration, community representatives offer evidence of cooperation and participation with the administration as well as resistance which is articulated through the exercise of language choice and as integral to sense of identity and citizenship.

## In search of new research practice

Although pre-colonial African traditions of literacy and education, particularly Coptic Christian and Islamic, predate developments in Europe, contemporary Western texts encode Ethiopian social systems as not simply poor, but dependent upon external aid, educational expertise, languages and legitimacy. Aid is provided in a vertical arrangement over horizontal practices, the effect of which is that few participants gain entry to the vertical axis and thus the material capital delivered. This structural arrangement places the researcher in an ambiguous position as of the 'centre', yet concerned with understanding participants of peripheried contexts who transverse horizontal systems. The researcher is spatially mobile, crossing from international–metropolitan–urban proximities to power, towards the contours of remote reaches. Physical and cognitive mobility, however, are often disconnected on a temporal plane. As suggested above, the researcher of the centre requires both a temporal and spatial journey in order to tune into what lies beneath intricate webs of social practices in remote settings. Purse strings determine whether the researcher moves within the vertical or between the horizontal axes. Short-term consultancies inevitably render predictable findings aligned with templates of the centre. These ultimately recommend solutions which overlay yet another set of vertical systems, to be implemented from the centre outwards. Litmus test solutions secured from consultants who are urged to collect data from settings easier to reach from urban centres are unlikely to reveal the intricacies of community participation or women's resistance, (in)audible linguistic repertoires, or the functional use of multilingual resources (Heugh, 1995) where citizens make judicious use of such resources and assert their own agency (Kerfoot, 2010).

Recent contributions which expand the anthropologist's essential toolkit, for example, peeling away or slicing through metaphorical layers of the onion (notably, Hornberger and Johnson, 2007; McCarty, 2011), have informed numerous studies of language and literacy practices (e.g. Shoba and Chimbutane, 2013). Such studies and other theories of ethnography correctly adopt ethical practice, however, the emphasis is usually towards methodologies which navigate protective coatings of the subject's position. The gaze, therefore, is towards the informant. The focus here shifts towards a conscious reflexive interrogation of the position of both the researcher and subject.

What has become evident are constraints of most consultancy-based 'research' or 'educational evaluations' in Africa (Heugh, 2011b). These serve to undergird asymmetrical relationships between international aid agencies and the administrative architecture of recipient countries; between national administrative centres and further flung regions and towns; and between 'researchers' and the 'researched'. Such fragilities demand new research methodology and theory. This researcher has learned to distrust centre positioning of remote communities where there is a significant distance (spatial, socio-economic, linguistic and sometimes also faith-related) between the two. Part of the findings of a 25-country study of language education programmes in Africa illustrates disturbing levels of evaluation malpractice (Heugh, 2011b). When the administrative voice speaks on behalf of communities positioned as silent, there is every reason not to take this at face value.

The methodological practice discussed here literally involves a passage of time and the arduous physical overland journey to difficult-to-reach spaces. The further one travels from the centre the more one is able to gather a multisensory experience of distance over time, and of the changing environmental, socio-economic and political landscapes. One is also more easily able to leave behind a cacophony of theory constructed elsewhere, conventional literature, and strongly held views of the powerful agents, all of which clutter the mind. The inner journey requires ongoing reflexivity which releases layers of preformulated and habituated notions of what may be discovered. A conscious unlayering and acknowledgement of the researcher's own habitus offers proximity to scripts which remote communities formulate. The more clearly one recognises one's own limitations, the more one may recognise filters which get in the way. Reflexive recognition of one's own linguistic citizenship and how one positions both oneself and others in relation to the linguistic ecology may increase proximity to that of others.

## Gathering ethnographic data

Educational researchers who reach the margins encounter several sets of respondents. These include local and/or regional government agents, community leaders, women's groups, teacher trainers, teachers, teachers-in-training and students. It is tempting to suggest that the regional and local officials facilitate negotiation between the community and administration. Local officials appear to have deft skills which facilitate mobility along the vertical channels of communication between the centre and the local, and simultaneously they cohabit horizontal spaces through which discourses of resistance travel.

Ethnographic data collected in the field (Heugh et al., 2007) reveal contradictory representations of voice, agency and relationships within language ecologies, over different points of time and space. The local education office is a setting in which official responses approximate those of the Regional Education Bureau, and the federal Ministry of Education. A respondent, who offers responses which approximate the official position when located in the education office, may offer significantly nuanced alternatives during a journey which results in a physical distance from the administrative space, for example en route to or from a rural school. The parachute consultant/researcher is unlikely to have the time to be in dialogue with respondents over different time frames, and/or in different physical settings. Data collected under such constraints are therefore likely to be one-dimensional and fixed in time and space. Given what we know of ethnographic and anthropological research in other settings, limited data samples need careful contextualisation.

## Education policy, provision and research terms of reference

The Ethiopian language education policy provides for eight years of regional or local language (often identified as home language/mother tongue) medium education (MTM); plus the teaching and learning of the federal 'working language' Amharic; plus the teaching and learning of English as a subject in primary school; and English as a medium of instruction from the ninth grade (beginning of secondary school). Implementation of this policy in the eastern, sparsely populated and arid regions of the country has been made more difficult than in the west. Afar Region is the only region which has not had the resources to develop the regional language for use in mainstream primary schools. Where resources are limited, the default position is to continue Amharic-medium education in primary, with private English-medium schools proliferating in large urban centres. Afar, Somali and Oromifa languages are used in alternative basic education (ABE) schools which offer a truncated three years of primary schooling to a few handfuls of pastoralist communities.

Most of the people in Afar and Somali Regions are pastoralists. While there has been a dramatic increase in primary school enrolment across the country over the last decade, reaching 84 per cent by 2010, only 24.4 per cent of children of school-going age are enrolled in primary schools in Afar, and 31.6 per cent in Somali Region (Engel and Rose, 2010). Fewer than 5 per cent of pastoralist children reach secondary. In one pastoralist zone in the better resourced Oromiya Region, there are only 5 schools for 50,000 people (PACT Ethiopia, 2008: 7); secondary schools are located only in the few urban hubs. Primary schools tend to be located in urban or village settings rather than along grazing routes or near water. Thus, neither the federal Ministry of Education nor the regional authorities actually make it possible for pastoralists to have easy access to school.

Owing to limited development or provision of home language medium, followers of Islam in particular in Afar are expected to study through the medium of Amharic, which has always been closely associated with both Coptic Christianity and oppressive administrative regimes. Not only is this practice contrary to educational policy but it effectively excludes pastoralist children even if they were able to access schools.

From the centre, however, pastoralists are represented as uncooperative and intent on keeping their children out of school owing to their nomadic lifestyle and practices of early marriage, and so on. The external perspective of pastoralist communities is predominantly characterised by pessimism, stigma and a static portrayal of people locked out of the whirlpool of globalisation. As mentioned earlier, in Afar, Somali and eastern Oromiya Regions, pastoralists are subjected to poverty and climate change. But this does not mean that they have inadequate knowledge of the environment, thus development advice and aid, based on such assumptions, are often misplaced (cf. Cohen, 2007). An alternative discourse includes critiques of a curriculum which makes few connections between pastoralist and mainstream systems and it is said to be inflexible and insensitive to rhythms of pastoral life (PACT Ethiopia, 2008).

The federal Ministry of Education and the United Nations Development Programme (UNDP) commissioned an evaluation of the medium of instruction policy in Ethiopian primary schools in 2006. The terms of reference included only 5 of 11 regions none of which were in the eastern or Islamic dominant part of the country. The research team insisted on including four additional regions, including Afar and Somali. UNDP expected the team to fly from one centre to another, partly because of civil unrest, border disputes with Eritrea, Somalia and Sudan, and an imminent invasion of Somalia by the Ethiopian military. After vigorous debate the team was given permission to travel overland with an extended time frame, in order to be able to reach rural villages and remote communities. The collection of data across the country stretched far beyond the original terms of reference. Table 5.1 indicates the scope of the research.

Owing to military action, limited and controlled access was given to the Somali Region: one day's hard travel over a poor gravel and rock-pitted road to Jijiga close to the border with Somalia, Ethiopia's eastern neighbour, one day for interviews limited to Jijiga and one day for return travel, with regular reporting of movements to UN headquarters. Official access to Afar was also limited. In Somali the Regional

*Table 5.1*   Summary of actual data collection

| | |
|---|---|
| Regions visited and sampled | 9 of 11 administrative regions |
| Schools visited | 38 schools |
| Classroom observations | 99 observations |
| Teacher training colleges/universities visited | 12 institutions |
| Interviews (individual and focus group) | 256 people (including education officials at all levels of governance from local and regional to federal; teacher educators, academics, teachers, students, parents, women's groups and community leaders) |
| Questionnaires completed | 353 questionnaires completed, plus one from each of the 11 regional education bureaus |
| Informal data collection | Researchers kept notebooks and records of casual conversations with members of the communities visited (in marketplaces, village shops and cafes, local eating establishments), and people encountered in the street, particularly where language education matters arose. Records of observed language practices were similarly recorded in notebooks |

Table adapted from Benson et al. (2010: 52, Table 1.6).

Education Bureau (REB) was visited, and local (*woreda*) education bureaus were visited in Afar and eastern Oromiya. A total of 9 school sites were visited and 34 interviews were conducted in this part of the country, under particularly difficult circumstances.

## Voice and agency

Jijiga is at a crossroads of pastoralist trading routes across Somali region and illicit trade with Somalia with the urban civilians largely engaged in trade or civil service. We found officials in the REB office in Jijiga forthright in their criticism of federal government:

> The Ministry of Education [MoE in Addis Ababa] is good at sending rules and regulations. It could channel resources to this region which is the second largest region in Ethiopia, but the contribution is too small. (Somali REB official)

Limited resources and lack of infrastructure meant that students would have to travel to Addis to go to university or teacher training college where they would be trained to teach in Amharic, not Somali. Even though teaching and learning materials had been developed in Somali, there were insufficient funds for printing. Parent–teacher associations were positioned as playing a significant role in curriculum development and in monitoring the performance of teachers. Interviews with parent committee members at Jijiga Senior Secondary School certainly seemed to confirm this. The school principal described the parent–teacher association as 'quite forceful and demanding', while the research team found that the strongest views regarding teacher competence and school administration were expressed by women committee members and students. An innovation in secondary schools was the use of video teaching of subjects across the curriculum in English from Grade 9 onwards. Teachers would attempt to explain confusing parts of the lesson – often at points when students had been instructed by the video teacher to engage in an activity or problem-solving exercise, but students found this disturbing: 'Students ask me to take the teacher out of the classroom because he is causing a disturbance while the Plasma [video] lesson is on' (Principal). The research team's discussion with students found that they expressed surprisingly strong views of the federal MoE and their teachers, for example: 'We feel neglected by the federal government and we need good quality teachers' (Grade 10 student). At the time of the visit to this school, the senior Grade 11 and 12 students staged a protest against a shortage of books and 'quality teachers' and refused to attend afternoon lessons.

The REB officials drew attention to the clan- and tribe-based structure of Somali society, and the role of traditional and faith-based leaders in conflict resolution and the mobilisation of communities. Traditional and religious leaders were said to play a significant role in organising the building of ABE schools in remote areas, a view somewhat contrary to the picture painted of these communities in Addis Ababa. Local (*woreda*) education officials in Afar and eastern Oromiya Regions also portrayed community participation in similar ways. However, whereas in Somali and Oromiya primary schooling is largely provided in the corresponding regional language this is not the case in Afar, except in the few ABE schools for pastoralists.

While the team found it relatively easy to locate urban and village schools in all regions, finding ABE schools in pastoralist communities was more challenging. We had not been permitted to locate such schools in the Somali region, and without any support from Addis, we set about finding one such school near Dudub pastoralist village in Afar. The local (*woreda*) education bureau located in the closest town, Awash, had assisted the community to construct a school building close to the hamlet. Since mobile communities are seldom accessible by a regular road and difficult to locate, official assistance would have been helpful. The education officer, however, refused to accompany or assist the team other than with vague directions, 'travel north along the dry Awash River bed'. The driver and Ethiopian researcher were apprehensive and reluctant to venture off the beaten track, however, we did find a pastoralist route with disused informal shelters that may have been temporary structures for meetings or Qur'anic schools. At one point an armed herdsman with a team of camels intercepted the researchers. Only after deft negotiations made it clear that none of the team was a native speaker of Amharic, or a government representative, were we able to continue. We eventually located the school, a teacher and a few students, none of whom were in class. After some persuasion they accompanied the researchers to the outskirts of Dudub hamlet. Women and girls were kept hidden away, perhaps because of a recent spate of abductions of young girls, and the team, including one *faranji* (foreigner), was viewed with suspicion.

The village chairperson and a number of representatives agreed to participate in a discussion with the researchers and the teacher in Afar with some use of Amharic and Oromifa (language of Oromiya). One researcher spoke Tigrinya, while the driver spoke Oromifa, and the teacher spoke Afar. All three were able to use Amharic as a vehicular language, as were several of the community representatives. Fardon and Furniss (1994) have argued that linguistic diversity in Africa means that multilingualism is the lingua franca of the continent, and the methodology here was to use the multilingual resources of the participants to collect narrative data; to negotiate meaning amongst informants, the intermediaries and the researchers; and to check and cross-check interpretations. The driver and Ethiopian researcher provided double interpretation into English for this researcher. The accuracy of translated transcripts in English was later verified by the Ethiopian researcher.

It became clear that the community had cooperated fully with education authorities in constructing the school, but the pastoralists believed that there had been insufficient reciprocity:

> The community ... supplied free service, labour for construction and stools for students, and water during construction. There is a water pump to provide water for the children at school – but no generator so the school is not open ... (Chairperson)

This explained why we had not found anyone in class earlier and the implication was that the *woreda* education bureau had not provided the necessary resources for the school to function. The chairperson was initially careful with his criticism, but his point regarding the generator was heavily laden. Water is essential for the students to drink in desert conditions. Water for toilets is a necessity, especially in order to retain girls in school. This, rather than uncooperative pastoralists, is a contributory explanation for the low attendance of girls. Other members of the village committee were also keen to volunteer information. 'We [adults] would also like to learn in the evenings but there is no electricity ...' (Spokesperson 1).

Villagers, who had participated in building the school, had hoped for some rewards and to participate in adult education. However, this wish had been dashed or delayed owing to poor planning or government ineptitude. Emboldened by the second criticism, another representative continued: 'We would like to learn to read and write Afar, Amharic, mathematics, civics and English ...' (Spokesperson 2).

First mentioned is the local language of Afar people, followed by the national 'working language', Amharic, probably because it has vehicular traction, even though the community associates this language with government-initiated linguistic violence. Mathematics is next, followed by civics, which suggests a willingness to participate in regional or national citizenship. Last is English – suggesting a desire for contact with the outside world. So the concerns here, in the middle of the desert, appear to be clearly articulated, demonstrating a connection between the local and the centre, and certainly not limited or disconnected from global discourses. The chairperson, however, was not in complete agreement, and he turned the discussion back towards the needs of children: 'The children should learn Afar and then English ...' (Chairperson).

The chairperson was careful to reveal his position, not through what he said, but through what he did not say. That omission of Amharic signalled his resistance towards the language. To ensure that the researchers had not missed this omission, the spokesperson who had earlier added to the chairperson's initial criticism of government continued: 'Those Amharas must learn English and we don't need Amharic ...' (Spokesperson 1). Here the matter is unambiguous, the use of 'those Amharas' signals a yawning sociopolitical chasm between the pastoralist community and those who govern them.

The chairperson and Spokesperson 1 took a highly political stance through a claim on citizenship expressed through language choice and linguistic identity. Secondly, they knew that the REB was contravening national language education policy, and they dismissed government-provided education as irrelevant, 'we don't need Amharic'. It is not surprising that pastoralist parents are reluctant to send their children to mainstream schools where there is an illogical language mismatch, assuming they are able to access such schools. Viewed from the centre this might be cast as uncooperative behaviour. Viewed from the margins, communities exercise passive resistance and voice dissent. However, they also express participatory citizenship in terms of linguistic affiliation and contributions towards building educational infrastructure. Spokesperson 2, furthermore, demonstrates a multifaceted pragmatic view of Amharic as part of the horizontal linguistic ecology of which each of the pastoralist informants made strategic use.

While pastoralists are frequently positioned anachronistically and accused of being sexist and paying less attention to their daughters' education, or keeping their daughters out of education, we found alternative claims:

> Girls should go to Grade 8 or beyond. We used to think foolishly that ladies should not get education – now we know that first ladies must get education ... in Afar for Grades 1–4 for the foundation. From Grade 5 it should be English ... (Chairperson)

> Actually we want Afar and English [medium] to the end of secondary. (Spokesperson 1)

The dialogue included several instances of the informants reinterpreting or reshading their responses. Spokesperson 1 continued a pattern of emphasising a key element in the chairperson's contribution. Here, he expresses an even stronger affiliation with, and confidence in, the viability of the Afar language in education. The claim for Afar and English signals a wish to establish equilibrium between local needs and access to the international context. Subsequent to a question from the Ethiopian researcher about the possible impact of English, this point was elaborated: 'If you have confidence in the language and culture … you should not be worried about loss of culture because of English …' (Chairperson).

This is interesting for several reasons. Firstly, the chairperson articulates the strength of the association between the Afar language, identity and agency of this small mobile community. Secondly, the stance towards English is remarkable. That the response is so clearly articulated suggests that the community had discussed this matter themselves and come to a clear decision about English in relation to their children's education. It also indicates that even remote communities are not immune to or disconnected from the symbolic capital of English as a proxy for access to participation in the contemporary world beyond Ethiopia.

The chairperson concluded with a statement in which he addressed a significant concern within the Afar community that, owing to the paucity of school provision for pastoralist communities, the regional government tries to persuade pastoralists to enrol their children in boarding schools in the closest town and thus to study through Amharic to the end of Grade 6: 'Our culture does not say we must send our children away [for primary or secondary education]' (Chairperson).

Of course, this last statement might be interpreted by agents of the centre as confirming the non-cooperative stance of the Afar communities. However, the community clearly sees this as an act of symbolic, linguistic, cultural and faith-based violence which is insensitive to Afar people. Disappointment and antipathy towards the authorities perhaps explain why it was that the education official had been reluctant to accompany the team to this community. In retrospect, this was fortunate since his presence may have dampened what the community members were prepared to reveal of their positions and voice.

These data are consistent with those of Krätli (2001), Brocklesby et al. (2009), and others, who find that pastoralists and remote communities adapt to and are aware of global challenges. Women's voices are not always silent, articulate positions are expressed, traditional and religious leaders play important roles, and communities contribute their labour and resources to building schools. Remote communities are aware of and wish to inhabit complex worlds which involve neither the loss of their language nor culture but which do offer expanded repertoires. However, government and development agencies 'do not understand the diversity and dynamics of pastoralist communities' (Brocklesby et al., 2009: 4).

## Conclusion

This discussion shows that the voices, position and agency of people in remote regions do not coincide with representations made of them from administrative centres. Citizens of the margins do have a clear set of priorities relating to their linguistic citizenship and this includes instrumental use of their local or regional language as well as a desire to have access to English which appears to offer access to global concerns. The one does not preclude the other. Scripts of the centre which claim that communities on the fringes are disconnected or uncooperative, or without voice and agency, may miscalculate and be requiring of revision. Such scripts, however, are disconnected from the needs of communities who have different occupational and faith-based traditions from those of the centre, and they inflict symbolic violence.

These matters have implications for short-term consultancies and evaluations in less developed settings. More specifically, however difficult, ethnographic research needs to take account of people in remote settings. Even where commissioning agents attempt to block access to remote communities, or limit access to representative samples, the researcher can find ways to stretch boundaries. As a researcher, one needs to uncover layers of habituated practices and pressures that have led to one's own linguistic citizenship, and this may take time and overland journeying. These may permit an easier understanding of the dialogic and recursive ways in which data are transmitted and interpreted amongst informants and researcher. The final point to be made is that communities of the centre appear to become immobilised by their own anachronistic scripts which are vulnerable to out-of-focus snapshots of mirages in the desert. The communities of the fringe, on the other hand, are quite capable of demonstrating their mobility along many different dimensions of time and space.

## References

Alidou, Hassana (2004). Medium of instruction in post-colonial Africa. In James Tollefson and Amy Tsui (eds), *Medium of instruction policies: Which agenda? Whose agenda?* (pp. 195–214). Mahwah and London: Lawrence Erlbaum.

Alidou, Ousseina (2005). *Engaging modernity: Muslim women and the politics of agency in postcolonial Niger*. Madison and London: University of Wisconsin Press.

Bamgbose, Ayo (2000). *Language and exclusion: the consequences of language policies in Africa*. Münster, Hamburg and London: Lit Verlag.

Benson, Carol, Heugh, Kathleen, Bogale, Berhanu, and Gebre Yohannes, Mekonnen Alemu (2010). The medium of instruction in the primary schools in Ethiopia: a study and its implications for multilingual education. In K. Heugh and T. Skutnabb-Kangas (eds), *Multilingual education works: from the periphery to the centre* (pp. 34–82). Delhi: Orient Blackswan.

Brocklesby, Mary Ann, Hobley, Mary and Scott-Villiers, Patta (2009). 'Raising voice – securing a livelihood'. The role of diverse voices in securing livelihoods in pastoralist areas of Ethiopia – a summary paper. Pastoralist Consultants International. www.pastoralists.org

Carr-Hill, Roy and Peart, Edwina (2005). *The education of nomadic peoples in East Africa. Review of relevant literature*. Paris and Tunis: UNESCO Institute for Educational Planning and the African Development Bank.

Cohen, Gideon (2007). Mother tongue and other tongue in primary education: can equity be achieved with the use of different languages? In Hywel Coleman (ed.), *Language and development: Africa and beyond* (pp. 62–75). Addis Ababa: British Council.

Coleman, Hywell (2011). *Dreams and realities: developing countries and the English language*. London: British Council.

CSA (Central Statistical Agency of Ethiopia). 2007. *Population and Housing Census of 1994 metadata and documentation*. http://www.csa.gov.et/surveys/ Population%20and%20Housing%20Census%201994/survey0/index.html

Engel, Jakob and Rose, Pauline (2010). Ethiopia's progress in education: a rapid and equitable expansion of access. Overseas Development Institute. Accessed 15/02/13. http://allafrica.com/download/resource/main/main/idatcs/0002025 7:ae9e77aeacf6cb4d8a886967f7390afe.pdf

Fardon, Richard and Furniss, Graham (1994). Introduction: frontiers and boundaries – African languages as political environment. In R. Fardon and G. Furniss (eds), *African languages, development and the state* (pp. 1–29). London and New York: Routledge.

Foucault, Michel (1977). *Discipline and punish: the birth of the prison*. Translated by A. Sheridan. New York: Pantheon Books.

Heugh, Kathleen (1995). Disabling and enabling: implications of language policy trends in South Africa. In R. Mesthrie (ed.), *Language and social history: studies in South African sociolinguistics* (pp. 329–50). Cape Town: David Philip.

Heugh, Kathleen (2011a). Discourses from without, discourses from within: women, feminism and voice in Africa. *Current Issues in Language Planning*, 12(1): 89–104.

Heugh, Kathleen (2011b). Theory and practice – language education models in Africa: research, design, decision-making and outcomes. In Adama Ouane and Christine Glanz (eds), *Optimising learning, education and publishing in Africa: the language factor. A review and analysis of theory and practice in mother-tongue and bilingual education in sub-Saharan Africa* (pp. 105–56). Hamburg and Tunis Belvédère: UNESCO, ADEA and African Development Bank. http://unesdoc. unesco.org/images/0021/002126/212602e.pdf

Heugh, Kathleen, Benson, Carol, Bogale, Berhanu and Gebre Yohannes, Mekonnen Alemu (2007). *Final report: study on medium of instruction in primary schools in*

*Ethiopia*. Addis Ababa: Ministry of Education. http://www.hsrc.ac.za/research/output/outputDocuments/4379_Heugh_Studyonmediumofinstruction.pdf

Hornberger, Nancy and Johnson, David (2007). Slicing the onion ethnographically: layers and spaces in multilingual language education policy and practice. *TESOL Quarterly*, 41 (3): 509–32.

Jaffe, Alexandra (1999). *Ideologies in action: language politics on Corsica*. Berlin: Mouton de Gruyter.

Kabbaj, Omar and Matsuura, Koïchiro (2005). Foreword. In R. Carr-Hill and E. Peart, *The education of nomadic peoples in East Africa. Review of relevant literature* (pp. 5–6). Paris and Tunis: UNESCO Institute for Educational Planning and the African Development Bank.

Kerfoot, Caroline (2010). *Changing perceptions of literacies, language and development*. Dissertations in Bilingualism 18. Stockholm: Centre for Research on Bilingualism, Stockholm University.

Krätli, Saverio (2001). *Education provision to nomadic pastoralists: a literature review*. Brighton: World Bank – Institute of Development Studies (IDS) http://www.eldis.org/fulltext/saverio.pdf

Kroskrity, Paul (ed.) (2000). *Regimes of language: ideologies, polities, identities*. Santa Fe: School of American Research.

Laitin, David (1993). The game theory of language regimes. The emergent world language system. Le système linguistique mondial en formation. *International Political Science Review/Revue internationale de science politique*, 14(3): 227–39.

McCarty, Teresa (2011). Entry into conversation: introducing ethnography and language policy. In Teresa McCarty (ed.), *Ethnography and language policy* (pp. 1–28). New York: Routledge.

Maxey, Kees (2004). *Education for all – is it feasible for pastoralists? Pastoralists and education: towards integrated education for sustainable community development in the Horn of Africa*. Indigenous Knowledge Systems Research and Development Studies No. 5. The Hague: PENNHA/LEAD-UL.

MoE (Ministry of Education) (1994). *Education and training policy*. Addis Ababa: St George Printing Press.

Ouane, Adama (2003). Introduction: the view from the linguistic jail. In Adama Ouane (ed.), *Towards a multilingual culture of education* (pp. 1–22). Hamburg: UNESCO Institute of Education.

PACT Ethiopia (2008). *Education for pastoralists: flexible approaches, workable models*. USAID and PACT Ethiopia. http://www.pactworld.org/galleries/ethiopia/Education%20for%20Pastoralists-A4.pdf

PCC (Population Census Commission) (2008). *Summary and statistical report of the 2007 Population and Housing Census*. Federal Democratic Republic of Ethiopia. Addis Ababa: UNFPA. http://www.csa.gov.et/pdf/Cen2007_firstdraft.pdf

Said, Edward (1979). *Orientalism*. New York: Vintage Books.

Shoba, Jo Arthur and Chimbutane, Feliciano (eds) (2013). *Bilingual education and language policy in the global south*. London and New York: Routledge.

Stroud, Christopher (2001). African mother-tongue programmes and the politics of language. Linguistic citizenship versus linguistic human rights. *Journal of Multilingual and Multicultural Development*, 2 (4): 339–55.

# Part II
# Teaching and Research with Diverse Students

# 6

# Marginalised Knowledges and Marginalised Languages for Epistemic Access to Piaget and Vygotsky's Theories

*Michael Joseph and Esther Ramani*

## Introduction

South African scholars such as Henning (2008) have argued that university students are unable to deal with theoretical concepts and that not much effort is being made to ground students in theoretical orientations to research and knowledge construction. Self-critically, she also acknowledges that very often, senior researchers like herself are unable to mediate abstract concepts for students. Henning's thoughtful reflections have launched us into an effort to theorise how we ourselves have been teaching theory or, more accurately, how we have brought about the learning of theory by our undergraduate students in a contextualised and empowering way.

The goal of learning from the earliest years of formal education should be the acquisition of theory but this is particularly crucial in university education. It has long been acknowledged that the place to begin in all formal education is the real-life experience of students, namely 'everyday knowledge' or EK. Educationists argue that it is this engagement with EK that will, through a process of transformation, lead to scientific knowledge (SK). However, among Vygotskyan approaches to theoretical learning, there appears to be an unresolved problem about the relation between EK and SK. Some scholars following Bernstein (1973) merely stop at making the distinction between the two and argue for the importance of the latter (SK) as the goal of education, dismissing overtly or covertly the role of EK. Others, mainly from the anthropological disciplines (such as Heath, 1983 and Moll et al., 1992) stress the role of EK as a way of expanding the knowledge pool of formal education. These approaches are unclear about the relationship between EK and SK, as Vygotsky conceptualised it.

We argue that the aim of teaching and learning in higher education should be the acquisition of theory by students. The challenge for university teachers therefore is to facilitate access to theory. What we present here is an ongoing pedagogic exploration that we have engaged in for the last eight years in making theory accessible to students in a historically black university (HBU) in the impoverished rural Limpopo province in South Africa.

A third-year module *CELS 302: Language and Cognition* is the context for this pedagogic research. This module is located within the BA degree programme in Contemporary English and Multilingual Studies (BA CEMS), a dual-medium degree in which six modules (in the CELS strand below) are taught and assessed in English, and the other six (in the MUST strand below) are taught and assessed in the language of the learners, Sesotho sa Leboa (also known as Sepedi). The degree has been much written about and more detail can be found in Ramani and Joseph (2002, 2008), Joseph and Ramani (2004) and Ramani et al. (2007).

African-language-speaking students from impoverished schools are forced to access disciplinary content through English. Nevertheless, such students continue to use their mother tongue as a language of learning, as they discuss academic ideas in their language, and use it as a resource in a context where English is the medium of both instruction and assessment. In our dual-medium degree, the students' own language is elevated to a medium of instruction and assessment, and through this move, we believe 'disadvantaged' students can gain epistemic access. The use of Sesotho sa Leboa, marginalised, like other African languages, in South African higher education, therefore facilitates epistemic access largely denied to students not competent in English.

As can be seen from Table 6.1, the module *CELS 302* is the final, third-year module offered in the English strand. The aim of this module is to introduce students to Piaget's ideas on private speech and Vygotsky's theories on the relation between language and cognition, especially on the cognitive function of private speech, the zone of proximal development, mediation and internalisation and more recently, fantasy play (Piaget, 1962; Vygotsky, 1934/1986).

## The curriculum framework

The curriculum framework for relating EK to SK is based on Vygotsky's epistemological distinction between the two, and the pedagogic connectedness of the two, which latter results in the transformation of EK into SK.

*Table 6.1* Structure of the BA CEMS degree and the location of *CELS 302: Language and Cognition* within it

| Modules in BA CEMS | |
| --- | --- |
| **Contemporary English Language Studies (CELS) modules: taught and assessed in English** | **Multilingual Studies (MUST) modules: taught and assessed in Sesotho sa Leboa (Sepedi)** |
| CELS 101: English in context | MUST 101: Matsentšhagae a bomalementši [Introduction to multilingualism] |
| CELS 102: A discourse approach to the structure of English | MUST 102: Dikgokagano ka go bolela setšhabeng bolementši [Spoken communication in a multilingual society] |
| CELS 201: Critical language awareness: the global spread of English | MUST 201: Mokgwa wa bolementši wa go ruta dingwalwa le mehuta ya dingwalwa [A multilingual approach to text and genre] |
| CELS 202: Language and literacy learning in multilingual contexts | Must 202: Bokgoni bja go bala le ngwalwa mešomong ka tsela ya bolementši [Workplace literacies] |
| CELS 301: Bilingual and multilingual education | MUST 301: Ditirelo tša bolementši ka Afrika Borwa [Multilingual services in South Africa] |
| CELS 302: Language and cognition | MUST 302: Go nyakišiša bomalementši [Researching multilingualism] |

The curriculum construct operates at two levels: the lecturers' selection of content for the module and the use of the content to develop procedures to tap learners' EK, some aspects of which may resonate, and others which may not with the content. This construct is similar to Hedegaard's concept of the 'double move' (1990): the first involves the selection of content (in our case, the key concepts) to be taught, and the second is the pedagogic process for enabling these concepts to be grasped. A recent paper (Joseph and Ramani, 2011) describes this process in detail.

The focus in this chapter is on the use of narratives (through which EK is encoded) as a resource for accessing dominant forms of knowledge, i.e. SK.

## Contextual background

The everyday knowledge of students and lecturers has emerged as narratives during the last eight years when the module *CELS 302* was taught to different cohorts of students. The rural background of these students is significant as it shows that the students' narratives are strongly located in their African cultures, in sharp contrast to the 'Western' scientific knowledge that they are expected to master at university. This contrast between the two kinds of knowledges is foregrounded symbolically in the university's perception of its being an 'African' university that needs to privilege indigenous knowledge (IK) and which does so through its annual Spring Lectures where Eurocentrism is challenged and Africanist knowledges celebrated.

Substantively, however, the everyday knowledges and African languages of the students are excluded from most of the university's curricula, resulting ironically in an Africanist university offering access to Western knowledge through the medium of English. Despite the government's National Language Policy for Higher Education (NLPHE, 2002), which mandates that all universities develop multilingual policies and develop African languages as mediums of teaching and learning 'in the medium to long term' (p. 5), such a policy even on paper has not yet been formulated by the University of Limpopo. Against this backdrop, the dual-medium degree BA CEMS is an example of practice going ahead of university policy, where the practice is nevertheless in line with the South African Constitution and the NLPHE. Though the degree was approved by the Council on Higher Education and the South African Qualifications Authority in 2001 its legitimacy is still contested within the university. We hope that this description of contextual factors, namely, the rural setting of a bilingual degree that remains contested to this day, will serve as a background to discuss the narratives elicited in the teaching and learning of the module *CELS 302* and their role in facilitating access to theory.

## What we are *not* doing in the dual-medium degree, BA CEMS

Our focus on students' EK is not to maintain or develop our students' African identity; nor is it to stimulate initial classroom discussions in order to create an affective climate within which theoretical learning can be launched. Such uses of everyday knowledge for identity development and achieving affective goals is familiar in South African classrooms both in schools and universities under the rubric of 'the learners' prior knowledge'. We are not using EK to level the playing fields, i.e. to challenge the hegemony of dominant discourses (SK) and their languages (such as English) and to replace them with marginalised varieties. We recognise these goals as belonging to the agenda of many critical ethnographers, such as Edelsky's critique (2006) of Cummins, or Hornberger's continua of biliteracy project (2003), and we do see their value in supporting forms of knowledge that can be brought into a more inclusive curriculum. However, our position is more in line with that of critical language awareness (CLA) scholars like Janks (2010) who argue for epistemic access to dominant knowledges and dominant languages (such as English) as the right of African students, even at the risk of further entrenching the hegemony of English. This is what Lodge (1997) and Janks (2004) refer to as the 'access paradox'. However, instead of relying, as CLA scholars do, on providing access through a 'right to English' approach, we believe students need to be exposed to the non-neutrality of dominant knowledges (and languages) and how they acquired their hegemonic status through historically constructed power struggles. Finally, instead of giving academic support through only English (either in stand-alone or integrated courses), we suggest dual-medium education for epistemic access as the most effective use of EK and SK for student empowerment. We aim to demonstrate this claim in the rest of this chapter.

The rural background of the Sepedi-speaking students doing our degree and their EK embedded within their African cultures are in strong contrast to the Western scientific knowledge they are expected to gain access to at university. This epistemic gap appeared initially as one that had to be bridged with difficulty especially when we argued that students need to *grasp* abstract concepts central to disciplinary knowledge. Concepts such as 'the zone of proximal development', 'mediation', 'internalisation', 'assimilation' and 'accommodation' all taken from Piaget and Vygotsky are difficult to grasp. These kinds of key abstract concepts are referred to as 'threshold concepts' by Meyer and Land (2006), as they are central to the mastery of the discipline.

In the first years of teaching *CELS 302*, before we used the double move (Hedegaard, 1990, explained earlier in this chapter) students engaged in rampant plagiarism in written assignments. They found texts on the Internet which they copied without understanding. Our search for a new way to enable students to grasp abstract concepts led us to see Vygotsky's notion of EK and SK as distinct (at the epistemic level) but related at another (pedagogic) level. Vygotsky's concept, made more powerful by Hedegaard's double move, thus served to help us construct a more effective curriculum, one in which learners' and teachers' EK, embedded in narratives, played a key role.

Once the key abstract concepts are selected (the first move), we can focus on the second move, which is to help students to grasp these theoretical concepts. As explained earlier, this second move involves the pedagogic connectedness between EK and SK and in our view, teaching and learning have to do with developing this connection. In Figure 6.1, we capture our understanding of the relation between EK and SK.

## Relation between EK and SK

The second pedagogic move, which is to integrate EK and SK, is captured in Figure 6.1.

As mentioned earlier, Joseph and Ramani (2011) describe this second move in great detail. It involves first of all tapping (eliciting, as shown in Figure 6.1) students' beliefs (in this case, on private speech or self-talk, identified by Vygotsky as a key stage in children's development). We accord these beliefs the status of data by referring to them as 'introspective data' and which are in fact expressions of their EK. These introspective data are juxtaposed with selected scholarly writings and then are transformed (transforming, in Figure 6.1) into hypotheses, when students are required to investigate them through empirical research on children in their own communities (researching, in Figure 6.1). Their findings are once again related to scholars' views, which enable students to revisit their beliefs and their findings. In this chapter, only the first two steps (eliciting and transforming) will be described in detail, as the third step (researching) has been dealt with in Joseph and Ramani (2011).

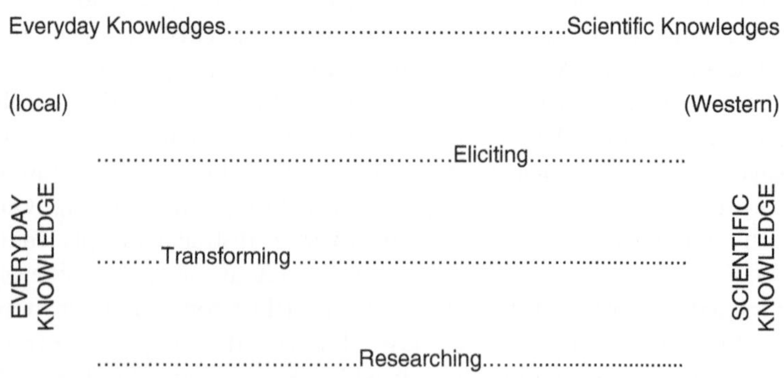

Everyday Knowledges..............................................Scientific Knowledges

(local)                                                                                        (Western)

..............................................Eliciting.....................

EVERYDAY KNOWLEDGE         .........Transforming..................................................         SCIENTIFIC KNOWLEDGE

..............................Researching...........................

*Figure 6.1*   The relation between EK and SK

## Narrativising everyday knowledge: autoethnography in action

In this section, we provide actual examples of students' introspective data (EK) that they gave in response to our questionnaire on private speech. The questionnaire contained questions such as the following:

- Do you find yourself talking to yourself?
- Do you observe very young children talking to themselves?
- At what age do you think this happens?
- Do you think all children talk to themselves?
- Does their self-talk have any purpose?

We found that students spontaneously provided narrative accounts of their own *private speech*, and childhood *play* (in which private speech was sometimes embedded). These narratives were rich in contextual detail and students' own beliefs, and moreover showed strong differences among students in beliefs and interpretations of each other's anecdotes of private speech and play. These anecdotes served as a rich reservoir of student-generated EK for the teacher to connect to scholarly texts (SK).

We now present some examples of narratives reported by students and lecturers from their own lives. The examples are based on two key genres: *private speech* and *make-believe play*, on which the module focused. Our main goal as teachers of this module was to first elicit the narrativised EK of students and teachers, and then reconstruct them as knowledge in relation to paradigm debates. For example, the question 'Do you think all children talk to themselves?' is related to the debate on whether private speech is universal or culture-specific and foregrounds the views of Piaget and Vygotsky and subsequent scholars who extended or challenged their theories.

## Narratives on private speech from students

Students had no difficulty at all in reporting on their experiences of private speech. Their memories came thick and fast. One of the students, Dorcas, reporting that she often used private speech as a child, says, 'If I was playing and they (parents) call me and send me somewhere may be to get something for them, they said I became angry and would talk to myself on the way.' Identifying self-talk with emotivity, Dina writes, 'Yes, I still talk to myself, when I am irritated, angry or stressed.'

Katlego points out 'We tend to think people are insane if they talk to themselves.' Sibongile claims, 'When I have to do a presentation, and I become nervous that I am going to stand in front of many people, I just tell myself aloud that I am going to succeed and I am a winner! After saying these words to myself, I become a bit calm and confident.' Katlego uses private speech to score goals on the soccer field. It is easy for students to recognise the emotive function of private speech (a theory first put forward by Piaget and extended by Vygotsky to also include the cognitive and self-regulative function of private speech for problem solving).

It is significant to note that the students of *CELS 302* not only observed the widespread use of private speech among young children, but pointed out how prevalent it is among the elders in their community. Their generalisation was that private speech declined during adulthood because of the social stigma attached to its public display. 'Children don't feel embarrassed or ashamed when they talk to themselves but adults do because people will think they are mad or crazy', writes Mpho, while Mosima recounts, 'My grandmother who is 67 years old talks to herself, especially when nobody wants to spend time with her. She says to herself, 'Le tla nkopola ke sule!' (You will remember me when I am dead).' These accounts show that students are capable of views similar to Piaget's that private speech is used to express emotion (namely, the emotive function of private speech referred to earlier).

Many students claim that private speech occurs in children's play. Delinah notes: 'I speculate that children from the age of 3 to 7 years do use private speech especially when they are playing with their toys; they would talk to the toys as if they are talking to some human being.'

In discussing private speech in fantasy play, debates broke out among students about whether a well-known Pedi game, *Masekitlana*, is a form of private speech or not. Various accounts of this game were provided, clearly showing that younger children engaged in a solitary form of this game, while older and more accomplished children played it socially with other children. Other differences relating to the geographic origins of the game, or whether it was played in more rural or urban settings, also emerged. All these accounts created a rich resource base of EK from which to draw on in the process of the transformation of knowledge to SK.

## Narratives on private speech from lecturers

Both the lecturers (the authors of this chapter) narrated incidents from their own experience which involved private speech. One of the authors clearly remembered her younger sister spending several minutes, on several different occasions, talking to a lamp post, in which she (the sister) recounted a story and even drew figures in the sand with a stick. It seems to ER that her sister was using the lamp post as an imaginary friend and talking to it, but clearly, her private speech was being used to clarify some ideas that were difficult for her to understand. The diagrams she drew in the sand were for her own self-clarification (what Vygotsky has termed as 'self-mediation').

ER herself engaged in private speech while playing teacher-teacher in a form of fantasy role play. She would cut out leftover pages from school exercise books, stitch them up into small books, write names on them (usually of her classmates) and then pretend to be a teacher and 'talk' to her imaginary students. She even wrote in these little exercise books and did sums in them. This was the kind of pretend play she enjoyed so much that she soon got her sisters and friends to role-play her students and spent several hours 'teaching' them and 'marking' their work in the little exercise books. Sharing such childhood memories of make-believe or pretend play demonstrated to students that a child growing up 50 years ago in a city in urban South India shared much with a child in rural South Africa, though separated in time and space. Students were enabled to see the power of Vygotsky's claim that private speech and pretend play may be universal stages in child development.

MJ's narrative on private speech was not about his own experiences of engaging in private speech but rather on a story that he was told at the university he worked in in India, Loyola Autonomous College. Sometime in the mid-twentieth century, the famous Indian physicist C.V. Raman (who won the Nobel Prize for Physics for his work in crystallography) visited the college. The story goes that Raman was invited to give a scientific lecture, but unfortunately and unexpectedly, the day of the lecture was declared a holiday for students and staff. However, Raman insisted he would deliver his lecture and requested the embarrassed organisers to round up whoever they could find so that he could deliver the lecture. The lecture theatre quickly filled up with cleaners, gardeners, cooks and office workers who were present at the college on that day. Raman delivered his lecture and at the end thanked his audience profusely because he had been grappling with a difficult conceptual issue in physics and talking to them had helped him resolve it!

Such stories vividly bring across to students the fact that talking (even to someone who does not understand you) helps to clarify one's thinking and to solve problems. Students are then able to identify the self-regulative function of private speech, a function they do not see as readily as they do the emotive function. Some students (such as a mature student we had a few years ago called Pinox) have extremely strong beliefs and maintain that children use only emotive private speech whereas adults use self-conscious and deliberate private speech for self-regulation and planning.

Such disclosures open up a space to create a fund of stories to share on the widespread phenomenon of self-talk, especially in pretend (or fantasy) play.

## The mobility of narratives

The anecdote about C.V. Raman's scientific lecture shows exploratory speech and private speech intertwined, but it also exemplifies a phatic function for the illiterate non-scientific audience. This anecdote coming from another time and country is possible because MJ carries these stories as part of the geographic migration of Indians to South Africa.

Another form of migration is illustrated by students who talk about *Masekitlane* mentioned earlier. It is a storytelling game in which players (usually female children) use stones to represent characters in a story. The narrator gives names to each stone (character) and plays out a drama in which she role-plays each character, taking on the voice, movements and gestures of the characters. Usually there is an audience of other children, listening to the story and awaiting their turn to be the narrator. The stories enacted are often based on children's observations of adult behaviour in their communities. Pamla talks about her daughter playing *Masekitlana*, which she learns at school from other children and then brings home. This shows a reversal from earlier generations of *Masekitlana* players, who first encountered it in their homes and communities and then took this game to school. In terms of the content of the stories enacted by the children, they often seem to be influenced currently by programmes they watch on TV or by stories in books and magazines, which players of earlier generations did not have access to.

The student Pinox introduced earlier in this chapter had a different account of the game from his classmates: in his village all the very young children play a solitary form of *Masekitlana*, even if they play it collectively. In other words, each child would play the game on its own, in the company of others similarly playing on their own. There is no interaction or communication between these children. Pinox used Piaget's concept of 'collective monologues' to capture his observations, and resisted the view that the children may have first encountered the game themselves as part of an audience watching someone else telling a story. He rejected the Vygotskyan view that the private derives from the social. Other students argued that the private and the social are different variants of the game. Staff researching this concluded that the social form of the game is the norm, and that very young children use the solitary form to rehearse for the social more mature play. Though the relationship between social and solitary play is not even resolved at the research forefront, these debates among the students show that variation is a cognitive resource that advances theory construction. The students' differences arise from their observations, based on their own sociogeographic origins and histories. Theory construction therefore also becomes more complex and infused with local knowledges, exposing the idea that ethnographic studies (SK) are also varied.

In other words, Western scientific knowledge (SK) of which ethnography is a part, is revealed to the students as not homogeneous and static but also diverse and dynamic. The students link their diverse sociogeographic local knowledges with the diversity in Western knowledge. Epistemic diversity therefore becomes a resource in the search for universality and thus allows for an authentic constructivist pedagogy. In the case of African-language-speaking students (such as in *CELS 302*) the local knowledges are embedded in their mother tongue, Sesotho sa Leboa/Sepedi. Since the CELS students are bilingual (but better versed in Sepedi than in English) they are better able to access local knowledges embedded in Sepedi. As they convert and interpret their EKs into English, they move closer to attaining the knowledge capital (modern scientific knowledge) and linguistic capital (CALP English) that we regard as genuine epistemic access.

That they do indeed acquire knowledge and linguistic capital can be shown through their writing, of which we give examples below:

> I disagree with Piaget's thinking when he says that egocentric speech is a symptom of weakness and immaturity in the child's thinking which will disappear when the child grows older. From Vygotsky's data I got a new comprehension of egocentric speech that it plays a specific role in the child's activity. It shows the child thinking. (Mpho)

> Private speech can also occur to serve a function of self-regulation, which involves planning and thinking aloud. It is also called the cognitive function. I have also experienced it. It happens to me usually when I have to write an examination, I would say to myself aloud the points I have learnt. (Sibongile)

Unlike Piaget, Vygotsky has rightfully noted that this phenomenon (private speech) cannot be viewed in isolation, but rather is part of both language and cognitive development in children. (Abram)

In my own experience, egocentric speech was never given much attention or recognition. When a person was found talking alone, s/he was considered to be out of their mind, especially at an elderly age. Even at school, students are not encouraged to speak while given work to do. No matter how difficult the task may be, they are never encouraged to use egocentric speech to solve the problem or to plan how to tackle the problem. Whenever a child was found talking to oneself, she will be seen as someone who is just playing and no attention will be paid to egocentric speech. (Mapelo)

External examiners of *CELS 302* examination scripts have been pleasantly surprised at the fluency, enthusiasm and engagement with which these Sepedi-speaking students write in English!

Moving back now to the stories, the mobility of these narratives is possible because of the convergence of students and teachers from different places and times (in the new South Africa) in spaces such as our university. We see these stories as a rich resource to draw upon in the acquisition of Western knowledge. These narrations help the students to become more confident of the scope and value of private speech, as shown in their writings above. Additionally, they also begin to make hypotheses about the universality of both private speech and fantasy play. However, these generalisations do not guarantee that students can move to scientific concepts. As Davydov (1988) notes, generalisations based on the inexplicit and intuitive articulation of EK is slow, and not as systematic as scientific generalisations based on SK. However, the students' EK enables them to generate hypotheses, as mentioned earlier. The value of hypotheses lies in increasing student motivation, and ability to generalise, a cognitive skill they deploy in their encounters with scholarly texts.

## The role of narratives in moving from EK to SK

The movement from SK to EK and back that we sketched (in Figure 6.1) is only possible because both local and Western knowledges move either via electronic media or through the actual movement of people who carry the stories of their childhood (and other experiences) in their heads. We need a pedagogy based on the mobility of knowledges across space and time to give value to these stories in education. We need to unlock the narratives of space and time by seeing them as valid knowledges (as well as the languages in which this knowledge is encoded) so that they can be deployed as a means to connect with Western knowledges. In this sense, our use of diversity of knowledges and languages is not primarily to affirm the identity of marginalised communities. Preserving this identity is often the goal of multilingual campaigns and research studies (such as the ecological approach of Hornberger). In our case, recovering stories from marginalised communities is primarily a means to epistemic access. A failure to enable students to gain epistemic access only results in a weak form of cultural identity (a notion of identity that does not empower students) coexisting with a strongly entrenched domination of (incomprehensible) scientific knowledge in English. Access to varieties of local knowledges embedded in local languages is possible, as we have shown, if autoethnographic methods of elicitation are used by the teacher.

## Autoethnography in pedagogy

Autoethnography is a relatively new method within ethnography used for researching any activity through self-report data. It has recently been used in research studies (Finley, 2005; Dyck, 2010; Davis and Davis, 2010; Skinner, 2010) of performance (such as drama, dance, play and sport). There is no reason why teachers should not use such methods as a pedagogic resource. The teacher's use of autoethnography to unlock the narratives embedded in time and space is an example of teacher appropriation of research methods directly into pedagogy. The famous teacher and researcher of child play, Paley (2004), provides a good example of the need for adults (teachers) to value their own childhood play as a resource to connect with children's play. As classrooms become more and more diverse, leading to teachers usually seeing diversity as a problem, we need a curricular principle that sees such diversity as a resource for epistemic access. Probing students' stories around a particular key concept could do this if the teacher recognises the diversity of the geographic and temporal origins from which stories emanate. In other words, a sociogeographic awareness on the part of the teacher, and its transference to students, legitimises the telling of stories across space and time.

Using narratives around the same genres (private speech and fantasy play) helps us to value these genres as knowledge-constructing episodes. Students' lives are rich with these episodes and treating them as a resource helps to illuminate abstract scholarly texts in the process, as we have shown. Students' EK becomes transformed into SK through their research, leading to a new view of EK. Teachers' sharing of their own EK leads to a view of research as a collective learning process. Needless to say, such processes are always highly motivating for students and teachers.

## Epistemic diversity in SK

The original research on private speech by Piaget and Vygotsky was performed with limited samples of European and Russian children respectively in limited experimental settings. These methodological limitations of Piaget and Vygotsky's research are recognised by scholars (such as Fuson, 1979) as a reason for doubting their claims of universality.

The contradiction between the students' introspective data (EK grounded in their intuitive knowledge of their communities' naturalistic practices) and the experimental methods used by scholars opened the way to looking at diversity in the key stages (private speech and play) in other societies. We also decided to include the teaching staff's own historic backgrounds of their childhood practices as a resource from another country (as both the teachers/authors are from India) and other stories from the metropolitan city of Johannesburg. We soon found that some of the students came from different villages or townships in Limpopo, each with variations in the particular make-believe game called *Masekitlana* referred to earlier. Most of these accounts were described narratively and this is not surprising as the childhood activities remembered by adult students or staff were performances, i.e. role plays.

The narrative accounts of private speech in play in everyday contexts gave us better access to the geographic and temporal dimensions of the people who engaged in the play. The travel of knowledges has increased due to globalisation in general, and in South Africa, due to the increased social mobility of black students in a post-apartheid context, and the mobility of non-South African teachers coming into this country.

## Conclusion

In this chapter we have shown that epistemic diversity arises from the transfer of everyday knowledges across space and time. The *CELS 302* module on language and cognition exemplifies how pedagogic criteria that link historically and geographically mobile EK with modern, Western SK can be further enriched by using autoethnographic elicitation techniques to stimulate student and staff narratives related to key concepts from the disciplines. Far from seeing diversity of EK and its local languages as a problem, or even as a goal to achieve local identity, we see the diversity of local knowledges as enabling marginalised students to gain access to SK and to dominant discourses, examples of which we have given in this chapter. At the same time the acquisition of dominant discourses through students' EK is shown to result in transforming these local knowledges, giving them an epistemic status that frees them from their original tacit moorings.

## Acknowledgement

The authors are grateful for the very helpful comments made by an anonymous reviewer.

## References

Bernstein, B. (1973). *Class, codes and control.* London: Routledge & Kegan Paul.

Davis, D. L. and Davis, D. I. (2010). Duelling memories: twinship and the disembodiment of identity. In P. Collins and A. Gallinat (eds), *The ethnographic self as resource: writing memory and experience into ethnography* (pp. 129–49). Oxford: Berghahn Books.

Davydov, V. V. (1988). The concept of theoretical generalization of L. S. Vygotsky. *Soviet Psychology*, 3: 44–55.

Dyck, N. (2010). Remembering and the ethnography of children's sports. In P. Collins and A. Gallinat (eds), *The ethnographic self as resource: writing memory and experience into ethnography* (pp. 150–64). Oxford: Berghahn Books.

Edelsky, C. (2006). *With literacy and justice for all: rethinking the social in language and education.* London: Routledge.

Finley, S. (2005). Arts-based inquiry: performing revolutionary pedagogy. In N. K. Denkin and Y. Lincoln (eds), *The SAGE handbook of qualitative research* (pp. 681–94). London: SAGE.

Fuson, K. C. (1979). The development of self-regulating aspects of speech: a review. In G. Zivin (ed.), *The development of self-regulation through private speech* (pp. 135–218). New York: Wiley.

Heath, S. (1983). *Ways with words: language, life and work in communities and classrooms.* Cambridge: Cambridge University Press.

Hedegaard, M. (1990). The zone of proximal development as basis for instruction. In L. C. Moll (ed.), *Vygotsky and education: instructional implications and applications of sociohistorical psychology* (pp. 349–71). Cambridge, UK: Cambridge University Press.

Henning, E. (2008). Theoretical struggles in the Zo-ped of research programmes. *Education as Change*, 12(2): 5–24.

Hornberger, N. (2003). *Continua of biliteracy: an ecological framework for educational policy, research and practice in multilingual settings.* Clevedon: Multilingual Matters.

Janks, H. (2004). The access paradox. *English in Australia*, 12(1): 33–42.

Janks, H. (2010). *Literacy and power.* New York: Routledge.

Joseph, M. and Ramani, E. (2004). Academic excellence through language equity: case study of the new bilingual degree (in English and Sesotho sa Leboa) at the University of the North. In H. Griesel (ed.), *Curriculum responsiveness: case studies in higher education* (pp. 237–61). Pretoria: SAUVCA: ISBN 0-620-33085-6.

Joseph, M. and Ramani, E. (2011). Researching one's way into Vygotsky. *Education as Change*, 15 (2): 115–29.

Lodge, H. (1997). Providing access to literacy in the Arts Foundation Programme at the University of Witwatersrand in 1996: the theory behind the practice. Unpublished dissertation, University of Witwatersrand, Johannesburg.

Meyer, J. H. F. and Land, R. (2006). *Overcoming barriers to student learning: threshold concepts and troublesome knowledge.* London: Routledge.

Moll, L. C., Amanti, C., Neft, D. and Gonzalez, N. (1992). Funds of knowledge for teaching: using a qualitative approach to connect homes and classrooms. *Theory into Practice*, 31 (2): 132–41.

National Language Policy for Higher Education (2002). Department of Education, Pretoria, South Africa.

Paley, V. G. (2004). *A child's work: the importance of fantasy play.* Chicago: The University of Chicago Press.

Piaget, J. (1962). *Play, dreams, and imitation.* New York: WW Norton & Co.

Ramani, E. and Joseph, M. (2002). Breaking new ground: introducing an African language as medium of instruction at the University of the North. *Perspectives in Education*, Special issue on Multilingualism, 20 (1): 233–40.

Ramani, E. and Joseph, M. (2008). Achieving academic excellence through higher-order thinking in an African language. *Perspectives in Education*, 26 (4): 42–56.

Ramani, E., Kekana, T., Modiba, M. and Joseph, M. (2007). Terminology vs. concept development through discourse: insights from a dual-medium BA degree. *Southern African Linguistics and Applied Language Studies*, 25(2): 207–23.

Skinner, J. (2010). Leading questions and the body memories: a case of phenomenology and physical ethnography in the dance interview. In P. Collins and A. Gallinat (eds), *The ethnographic self as resource: writing memory and experience into ethnography* (pp. 111–28). Oxford: Berghahn Books.

Vygotksy, L. (1986). *Thought and language.* Cambridge, Mass.: MIT Press. (Original work published 1934.)

# 7
# Reassembling the Literacy Event in Shirley Brice Heath's *Ways with Words*

*Kimberly Lenters*

> After typing out the stories just as they were told into the
> tape recorder, some teachers found that a few students
> would reject their oral version in written form. (Heath,
> 1983: 304)

Shirley Brice Heath's work in the Carolina Piedmonts resulted in an ethnographic study covering a span of ten years from 1969 to 1978, in which she chronicled language use in three communities, Roadville, Trackton and Maintown. Her rich accounting of the literate practices of three culturally diverse groups living in close proximity to one another was groundbreaking in redefining literacy.

The pedagogical context of *Ways with Words* is reminiscent of urban classrooms worldwide, where children of diverse linguistic, cultural and social backgrounds are educated. In these transcontextualised settings, students frequently have limited familiarity with the pedagogy employed or find that their personal practice of literacy falls outside the school 'mainstream'. In *Ways with Words*, Heath pioneered the use of the *literacy event* as a means of examining the language and literacy practices in the homes, communities and school of Roadville, Trackton and Maintown. However, with its 'here and now' orientation, the literacy event may not be the best means for understanding literacy practices in contexts, such as schools with diverse populations, where multiple local and global agents have an interest in determining literacy curricula. In this chapter, I engage with Heath's account of literacy practices in the Piedmont communities to ask how bringing concepts of materiality into the literacy event – through *literacy-in-action* – can open up theoretical possibilities for transcontextual literacy studies in pedagogical contexts.

## The literacy event

Heath's *Ways with Words* (1983) is viewed as one of the most influential works contributing to our understanding of literacy within the body of work known as the new literacy studies (NLS) (Baynham, 2004; Cook-Gumperz, 2006; Collins and Blot, 2003; Street and Lefstein, 2007). Heath is credited with providing sociocultural or social practice studies of literacy with a new unit of analysis: *the literacy event*. The introduction of the literacy event was a significant stage in the theorisation of literacy as a social practice, as it provided a common unit of analysis, allowing for a comparison of literacy practices across a variety of contexts when it was subsequently taken up by numerous ethnographic studies of literacy.

In *Ways with Words*, Heath documents the myriad oral and written language practices of members of three communities. The ten-year-long ethnographic study began with Trackton families in 1968, added Roadville families in the mid-1970s and subsequently included the Maintown families to provide a contrast to language use in Trackton and Roadville. Roadville represented a white working-class neighbourhood; Trackton, an African-American working-class neighbourhood; and Maintown represented a middle-class, mixed race group dispersed throughout the town known as Gateway. In two parallel articles (1982a, b), Heath more explicitly describes the data analysis connected to the ethnographic study. These two articles were later reprinted in several edited volumes as late as 2009, attesting to the conceptual longevity of the ideas contained therein.

Building on the concept of speech events (Hymes, 1977/1994) and borrowing from Anderson et al. (1980), who briefly used the concept, Heath defined the literacy event as 'any occasion in which a piece of writing is integral to the nature of participants' interactions and their interpretive processes' (1982a: 350). Within a social practice perspective, *literacy practices*, which are not observable in the same way as a literacy event, given that they involve values, attitudes, feelings and social relationships (Street, 1993), are inferred by observing instantiated literacy events over a period of time (Barton et al., 2000).

Baynham (2004) divides the 30-year history of sociocultural studies of literacy into three generations. In early studies, such as *Ways with Words*, local situated studies of the way literacy is practised were undertaken. Second-generation literacy studies explored the relationship between the literacy event and literacy practices. One of the legacies of first- and second-generation literacy studies has been a naturalisation of the literacy event, as frequently evidenced in studies where it is seen as requiring no introduction or citation. For example, Rowe and Leander (2005) analyse the production of material and embodied features of third space in classroom literacy events. While they utilise the literacy event as a unit of analysis they neither cite its origin nor define it.

## Third-generation literacy studies

Recent work in the NLS has come to re-examine some of the concepts once considered fundamental (Barton and Hamilton, 2005; Baynham and Prinsloo, 2009; Collins and Blot, 2003; Kell, 2006; Reder and Davila, 2005). Teased apart, the interconnecting concerns question ideas of situated context and agency in literacy studies, the adequacy of the literacy event as a unit of analysis, and the anthrocentric point of view taken in literacy studies research.

In first- and second-generation literacy studies, how can we call literacies purely situated or local when, particularly in a world connected by media, so many outside influences mediate those literacies? With regard to agency, how much of the literacy practised by individuals and communities in their uses of literacy is shaped within and how much is shaped by others? The question thus becomes: is the literacy event, with the way it conceptualises particular instantiations of literacy as bounded events, sufficient for deriving literacy practices when issues of situated context and agency are taken into account?

And finally, questions have arisen regarding the anthrocentric point of view literacy studies have fostered. With the important work of the NLS in shifting the focus from literacy as a technical skill to an understanding of what people do with literacy, have we come to a point of disregarding an inherent aspect of literate interactions, the various texts that are inevitably involved (Brandt and Clinton, 2002; Michaels and Sohmer, 2000; Omerod and Ivanic, 2000)?

Recent work incorporating concepts of materiality in literacy studies shows promise for dealing with issues of situated context, agency and anthrocentricity. For example, current work utilising object ethnography (Carrington, 2012), multimodality (Pahl and Rowsell, 2006, 2010), activity theory (Bomer, 2007; Kell, 2006) and actor-network-theory (Hamilton, 2001; Leander and Lovvorn, 2006; Michaels and Sohmer, 2000; Nichols, 2006) considers the material forms of literacy and what those who interact with those texts invest in them.

Actor-network-theory (ANT) (Latour, 2005) and the work of Brandt and Clinton (2002) provide a helpful approach to investigating materiality in literacy studies, particularly those that seek to account for transcontextual literacy practices. ANT uses an ethnographic approach to trace material and human resources to understand social processes. In this sociology of associations, humans are seen as delegating roles and responsibilities to objects (labelled as *actants*), which often endure long after humans have left the scene. Latour contends that by tracing the objects that circulate within and between sites of human social interaction, that is, by following *all* of the actants, human and non-human, an accounting of the social becomes possible. ANT does not ascribe causal agency to objects, but it does argue that objects, through the roles and responsibilities delegated to them by humans, play an agentive role in creating or maintaining power relationships.

## Literacy-in-action

Drawing on the work of Latour, Brandt and Clinton (2002) propose replacing the main unit of analysis in literacy studies, the literacy event, as one means for addressing challenges to the NLS. In the literacy event, the written materials or texts tend to be primarily viewed as contextual features, something participants act upon. What this concept ignores is the fact that the texts involved are very often constructed outside of the particular literacy event. And, therefore, the meanings those distantly constructed texts carry may be mediating that literate interaction. Brandt and Clinton's proposal brings these texts into the central action of the literate encounter – it gives objects a seat at the table, as it were. Rather than being objects only acted upon by the participants in a literate interaction, the texts become 'actants' through the agency delegated to them by human actors – at times they, in effect, push back on the participants in the interaction. By bringing objects such as texts or other technologies of communication into the analysis – by seeing them as having a place in the literate interaction and not just as contextual features or inactive bystanders – it becomes possible to understand literate interactions more fully.

The unit of analysis, literacy-in-action, allows for an examination in literacy studies that can follow 'objective trace[s] of literacy in a setting (print, instruments, paper, other technologies) whether they are being taken up by local actors or not' (Brandt and Clinton, 2002: 349). These objective traces, or literacy objects, may be constructed in distant places and yet be co-opted to play a role in local literacy practices. According to Brandt and Clinton, the construct of literacy-in-action intentionally carries a double meaning, 'The construct orients us to ask: What part does literacy play in the action and what does it look like in action?' (2002: 349). Or more simply, this new unit of analysis allows us to look at what people are doing with literacy and how literacy, in its material form, may be mediating that activity.

In recent studies examining literacy practices in elementary school classrooms, a colleague and I have used literacy-in-action to trace the way pedagogy conceptualised in the academic spaces of literacy pedagogy researchers made its way into a local classroom (Lenters, 2012; Lenters and McTavish, 2013). We were able to successfully demonstrate ways that literacy objects created in distant spaces, travelled through numerous connected spaces to be taken up by human actors in a local classroom to mediate children's classroom literacy practices. The work provided a helpful exploration of one means by which pedagogies and practices viewed as rich in the ivory tower come to be distorted in practice in local classrooms.

The concept of literacy-in-action is somewhat contested, however. Kell (2006) and Street (2003) express concern that, in ascribing any form of agency to literacy objects, we run the risk of reinscribing autonomous notions of literacy. To be certain, this is a matter of concern. When working with the concept of literacy-in-action, researchers must always be mindful that objects only take on agency, or the appearance of agency, through the roles and responsibilities delegated to them by human agents. In and of themselves, they have no agency, deterministic abilities or capacity for causality. Nonetheless, as I argue in this chapter, the role of literacy objects cannot be ignored in studies that wish to examine the transcontextual nature of literacy as as social practice.

## Method

I catalogued literacy events located in the three original publications (1982a, b, 1983). For this chapter, I use two literacy events in the lives of Roadville and Trackton families and one aggregated literacy event that took place in the Maintown school with Roadville, Trackton and Maintown students to elaborate the way literacy-in-action can be used to deepen the analysis of what took place in local sites of literate activity. In this enterprise my goal is to take exemplars familiar to ethnographic researchers and examine them through a new lens. By doing so, we are enabled to take a more focused look at the theoretical possibility of ANT and literacy-in-action as a unit of analysis in literacy studies.

After presenting Heath's literacy event analysis, I use the concept, literacy-in-action, with its dual focus of examining what people are doing in an interaction involving text and how those texts mediate that literate activity, to provide a sense of what may be gained by including a notion of textual 'agency' at the fundamental level of unit of analysis. To further guide the analysis, I follow the steps outlined by Latour (2005) for employing ANT. By following the actors, as they present themselves in observational research or in inscriptions, the researcher assembles what are termed 'actor-networks'. In these actor-networks, who and/or what is participating in the action is carefully plotted by laying down plausible or traceable connections between actors and sites (chains of actors). Next the network is examined, and questions such as the following may be asked: How do these actants work together as a durable whole in this moment of interaction? How is the local itself being generated? What circulates from site to site? And finally, once these associations have been laid out and considered, the matter of political relevance is addressed. At this stage, the ethnographer has a strong sense of what the actants – distant and local – are doing, and is able to realistically make observations, posit explanations and draw conclusions about what is happening.

## Writing a thank you note in Roadville

In this literate interaction (Figure 7.1), Mrs Macken is apprenticing seven-year-old Kim into the practice of thank you note writing. Kim

*Staying in Touch*

Mrs. Macken, while kneading bread, kept one eye on Kim, who was studying a single sheet of lined stationery at the kitchen table. Kim twisted and turned, chewed on the pencil, while Mrs. Macken said, "Just ask how they are, and tell them what you've been doing. Then tell them 'thank you' for the nice birthday present." Kim wrote slowly and laboriously using her best second-grade writing for several lines, carefully forming the letters, and then asked, "How do you spell *basket*?" Mrs. Macken lifted her hands out of the dough, dusted them off and walked to the table to look over Kim's shoulder: "Why do you want that word?" "I wanted to tell 'em what I made at Bible School." Mrs. Macken smiled and said, "That's not necessary, just say you went to Bible School. That's enough, and don't forget to thank them." Kim erased the last line she had written, wrote "Thank you for the present.", signed her full name with a flourish of triumph as her pencil point broke. Mrs. Macken reminded her to add "Love," above her signature and released Kim to go outdoors to play.

(Heath, 1983, 211–12)

*Figure 7.1*   Field notes of interaction in which seven-year-old Kim is being apprenticed into thank you note writing in Roadville

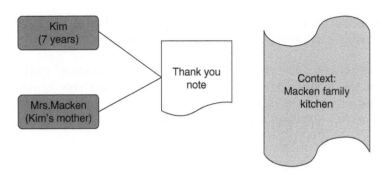

*Figure 7.2*  Literacy event – learning to write a thank you note

appears to be somewhat unengaged with the process – whether this is because she has other things she would prefer to do, or because she does not know how to get started with the thank you note, is unclear. Mrs Macken gives her directions, 'Just ask them how they are, and tell them what you've been doing. Then tell them "thank you" for the nice birthday present', a direction she later reverses when Kim writes what she has been doing (making baskets at Bible School) and Mrs Macken tells her this is an unnecessary addition.

Heath presents this as a literacy event exemplifying the note writing that 'takes place in connection with holidays, family celebrations, and crises in personal lives, such as sickness and death' (1983: 212) amongst female members of Roadville homes. The literacy event analysis does not query the preciseness of the apprenticeship that Kim receives from Mrs Macken in regard to what was acceptable content for the note and what should be excluded or the fact that Mrs Macken seemed to have predetermined ideas of what belonged in the note that she herself was unable to articulate. As a literacy event, this interaction can be represented as in Figure 7.2.

## Thank you note writing as literacy-in-action

By looking at a further observation Heath makes regarding the purpose and content of thank you notes in Roadville and employing literacy-in-action, which brings the thank you note into the action as an actant, a deeper analysis of this literate interaction becomes possible. Heath states that the women of Roadville write fewer letters as their families grow, citing 'no quiet time to themselves' (Heath, 1983: 215) in which to write letters. But the practice of writing greeting cards and thank you notes is one with which they continue in spite of being busy,

> for these are strongly tied to courtesy and 'good breeding.' The brief notes on these carry little news though, and their only conversational gambit is the 'how are you opener.' The remainder of the message is without conversational character and carries a minimum of content. (p. 215)

Here we gain a sense of the importance of the thank you notes and the expectations regarding tenor and content. Not only are thank you notes a means for connecting with family in distant places, as they are circulated between actors, they carry the meaning that the author of the note is courteous and well-bred. Understanding the meaning with which this literacy object is imbued helps shed light on why it was important to Mrs Macken that Kim should be apprenticed into the proper conventions for writing a thank you note. While Mrs Macken may not have been able to articulate these conventions, as evidenced in her reversal of directive regarding the content of the note, she appears to be certain of them when she says, 'That's not necessary; just say you went to Bible School. That's enough, and don't forget to thank them' (Heath, 1983: 212). Sending a thank you note would demonstrate Kim's good upbringing, but for her to send a thank you note to her relatives that may not have adhered to thank you note conventions, as understood by the Macken adults, may have conveyed the wrong impression to the Macken relative to whom Kim was writing. This literacy object, as it was circulated, may be seen to have the capacity, in Mrs Macken's understanding, to convey an impression that could either reflect well or poorly on her as a mother (see Figure 7.3).

This interpretation of an agency-laden thank you note, used not only to socialise a young girl into demonstrating good manners but also to display the good parenting she has received, is supported by the three storybook reading events Heath highlights (1982a, b, 1983). Heath demonstrates the way Roadville adults 'initiate their children both into pre-scripted discourse around printed material and into passive listening behavior' (1983: 227). She concludes that adults in Roadville believe 'the proper use of words and understanding of the meaning of written words are important for their children's educational and religious success' (1982b: 61).

Literacy objects are used assiduously in Roadville for socialising young children, and as such may also be seen as actants in Roadville children's

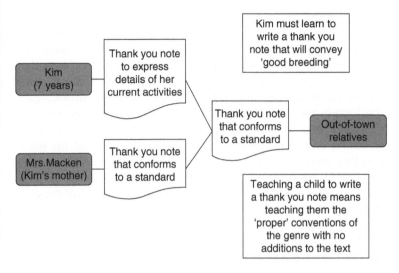

*Figure 7.3* Literacy-in-action – learning to write a thank you note

interactions with literacy. The agency carried by thank you notes and storybooks does not go unnoticed by Roadville children who have to be 'forced' into writing thank notes and come to find storybook reading sessions where they are expected to passively sit and listen 'troublesome' and to be avoided (Heath, 1982b: 60). Some Roadville children learn at an early age to push back against the socialising responsibilities their parents delegate to certain literacy objects.

## Using the language experience approach with Roadville and Trackton students

One aspect of the pedagogy employing ethnography in the classrooms Heath researched is the use of a form of the language experience approach (LEA) for literacy instruction (Ashton-Warner, 1963; Hall, 1970). In LEA, learners orally relate their experiences or stories to a teacher, who transcribes them as they are spoken. These transcriptions are generally written word for word in order to help learners see the connections between their spoken words and the symbolic representation the teacher is constructing. In this pedagogy, the transcriptions are subsequently used as the basis for further reading and writing activities.

Non-mainstream (i.e. Roadville and Trackton) and mainstream (i.e. Maintown) children would have been involved in the LEA activity. One of the difficulties the teachers encountered with the Roadville students was their difficulty producing elaborated or fictional stories (see Heath, 1983: 304). As one means of assisting them with this mainstream school literacy practice, some teachers asked young students to dictate their stories into a tape recorder. The teacher then transcribed the students' stories verbatim and produced multiple copies that were distributed to all students in the class. Heath describes this activity and an associated complication as follows: 'In the primary grades, teachers used these oral story-telling activities for several purposes. After typing out the stories just as they were told into the tape recorder, some teachers found that a few students would reject their oral version in written form' (p. 304).

In her analysis of the situation, Heath does not engage with the question of why the students might 'reject' the written form of their oral stories but instead endorses the LEA practice as one that developed in students' new understandings of their classmates' reading preferences. She states: 'Since the written versions of the stories were often distributed on the desks of class members when they came into language arts class, students began to develop sensitivities about what their classmates liked to read' (1983: 304–5).

## The language experience approach and literacy-in-action

What might be behind the students' rejection of their spoken words in print? By using literacy-in-action as the unit of analysis, we can examine not only the participants' activity in this particular interaction; we can also look at the way the literacy objects involved (voice recordings and multiple print copies of students' stories) may have played a role in the students' uneasiness with the practice.

Focusing on the transcription and the multiple copies that a student's peers could now read as a group and asking what part the multiplied literacy objects are playing in this activity brings out other possible interpretations for the students' discomfort. Their non-standard English with its grammar and word choice differences is now crystallised in written form, not only audible to fellow students but visible and durable. Their story may not follow mainstream construction of a story and this is now made more apparent to their peers. These objects, circulated and studied by all in the classroom, draw further attention to students who differ from those whose discourse fits the mainstream.

Literacy-in-action allows the examination to look beyond the temporal moment of the literacy event. The oral stories, in durable print form, now have the capacity to endure, to 'hang around' and serve as reminders, beyond the moment of the immediate literacy event, of the non-mainstream students' language differences. Given the centrality of language in personal identity, looking at the activity of the objects also allows us to ask questions related to identity formation and how those printed stories might inadvertently function to negatively position students before their classmates.

Corroboration of this new understanding of the difficulties associated with using LEA with the Roadville and Trackton students may be found in a statement regarding a 'students as ethnographers' project used by the teachers. Students in one class had prepared a videotaped 'program' explaining some of the ethnographic language arts projects in which they were involved. Their teachers were concerned the video might be accidentally erased and asked that a transcription be made. 'When the students saw in print what they had said on tape, they were uneasy; several recognized that their choice of words and ways of talking "didn't look right"' (Heath, 1983: 313).

These students' response to the transcript may shed light on the LEA students' reaction to their printed stories. Rather than engaging with the uncomfortable position in which the non-mainstream students were put when they saw their 'choice of words' in print, the literacy event analysis moves on to explain how the teachers, instead, adapted their pedagogy to have the students write a summary of the video. But here again, it is the production of the literacy object, a material reminder of their language difference, that plays a role in the students' uneasiness.

## Applying for childcare in Trackton

In the transcript in Figure 7.4, one of the young mothers in Trackton, Lillie Mae, has just received a letter in the mail. The letter invites her to apply to have her child receive childcare at a local daycare facility. She opens the letter outside on her porch and shares it with neighbours and a visiting friend (see Figure 7.4).

As a literacy event, the interaction can be diagrammed as shown in Figure 7.5.

Heath's analysis of this interaction centres on three areas: literacy as an occasion for social activity; group negotiation of meaning of the text; and reading comprehension. 'On all of these occasions for reading and writing, individuals saw literacy as an occasion for social activities' (Heath, 1982a: 356). Elsewhere she states, 'The question, "What does this mean?" was answered not only from the information in the print, but from the

---

### TRACKTON TEXT X

Lillie Mae:    You hear this, it says Lem [then two years old] might can get into Ridgeway [a local neighbourhood center daycare program], but I hafta have the papers ready and apply by next Friday.

Visiting Friend:    You ever been to Kent to get his birth certificate? [friend is mother of three children already in school]

Mattie Crawford:    But what hours that program gonna be? You may not can get him there.

Lillie Mae:    They want the birth certificate? I got his vaccination papers.

Annie Mae:    Sometimes they take that, 'cause they can 'bout tell the age from those early shots.

Visiting Friend:    But you better get it, 'cause you gotta have it when he go to school anyway.

Lillie Mae:    But it says here they don't know what hours yet. How am I gonna get over to Kent? How much does it cost? Lemme see if the program costs anything. (She reads aloud part of the letter.)

---

*Figure 7.4*   Transcript of Trackton parent reading invitation to apply for childcare

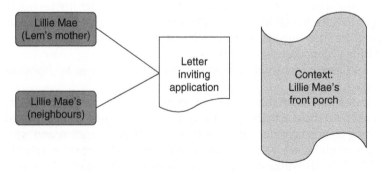

*Figure 7.5*   Literacy event – reading childcare invitation letter

group's joint bringing of experience to the text' (Heath, 1983: 197). She also notes that the interaction resembles the way individual readers who are categorised as strong readers use three levels of comprehension to extract meaning from the text (text level, utilising background knowledge, and synthesising information from the text and background knowledge). She states: 'Trackton residents as a group use these methods of extracting meaning from print on some occasions' (p. 392).

## Enrolling in a public institution as literacy-in-action

Literacy-in-action allows us to take an analysis like this a bit further by looking at the agency sedimented in the associated literacy objects and the institutions from which they emanate (see Figure 7.6). Civil rights legislation had recently opened previously segregated institutions to African Americans. Therefore, all of the forms and certificates brought out in the meaning negotiation process were official documents that would have been new to this generation of parents just placing their children in public educational institutions. While reading level may have been an issue associated with deciphering texts such as these letters, equally important is the negotiation of the bureaucratic maze such letters require. Taking one's child to daycare or school was not solely a matter

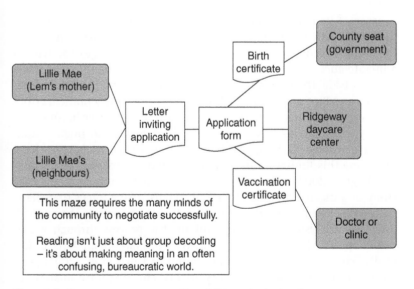

*Figure 7.6* Literacy-in-action – reading childcare invitation letter

of ensuring the child had a place in the programme and got there on time. Enrolling in daycare and school meant requiring an adult to prove the age of the child through a birth certificate. With another document, the adult had to prove that the child had received certain requisite vaccinations. If the child had not had been vaccinated, this regulation was one way of enforcing this public health initiative with families.

The intricate bureaucratic maze of institutions and documentation, brought into Lillie Mae's world through literacy objects, such as the childcare letter and application form, required the many minds of the community to negotiate successfully. In this example from Trackton, reading was not just about group decoding, group contribution of prior experience to text or an opportunity to socialise; it was about making meaning in an often confusing, bureaucratic new world that relied heavily on written documentation.

## Literacy-in-action, power, pedagogy and mobility

> We want to understand literacy's transcontextualized and transcontextualizing potentials. We are in search of new analytical concepts that can more readily explain how literacy, always locally manifested, nevertheless can function to delocalize or even disrupt local life. (Brandt and Clinton, 2002: 338)

Because of its bounded nature, its framing of literate interactions as discrete, locally situated events, bracketed off from outside influence, the literacy event is not able to account for the full range of activity in a literate encounter or address important power dynamics that come from 'outside' the local site, sedimented in travelling literacy objects. Collins and Blot state, 'Although *Ways* has been widely praised, critics have also noted that it avoids central questions of power in American society....' (2003: 44). As second- and third-generation literacy studies have worked to grapple with this issue, several researchers have overcome this limitation by layering analytical processes. For example, Rogers (2007) isolated literacy events in her ethnographic case study of a mother and daughter and the discursive forces that shape their lives. Recognising that the second layer of analysis she applied, discourse analysis, did not account for the process through which power operates in discourse, she added a third later of analysis, orders of discourse. Similarly, the studies found in Lewis et al. (2007) layer lenses of cultural studies, activity theory and discourse analysis to address issues of power.

Does changing the unit of analysis provide an alternative for addressing this issue? The foregoing reanalysis of the literacy practices derived from literacy events in the lives of Roadville and Trackton residents suggests that, indeed, a unit of analysis that takes into consideration the mediating influence of literacy objects provides the analytical means for looking at questions of power that is not possible using the literacy event.

## Power

As it traced literacy objects introduced into the lives of Trackton and Roadville residents, the analysis laid out in this chapter has shown the way objects, such as records and forms, are used for a variety of purposes in the exercise of power by people and institutions present in local literate interactions and those more distant. It has also demonstrated the way a power differential may be inadvertently reinforced, as in the cases of the transcriptions of students' oral stories and videos.

Situating ANT in literacy studies, literacy-in-action provides the means for seeing the ways local literacy practices, such as introducing a pedagogical innovation in school or using documents as gatekeepers to social services, such as childcare, may be mediated by policies and practices in distant locales: through the circulation of literacy objects. Glimpses of the notion that agency is deposited in, or responsibility is delegated to, literacy objects are found in some of Heath's observations. For example, the finding that Roadville women engage in the practice of writing greeting cards and thank you notes, in spite of having little time to do so, because 'these are strongly tied to courtesy and "good breeding"' (Heath, 1983: 215) suggests these cards and notes carry with them far more than a greeting or a thank you. Likewise, the statement 'written materials have determined the outcome of the request' (Heath, 1982a: 107) demonstrates an acknowledgement of the power vested in literacy objects. But the idea that these are literacy objects, whose activity can be examined to deepen the analysis of local literate practice, is not present. A sociological stance, such as that framing ANT, which acknowledges the activity of objects vested with authority or responsibility, is necessary for such an analysis.

Bringing a concept of materiality into literacy studies through literacy-in-action also enables us to see the way people extend their literacy practices into more distant locales to achieve specific goals. In Roadville, families use literacy objects not only as pedagogical tools to teach their young members how to display good manners, but as a means for parents to demonstrate the effectiveness of their parental socialisation skills to distant relatives or classroom teachers. In Trackton, parents learn to utilise literacy objects they know to be gatekeepers to their children's participation in distant institutions, such as daycare and schools, with the help of their friends and neighbours.

## Pedagogy

What went on to be taken up as innovative and useful pedagogy – the use of ethnography in the classroom to connect home, community and school literacies (e.g. Egan-Robertson and Bloome, 1998; Pahl and Rowsell, 2010) – can be seen, via literacy-in-action, to require certain caution in its implementation. The potential for some of the literacy objects produced by teachers and students in the Maintown classrooms to connect Roadville and Trackton students' home and community literacies to their classroom learning was enormously important. It came to be considered exemplary pedagogy for 'mainstream' classrooms with 'non-mainstream' students in contexts worldwide, from that point forward.

However, as the foregoing analysis has shown, the possibility for some of these seemingly neutral literacy objects (students' non-standard speech transcribed verbatim created as part of the ethnographic project) to further marginalise students must be seriously considered. Even pedagogies considered exemplary from a sociocultural or new literacies perspective, must be examined with regard to the agency carried by inscriptions of children's words. Engaging in such interrogation of pedagogy enables educators to provide the human mediation necessary to mitigate potential, unwitting alienation of non-mainstream students.

## Pedagogy and mobility

As the scholarly work in this volume illustrates, more people are 'on the move' globally than at any other time in human history. As a result of this translocation, classrooms worldwide are more culturally and linguistically diverse than ever before. And so, the very pedagogical context in which Heath conducted her research is one that is familiar worldwide: globally, non-mainstream children, some of them completely unfamiliar with formal learning institutions, are receiving their education in mainstream classrooms. Frequently taught by teachers whose own background is the dominant cultural or linguistic group of a particular society, following a curriculum written by educators of that same dominant group, these classrooms experience many of the same kinds of issues faced by the children of Trackton and Roadville as they were educated by their Maintown teachers in the Maintown school.

While in some local contexts, educators strive to develop culturally and linguistically relevant curricula and pedagogical styles that are inclusive of all members of the groups they teach, in other contexts the opposite occurs. 'Standards' requiring pedagogical approaches that promote the literacies of dominant groups and discount the literacies of non-mainstream groups often serve as gatekeepers, holding some students back until they can attain the literacies of the dominant group.

Sociocultural studies of literacy have looked at these phenomena for decades now. However, I argue that with the strong focus on agency of human participants in the new literacy studies, it is often difficult for a social practice perspective to adequately research literacy practices in formal learning institutions. In schools ... those that seek to be culturally and linguistically diverse and those that choose to ensure all students attain certain standards ... literacy objects abound. State-funded schools worldwide are feeling the pinch of shrinking government funding, leading to larger teacher : student ratios. In this context of large enrolments, educators frequently turn to the use of literacy objects, such as worksheets or digital reading tutors, to stand in their place. Furthermore, as the material possibilities for engaging with literacy open up to increasing numbers of students through the use of the Internet and mobile technologies, literacy objects are ubiquitous and ever-present.

Thus, utilising a concept such as literacy-in-action, which allows us to form an understanding of literacy practices through investigation of the activity of human actors and the role of literacy objects, can give us the theoretical means to more effectively examine literacy practices in school settings. Numerous literacy objects – projects, essays, tests, report cards, notices/letters to parents, and the technologies used to produce them, to name a few – have vested in them the power to shape students' social futures. For some students and their families, positive interactions with these objects will open doors and for others, the opposite will occur.

With its emphasis on the circulation of literacy objects, literacy-in-action can also help us to understand the way out-of-school literacy practices make their way into school. By following the circulation of literacy objects across the ever more permeable in-school/out-of-school boundary, our ability to trace literacy practices, and better understand and theorise what students are doing with literacy, is enhanced. It also allows us to better understand the way literacy objects play various roles in students' lives – roles that may be opening possibilities for students and roles that may be detrimental.

## Conclusion

The ethnographic work of Shirley Brice Heath in the Carolina Piedmonts left us with an important legacy in the field of language, literacy and cultural studies. Heath's analysis utilising the literacy event provides an important and remarkable understanding of the interplay between spoken and written language; however, this work also left us with the legacy of a limited unit of analysis. The very nature of the literacy event leaves little space for acknowledgement of the texts in the literacies people and communities practise, which so often come from some-where else or may be constructed with the intent of going somewhere else. Whatever direction they are travelling, these texts are imbued with meanings that cross into and out of local sites, and as such mediate the literacy practices of those who put them into circulation and those at the receiving end.

As this study has demonstrated, viewing objects as actants alongside of humans and following their traces in chains of connected literate activity, i.e. literacy-in-action, allows researchers to examine: translocal literacy interactions; trajectories for following situated literacy practices within and outside of local contexts; and traced associations between people's use of literacy at the local level and the people and institutions that mediate those literate practices from afar. The need for a unit of analysis with this kind of theoretical flexibility and scope is particularly important in today's global educational contexts, in which circulation of texts via multimedia networks is widespread.

## References

Anderson, A. B., Teale, W. B. and Estrada E. (1980). Low income children's pre-school literacy experiences: Some naturalistic observations. *Quarterly Newsletter of the Laboratory of Comparative Human Cognition*, 2: 59–65.

Ashton-Warner, S. (1963). *Teacher*. New York: Simon & Schuster.

Barton, D. and Hamilton M. (2005). Literacy, reification, and the dynamics of social interaction. In D. Barton and K. Tusting (eds), *Beyond communities of prac-tice: language, power and social context*. Cambridge: Cambridge University Press.

Barton, D., Hamilton, M. and Ivanic, R. (2000). *Situated literacies: reading and writ-ing in context*. London: Routledge.

Baynham, M. (2004). Ethnographies of literacy: introduction. *Language and Education*, 18: 285–90.

Baynham, M. and Prinsloo, M. (2009). *The future of literacy studies*. New York: Palgrave Macmillan.

Bomer, R. (2007). When writing leads: an activity-theoretic account of the liter-ate activity of first-graders stronger at writing than reading. In D. W. Rowe, R. T. Jimenez, D. L. Compton, D. K. Dickinson, Y. Kim, K. M. Leander and

V. J. Risko (eds), *56th Yearbook of the National Reading Conference* (pp. 151–63). Oak Creek, Wis.: National Reading Conference.

Brandt, D. and Clinton, K. (2002). Limits of the local: expanding perspectives on literacy as a social practice. *Journal of Literacy Research*, 34: 337–56.

Carrington, V. (2012). 'There's no going back'. Roxie's IPhone®: an object ethnography. *Language and Literacy*, 14(2): 27–40.

Collins, J. and Blot, R. K. (2003). *Literacy and literacies: texts, power, and identity.* Cambridge: Cambridge University Press.

Cook-Gumperz, J. (2006). *The social construction of literacy.* New York: Cambridge University Press.

Egan-Robertson, A. and Bloome, D. (1998). *Students as researchers of culture and language in their own communities.* Cresskill, NJ: Hampton.

Hall, M. A. (1970). *Teaching reading as a language experience.* Columbus, Ohio: Charles Merrill.

Hamilton, M. (2001). Privileged literacies: policy, institutional process and the life of the IALS. *Language and Education*, 15: 178–96.

Heath, S. B. (1982a). Protean shapes in literacy events: ever shifting oral and literate traditions. In D. Tannen (ed.), *Spoken and written language: exploring literacy and orality.* Norwood, NJ: Ablex.

Heath, S. B. (1982b). What no bedtime story means: narrative skills at home and at school. *Language and Society*, 11: 49–76.

Heath, S. B. (1983). *Ways with Words.* Cambridge, UK: Cambridge University Press.

Heath, S. B. (2009). What no bedtime story means: narrative skills at home and at school. In A. Duranti (ed.), *Linguistic anthropology: a reader* (pp. 343–63). Chichester, UK: Wiley-Blackwell.

Hymes, D. (1977/1994). Toward ethnographies of communication. In J. Maybin (ed.), *Language and literacy in social practice.* Clevedon, UK: The Open University.

Kell, C. (2006). Crossing the margins: literacy, semiotics and the recontextualization of meanings. In K. Pahl and J. Rowsell (eds), *Travel notes from the new literacy studies: instances of practice* (pp. 147–69). Clevedon: Multilingual Matters.

Latour, B. (2005). *Reassembling the social: an introduction to actor-network-theory.* Oxford: University Press.

Leander, K. M. and Lovvorn, J. F. (2006). Literacy networks: following the circulation of texts, bodies, and objects in the schooling and online gaming of one youth. *Cognition and Instruction*, 24: 291–340.

Lenters, K. (2012). Enhancing and displacing literacy practices: examining publishing in a writer's workshop. *Language and Literacy: a Canadian E-Journal*, 14: 125–51.

Lenters, K. and McTavish, M. (2013). Student planners in-school and out-of-school: who's managing whom? *Literacy*, 47(2).

Lewis, C., Enciso, P. and Moje, E. B. (eds) (2007). *Reframing sociocultural research on literacy.* Mahwah, NJ: Lawrence Erlbaum.

Michaels, S. and Sohmer, R. (2000). Narratives and inscriptions: cultural tools, power and powerful sense-making. In B. Cope and M. Kalantzis (eds), *Multiliteracies: literacy learning and the design of social futures.* New York: Routledge.

Nichols, S. (2006). From boardroom to classroom: teaching a globalised discourse on thinking through internet texts and teaching practices. In K. Pahl and J. Rowsell (eds), *Travel notes from the new literacy studies: instances of practice.* Clevedon: Multilingual Matters.

Omerod, F. and Ivanic, R. (2000). Texts in practices: interpreting the physical characteristics of children's project work. In D. Barton, M. Hamilton and R. Ivanic (eds), *Situated literacies: reading and writing in context*. London: Routledge.

Pahl, K. and Rowsell, J. (2006). *Travel notes from the new literacy studies*. Clevedon, UK: Multilingual Matters.

Pahl, K. and Rowsell J. (2010). *Artifactual literacies: every object tells a story*. New York: Teachers College Press.

Reder, S. and Davila, E. (2005). Context and literacy practices. *Annual Review of Applied Linguistics*, 25: 170–87.

Rogers, R. (2007). *A critical discourse analysis of family literacy practices: power in and out of print*. Mahwah, NJ: Lawrence Erlbaum.

Rowe, D. W. and Leander, K. M. (2005). Analyzing the production of third space in classroom literacy events. In B. Maloch, J. V. Hoffman, D. L. Schallert, C. M. Fairbanks and J. Worthy (eds), *54th Yearbook of the NRC*. Oak Creek, Wis.: National Reading Conference.

Street, B. V. (1993). Introduction: the new literacy studies. In B. V. Street (ed.), *Cross-cultural approaches to literacy* (pp. 1–21). Cambridge, UK: Cambridge University Press.

Street, B. V. (2003). What's 'new' in the new literacy studies? Critical approaches to literacy and practice. *Current Issues in Comparative Education*, 5: 1–14.

Street, B. V. and Lefstein, A. (2007). *Literacy: an advanced resource book*. New York: Routledge.

# 8
## Recontextualising Research, Glocalising Practice

*Elsa Auerbach*

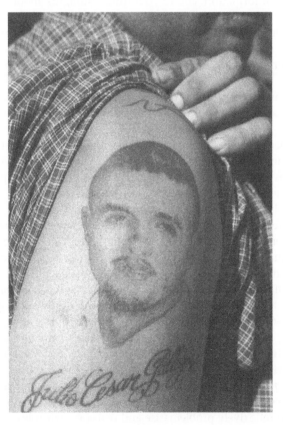

*Figure 8.1* © Mizue Aizeki. Reprinted by permission of City Lights Books

What comes to mind when you look at the photo in Figure 8.1? What is interesting to you about it in the context of your own work? What questions does it raise for you?

Julio Cesar Gilegos, the man depicted by this tattoo, and six other Mexicans were found dead of hyperthermia in the desert that connects California with Mexico. Gilegos was on a return trip to the US to reunite with his wife, who is a US citizen, and his son in Los Angeles. The tattoo is on the arm of Julio Cesar Gilegos' brother. The photo comes from a book entitled *Dying to Live: A Story of US Immigration in an Age of Global Apartheid* (Nevins, 2008) which explores the Gilegos family's struggle in the context of 'the deeper story of global migration, ... and the dynamic connections between peoples and places' (back cover).

With this information, add to your initial thoughts about the photo: what does it suggest in terms of language, literacy, transnationalism or mobility? Jot down a few thoughts you may have in response to the photo.

Now think about what identity or identities you brought to your response to this photo. Did you look at it through the lens of a researcher? Through the lens of a teacher? Through the lens of an activist? Through the lens of a migrant? Through the lens of a learner? Through some other lens/es?

The underlying question here is: how does your positioning shape your interpretation of the photo? And whom does this response privilege?

I use this example and series of questions to illustrate the point that as researchers, we always need to start by interrogating the identities that we bring to our work and think about how this work relates to the struggles confronting those who are the objects of our gaze. Just as current literacy theory posits that all definitions of literacy and literacy practices are situated, socially constructed, interested and ideological (e.g. Barton, 1994) – that they cannot be investigated without taking relations of power into account – so too, sociolinguistic research itself is situated and embedded in relations of power. It always is grounded in a view of the world and the researcher's place in it. It always is *about* something and *for* something; it always benefits someone and serves specific interests. The *where, how, with whom, why* and *when* of research are ideological. As such, a key question any researcher must consider is: who benefits from this research? Just as our work requires methodological rigour, it requires ethical rigour. As Lin (2005) says, academic research-ers need to reflexively problematise and revision their roles researching language in education policies and practices (p. 38). Not to consider whose interests our work serves risks abrogating ethical responsibility.

So while some researchers might say that the tattoo photo illustrates an interesting translocal literacy practice that is (literally) an embodied inscription of migration, I would focus more on the underlying economic and political struggles that contextualise the Gilegos brothers' migration and how language/literacy pedagogy can be positioned in service of the struggles that marginalised and brutalised migrants face. For me, the key questions in relation to the photo are: how can we draw on our resources as academics in order to align ourselves with the struggles of people like Julio Cesar Gilegos? How does discourse about global flows and ethnoscapes benefit the migrants who are the subjects of research on mobility? What does research about global, transnational and translocal processes mean for students and teachers as they work with each other inside and outside the classroom?

In this chapter, I will argue that ways of addressing these questions depend in part on how we conceptualise globalisation and in part on how we conceptualise our own positioning as scholars. First I will present a view of globalisation that creates space for academic activists to engage with the struggles of migrants like Julio Cesar Gilegos. Then I will suggest ways of recontextualising research so that it can be harnessed in service of building analysis, skills and practices to enable people to participate in organising for change as part of global networks, in what has come to be called 'glocalised' action for change. Finally, I will present examples of initiatives that recontextualise language/ literacy pedagogy in service of transformation processes; because my own engagement has been with adult learners, these examples will be drawn from the field of critical adult literacy. Underlying my argument is the notion that we need to turn the question of mobility back on ourselves and imagine ways of moving, as Lin and Martin (2005: 15) say, between 'roles as academic knowledge-producers/consumers and political participants in a world still full of both blatant and subtle forms of social injustice and relations of domination and subordination'.

## Reframing conceptualisations of globalisation

Globalisation is often seen to be the restructuring of the world economic order so that giant transnational economic institutions consolidate power and wealth in the hands of the few. This formulation frames globalisation as the all-encompassing engine of corporate world domination in which capital is free to go wherever it wants, fostering global markets for buying/selling of goods, labour and services. The transnational financial system is regulated by global institutions such as the IMF, the WTO and the World Bank. This system produces ever stronger pressures toward privatisation and deregulation, trade and tariff agreements (such as NAFTA), open markets, and a global assembly line linking the North and the South. In this view, global macroeconomic forces are seen to both require and force global migration or transnationalism, with the movement not just of capital but of people, technology, goods and labour; the consequences of globalisation are seen to include increased poverty and inequality, a widening divide between rich and poor, the intensificiation of global ecological and environmental damage, economic volatility, and the decimation of human rights – a system that has come to be called 'global economic apartheid' (Ciobanu and Naidoo, 2009).

In this conceptualisation of globalisation, critics on the Left often pit the local and the global against each other, with the local seen as virtuous and the global seen as menacing or evil. Within literacy studies, this sometimes takes the form of what Luke calls 'the sanctification of the local by opponents of globalization' (Luke, 2005: xv). So, for example, Warschauer points to 'an overriding contradiction between the power of global networks and the struggle for local identity' (2000: 512), implying, it seems, that the former is oppressive and the latter virtuous.

For the last ten years or so, this simplistic dichotomisation of the local and the global has been challenged in language and literacy studies; researchers have examined the interconnections between the local and global, with a focus on the ways that global processes are enacted in local contexts, engaging with what Baynham calls 'the perennial issue of theorizing the impact of large scale social processes on small scale interactions' (2007: 336). Many of the presentations for the *Mobility Language Literacy* conference in Cape Town (January 2011) on which this volume is based explored how the macro is enacted through the micro (with phrases in the abstracts like 'locally relevant, globally influenced' and 'the global transnational moves and conditions influence local contexts and get infused into the local contexts through local appropriation'). These formulations imply a directionality from the global to the local; the underlying question for researchers investigating language, literacy and globalisation is often framed as, 'What are the impacts of globalisation *on* local languages, literacies, and discourses?'

But across social movements around the world, conversations about globalisation problematise this directionality, seeing globalisation as a dynamic multifaceted process entailing complementary aspects: globalisation from *above* and globalisation from *below*. In other words, top-down forces of economic apartheid and interconnected grass-roots resistance to these forces are part of a whole, existing in dialectical relationship. In this formulation, globalisation from below is constituted by the vast network of local organisations that act in their own spaces and sites, but do so in alliance with other organisations around the world; as such they aim to create an alternative to corporate globalisation, recognising the inevitability (and potential benefits) of an interconnected world, but working to shape it in the interests of the poor. The globalisation from below movement is premised on the notion that the combined force of the local movements is greater than the sum of individual forces, invoking what has come to be called the Lilliput Strategy, with hundreds of local struggles banding together to take on globalisation from above. The term *glocalisation* is used to represent these networks of local movements with diverse interests and geographically diverse starting points that converge to work for social change in service of various forms of justice. Glocal struggles (with both local and global aspects) include movements for food security, environmental protection, water reclamation, human rights, health care access, women's rights, reproductive rights, and so on. A pre-eminent example of glocalisation is Via Campesina, which describes itself as

> the international movement which brings together millions of peasants, small and medium-size farmers, landless people, women farmers, indigenous people, migrants and agricultural workers from around the world. It defends small-scale sustainable agriculture as a way to promote social justice and dignity. (Via Campesina, no date)

It was formed in 1993 by a group of farmers' representatives from four continents; according to its website,

> At that time, agricultural policies and the agribusiness were becoming globalized and small farmers needed to develop and struggle for a common vision. Small-scale farmers' organizations also wanted to have their voice heard and to participate directly in the decisions that were affecting their lives. (Ibid.)

Via Campesina now consists of of 'about 150 local and national organizations in 70 countries from Africa, Asia, Europe and the Americas. Altogether, it represents about 200 million farmers' (ibid.).

Such struggles are enacted both in local sites and collaboratively across sites (even internationally) against the same forces. Local struggles are seen to be different facets of a broader movement based on solidarity that crosses boundaries of nations, identities and narrow interests. This glocalisation analysis recognises not only that what happens globally has local implications, but that what happens locally and translocally can have global implications. Globalisation from below and globalisation from above are seen as dialectically related.

## Repositioning language/literacy studies

What are the implications of the glocalisation framework for academics interested in language, literacy and mobility? First, seeing the role of grass-roots organisations in this global dialectic forces us to shift our questions, so that, in addition to asking how globalisation and mobility shape language/literacy practices, we now also must ask the inverse: *how can language and literacy practices contribute to reshaping globalisation in the interests of the poor? How can the field of literacy studies align itself with glocal struggles?*

This, in turn, opens new spaces where academics can reposition themselves, and recontextualise our work: it allows researchers to go beyond examining how the forces of top-down globalisation impose themselves at the local level, or how the grass-roots forces work to enact local practices. This perspective yields additional possibilities for academics to harness their work in service of social change through the ways we conduct research, the ways we engage with pedagogical initiatives, and the ways we connect with glocal struggles. In other words, it opens new spaces for ethical responses to the 'who benefits?' question.

Of course, literacy researchers and practitioners have long aligned themselves with struggles for social justice (Freire, 2007; Horton, 1998). All too often, however, we/they (I include myself here) have fallen into various traps. One trap is that of pontificating social justice perspectives without actually engaging in any struggles for change. The field of critical literacy certainly has its own versions of the proverbial ivory tower academics who draw high salaries without having any base in practice or engagement with on-the-ground struggles.

Another trap, however, is that of overstating the power of critical language and literacy practices or pedagogy. *Any* analysis of globalisation tells us that it is macroeconomic forces and collective movements, not individual competence or practices (linguistic or literate), that shape life possibilities. In the same way, the work of educators, researchers and even individual activists can do little more than contribute to larger initiatives for change. So I do not want to suggest that critical literacy education itself is the key to triggering change, as so many educators (myself included) have implied in the past. Michael James, an educator and activist who works with youth in the Bay Area, argues that such a view is naïve and counterproductive, saying that,

> literacy alone rarely guarantees privilege, access, or political leverage. When practitioners naively accept this idea, they sabotage their credibility with their students, who, in many cases, have an ability to recognize such idealism and know when to reject it. (James, 1990: 15)

In his analysis, the antidote to problems of equity and oppression is organising for change through concerted political action, rather than through educational interventions per se. This is certainly the lesson of the civil rights movement in the US and the struggle against apartheid in South Africa. In each of these movements, language/literacy practices/pedagogy may have played a role, but they were not the structural framework out of which the struggles emanated. What James called for is not educational activity with 'relevant content', but, as he says, 'political processes with an educational character' (ibid.: 18).

James' perspective suggests that change is possible, not when individuals improve their skills or expand their repertoire of literacy practices, but when they join with others in challenging specific conditions and forms of oppression. In other words, it is the context in which literacy education takes place and the struggles in which it is embedded that are the forces for change. I think this is also what Makoni and Makoni (2007: 112) imply when they say '... the intervention has to be at the level of society ... and not begin and end at the level of language'.

I want to focus now on two ways of aligning our work with struggles for a more just world. The first relates to research, the second to pedagogy. In terms of research, I will suggest a framework for interrogating research in order to think through its ethical implications and then give examples of work in which the repositioning of participants challenges traditional researcher/subject roles. In terms of the second, I will offer examples of ways of infusing pedagogy with an ideological orientation that includes learners in conversations about globalisation and connects pedagogy to glocal initiatives. I will suggest ways to inform pedagogy with a glocalisation analysis so that sites of struggle can become sites of learning and sites of learning can become sites of struggle. The examples presented here are certainly not the only ways that researchers can position themselves as activists; rather, they are drawn from work I am familiar with in the fields of adult second language and literacy. Each of the examples represents an attempt to take up Lin and Martin's call for us to travel 'between the roles as academic knowledge-producers/consumers and political participants in a world still full of both blatant and subtle forms of social injustice and relations of domination and subordination' (2005: 15).

## Recontextualising research

It is not unusual for researchers to become so immersed in theoretical discourses and research agendas that promote their academic trajectories that they neglect (or even refuse) to consider whose interests their work serves. Sometimes even research with a self-proclaimed transformative agenda (in terms of the content of the research) can enact colonising processes and relationships. This may happen when researchers enter communities, collect data and produce papers, without considering how the research can address issues that the research findings raise. In some cases, this even takes the form of academic opportunism where research-ers develop networks that enable them to access the communities of 'others' in order to mine data for export and 'sell' it in the global academic 'marketplace'. At a research-planning meeting that I attended in Cape Town in 2011, the convener (a European scholar proposing research in South Africa) framed the goal of the project as being to produce 'the most sophisticated empirical account of identity, practice and ideology on the social science market' (oral remarks) and explicitly refused to allow discussion of who might benefit from such research. Dictating research priorities from afar (from European funding insti-tutions) does little to promote transformation or change traditional power relations.

More often, though, failure to consider the 'who benefits?' question is the result of taken-for-granted practices engendered by institutional pres-sures to evaluate research in terms of how well it is grounded in the latest theoretical models, how rigorous it is, how it moves a body of knowledge forward, how it contributes to a theoretical debate and, more materially, where it gets published or how it promotes a researcher's professional status. Even research that situates itself within a 'critical' paradigm often neglects to interrogate taken-for-granted dynamics that may benefit researchers or 'the field' but do nothing to benefit the subjects of the research. Researchers exist within institutional power relations that position them as work-ers subject to constraints regarding job requirements; their livelihoods depend on conforming to standards imposed by these institutions.

Nevertheless, I believe it is necessary and possible to challenge some of the taken-for-granted assumptions and to work toward an ethically rigorous approach to research. We can doing this by intentionally and explicitly addressing questions like the following at the outset of language/ literacy research on language, literacy and mobility:

- *Rationale for research:* Why are we conducting this research? What is it for?
- *Research questions:* Where do they come from? How were they developed? Who participated in developing them? How are the subjects/ objects of the research positioned in the research? Whose voices articulate the research questions?
- *Research participants:* Who is setting the research agenda? Who are the stakeholders in the research? How are they positioned? What will the various stakeholders get out of their participation? Why are they participating? What are the relationships between participants?
- *Research findings and outcomes:* What will be done with the research findings? How will the findings be used? Whose interests do they serve? Who is the audience for the research? Who will benefit from the research?

Of course, nothing I am proposing here is original or new. A tradition of critical applied research in sociolinguistics, anthropology, educational linguistics and sociology goes back at least 25 years, including, for example, critical ethnography, action research and participatory action research paradigms (e.g. Anderson, 1989). In each of these paradigms, power relationships in research, practice and the broader social context are problematised. So, in the case of critical ethnography, larger contexts of social relations and structures of inequality are integral, and findings are applied in service of change. In action research, practitioners investigate their own teaching contexts in order to inform further practice. In participatory action research, community participants (however community may be defined in a particular context) are the ones who develop the research questions for their own purposes, participate in conducting the research and take action for change based on their findings.

Despite these long-standing traditions, the questions continue to be timely. In fact, just as I was finalising this manuscript, I came across an article on South Africa's *Mail & Guardian* website (Martin, 2012) that underscores the relevance of these questions within a larger social science conversation about whose knowledge counts. The article cited the work of the Mapungubwe Institute for Strategic Reflection in South Africa, which poses questions like the following:

Has the South African knowledge economy been permitted to drift without sustainable vision and purpose? Whose agenda and purpose do the current sites of knowledge production serve? Has education in South Africa successfully managed to shake off the shackles of colonialism and apartheid and the self-centredness of a market-dominated economic system? Can we forge ahead without a clear strategy for the transformation of what constitutes 'knowledge'? (Martin, 2012)

As these questions suggest, recontextualising research entails nothing short of examining the underlying question of what constitutes knowledge. The European sociolinguist (referred to earlier) who refused to engage with the 'who benefits?' question at the Cape Town meeting (preferring instead to align himself with 'the most sophisticated empirical account of identity, practice and ideology on the social science market') was falling into exactly the kind of colonising dynamic that the Mapungubwe Institute is challenging.

What are the alternatives? The following examples represent just a few of the many possible ways of enacting ethically rigorous research agendas. One example in the area of language/literacy education is the work of educational anthropologist Janise Hurtig (2008) and a group of Latina mothers who collaborated in a participatory research project in Chicago. Hurtig had an eight-year history of working with parents from Chicago's poor and immigrant neighbourhoods in community writing and publishing workshops through the University of Illinois' Community Writing and Research Project (CWRP). In the workshops,

[participants] have the opportunity to write and share stories based in their experiences, draw on their writings to examine their lives, and develop the art of writing. ... Because the writing prompts emerge from group discussion of the previous week's writing and often respond to issues of pressing concern to the writers, the group is frequently led to consider and challenge everyday forms of cultural and social oppression. (Hurtig, 2008: 93)

Thus, the content for literacy work arises organically from local issues confronting the participants. In some cases, the writing groups undertake social action related to these themes.

What is more relevant to the point about community participation in research agendas is that the CWRP provides training in the methodologies of participatory research to parents, community groups, teachers and others with the aim of 'contribut[ing] to the collective capacity of community folks to educate, defend, and develop themselves and their communities on their own terms' (ibid.: 93). Following this model, a research project with Latina parents grew out of a writing workshop based at a local bilingual elementary school in a Mexican immigrant neighbourhood. In this case, as Hurtig says, 'the writing workshop became one facet of a school–community organising campaign that had as its goal the creation of a community arts and education center that would be designed, organised and directed by community residents' (ibid.: 94).

When Hurtig applied for funding to study these writing workshops, she incorporated parents as researchers into the proposal since, as she said, 'the only appropriate way to study a writing group that supported participants as experts of their own experience was for the members of the writing group to participate as co-researchers ...' (ibid.: 95). Participants learned how to formulate research questions, develop activities to collect data, conduct surveys with parents and interview teachers. They created their own research processes, such as collectively monitoring their work through a tool they called *compromisos* (a set of commitments to hold themselves accountable) and drawing on the writing workhop methodology to process and analyse data. They debated the kinds of questions that social scientists grapple with (e.g. the challenges of simultaneously participating and observing, and the ways that participant observation shapes the data). Specific recommendations for improving the writing workshops arising from this research were 'useful and realistic' (ibid.: 99). More importantly, though, the women developed a sense of agency that transcended the specific project; as they wrote in the introduction to their report, 'through this process of researching the writing workshop we have been able to apply our abilities as writers to take on new challenges, and in this way develop ourselves collectively as leaders in our community' (ibid.: 100). As a result of this project, the community arts and education centre set up 'a standing research committee charged with documenting and evaluating the quality and effectiveness of the organizations' programs ...' (ibid.: 100).

Another tool that is widely used to engage marginalised people in research and action for change in their own communities is the photovoice method. Photovoice entails a process in which community participants photograph challenging realities in their work, community or day-to-day environments. These photos then trigger a process of storytelling, dialogue and analysis about the issues codified in the photos. The process leads to public representations of the issues and analysis geared toward a wider audience – community members, policy-makers, the media and others who may participate in addressing the concerns. So, for example, a photovoice project in Ann Arbor, Michigan (Wang,

2003), was designed to create public awareness and influence policy about issues confronting homeless people. Through a series of workshops, homeless participants discussed the concept of photovoice, issues of ethics and power, photography techniques and more. Participants discussed concerns like 'participants' safety, the camera as a tool conferring authority as well as responsibility, ways to approach people when taking their picture ...' (p. 185). After taking pictures, community members selected those that they felt were most significant and wrote about them, using a Freirean analytical process in which they described the photos, analysed themes represented in them, explored underlying causes of the conflicts, and strategised ways of addressing them (Wallerstein and Auerbach, 2004). They also discussed their photos in audio-taped interviews. Then, according to Wang, they made presentations to community leaders and the public, selected the most powerful photos and 'wrote descriptive captions for a series of articles that appeared in local newspapers, in a gallery exhibition, and in a major public forum' (ibid.: 188). The yield from this project included not only greater perspective for policy-makers and the public, but an increased sense of self-respect, dignity and agency among the photographer-researchers. One participant said that 'photovoice gave her the opportunity to define her life as she, not outsiders, understood it' (ibid.: 189).

## Glocalising pedagogy

Another way to align language/literacy work with glocalising agendas is to participate in political processes with an educational character (in Michael James' terms). This entails engaging with learners/migrants/activists in the kinds of substantive conversation about migration, globalisation and language/literacy that are addressed in this volume, as well as harnessing literacy work to struggles for a more just world. Contributions to this dialogical process may take a number of forms: (1) language/literacy educators may physically recontextualise this work (that is, move contexts of practice out of the academy or classroom into spaces where struggles are taking place); (2) pedagogical processes may become tools for activism; and (3) texts may create a space to explore glocal struggles through content-based lessons that foster analysis and contribute to those struggles. Each of these moves entails applying the notion of mobility to our own identities as we shift from 'knowledge producers' to 'political participants'.

The 'sites of struggle as sites of learning' model entails embedding language/literacy work in existing glocal grass-roots organisations like those struggling for tenants' rights and access to health care, or against environmental pollution and domestic violence. These struggles are shaped by local conditions, and their structural/institutional location may not be educational at all. Rather than adult education classrooms where language/literacy acquisition is an end in itself, in this model, learning takes place in women's centres, union halls or community gathering places. Instruction may focus on analysis, skills, practices and discourses that enable people to participate in organising for change (Kerfoot, 1993).

Grass-roots initiatives where literacy work is contextualised within globalisation from below are not uncommon in countries of the South. Gale Goodwin Gomez (2007), a US-based anthropologist, writes about one such initiative among the Yanomami people in the Amazon rainforest of northern Brazil. In this case, the Yanomami, whose engagement with written text was minimal until recently, have been learning to use computers so that they can communicate across vast distances with each other as they struggle against the logging companies in the Amazon; they have also been learning Portuguese so they can negotiate with the logging companies. As Gomez says,

> In the case of the Brazilian Yanomami, IT represents simply the latest stage in the process of acquiring Western means, such as written language, to strengthen their languages and culture and to provide access to information and knowledge of the outside world. IT is a potentially very powerful tool in their struggle to preserve their economic, political and cultural autonomy and ultimately to ensure their survival in a rapidly changing, globally interconnected world. (2007: 118)

An example of a project where pedagogical processes become tools for activism comes out of the Alternative Information Development Centre (AIDC) in Cape Town, South Africa. AIDC's mission is 'to strengthen the movement for social justice through the production of alternative knowledge and by enhancing the institutional capacity of Peoples' Media Organisations and the communication capacity of progressive civil society organisations' (no date). One of AIDC's projects, called Communication Capacity-Building for Dialogue, 'aims to strengthen the analytical and communication skills of civil society and community media activists. The programme resonates with the adult learning cycle of action and reflection, thesis and praxis' (ibid.). In this project, community activists from various grass-roots organisations participated in training designed to enable them to speak for themselves about the struggles they are engaged in, developing writing, speaking and multimodal literacy skills to advance their social justice work (see Figure 8.2).

*Figure 8.2*   Photo of activist in AIDC network (photo by Elsa Auerbach)

Finally, language/literacy texts may incorporate content that engages learners in analysis, reflection and action that focus on glocalisation. *Problem-Posing at Work: English for Action* (Auerbach and Wallerstein, 2004), for example, invites students to investigate local manifestations of global issues, contextualising these issues through narratives, as well as historical, economic and legal information. Rather than leaving issues of mobility, language and literacy for the 'experts' to explore, this book creates a context for exploring these issues *with* immigrant learners, valorising their experiences, concerns and expertise in service of supporting their struggles to address the issues. It is geared toward workers in the US and Canada.

The graphic in Figure 8.3 is part of a chapter that explores migration journeys, inviting students to situate their personal experiences within the broader dynamics of economic and political forces; relationships between individual life trajectories and macro forces are explored. The graphic, coming at the end of the chapter, invites learners to write a letter to North Americans (e.g. a letter to the editor) explaining conditions that push people to leave their countries.

**6. Practicing for action: Writing a letter to the newspaper**

*Figure 8.3* 'Practicing for Action' (Auerbach and Wallerstein, 2004: 38, reprinted with permission from Grass Roots Press)

Another lesson asks students to compare their work experiences in their home countries and their new countries, exploring the reality that immigrants and refugees are often forced to take jobs far below their skill levels. A lesson called 'Finding Jobs' invites students to explore social obstacles that may impede their efforts to attain their goals, relating individual struggles to dynamics like racism and discrimination against women. It also introduces legal information and invites critical analysis of when and how legal information may be useful (as well as its limitations). A later lesson explores various types of discrimination as well as legal protection against discrimination. It situates issues of racism and discrimination within a broader economic context, exploring who benefits from them and how.

A lesson about deportation discusses the ways in which both documented and undocumented workers are affected by fears of deportation. It explores the rights of those without legal status and what any foreign-born worker can do if approached by government authorities. It presents information about ways that organisations are advocating for the rights of undocumented workers in the US and Canada.

A lesson on plant closings and the movement of industries to other parts of world examines what is happening on a global level with plant closings, the migration of jobs, and the effects of the new economic realities for workers. It looks specifically at the effects of NAFTA for workers in Mexico, the US and Canada. It explores issues that confront displaced workers and the organising that is taking place across North America in the face of plant closings.

A key aspect of each unit in the book is applying the information and analysis emerging from exercises and readings to strategise ways of changing oppressive conditions. The template in Figure 8.4 is offered as a procedural tool for strategising.

The book ends with the notion that 'a better world is possible' as networks of groups and movements link together to challenge injustices and inequities. It invites participants to envision their hopes and goals for a better future. This process entails identifying allies and looking at how groups can join with each other to increase their power. A lesson in

Here are some suggestions that may help you decide how to respond to a workplace problem.

1. First, describe the problem in detail.

2. Then look over all the strategies and information you discussed related to this problem.

3. As a group, brainstorm possible actions and steps to address the problem.

4. Use one of these charts to evaluate the strategies. Be sure to discuss what the results of these steps might be. What might make it hard to act on this problem?

| | **What?** (possible strategy, action, or steps) | **Why?** (reason for this action, or expected outcome) | **Who** could help? (people, groups) | **How** would you go about doing this? | **Dangers** or difficulties? |
|---|---|---|---|---|---|
| 1 | | | | | |
| 2 | | | | | |
| 3 | | | | | |
| 4 | | | | | |

| | **What?** (possible strategy, action, or steps) | **Advantages** | **Disadvantages** |
|---|---|---|---|
| 1 | | | |
| 2 | | | |
| 3 | | | |

*Figure 8.4*  Responding to a workplace problem (Auerbach and Wallerstein, 2004: 304, reprinted with permission from Grass Roots Press)

the final unit explores the ways in which identities can become a basis for connection and solidarity (see Figure 8.5).

Worker narratives are integrated throughout *Problem-Posing at Work: English for Action* to provide real-life examples of how people join with each other to address problems. In every lesson, individual and local realities are connected to larger dynamics. The local and the global are in dialogue; acquiring literacy practices is linked to analysis, which, in turn is linked to strategies for action. Local actions are, in turn, contextualised within broader struggles.

The text is designed to be a tool for groups of immigrants as they confront the challenges of living and working in new contexts. It was

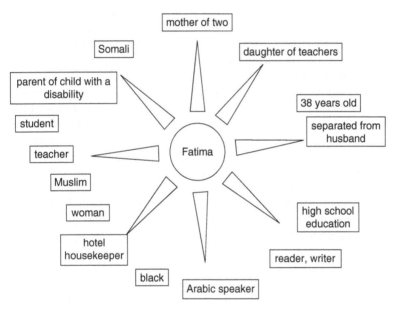

Kinds of organization or group:

1. *Somali immigrants organization* 5. *religious groups*

2. *Women's groups* 6. *student groups*

3. *hotel workers group:* 7. _____

   *labor organization* 8. _____

4. *immigrant groups* 9. _____

*Figure 8.5* Kinds of organisation or group (Auerbach and Wallerstein, 2004: 293, reprinted with permission from Grass Roots Press)

used in precisely this way by English as a Second Language (ESL) classes formed in the wake of the September 11, 2001 attacks on the World Trade Center (WTC). Immigrant workers who had cleaned, worked in restaurants and done maintenance work at the WTC formed an organisation to support each other, fight for their rights, set up ESL classes and find new work. This struggle is documented in a book called *The Accidental American: Immigration and Citizenship in the Age of Globalisation* (Sen with Mamdouh, 2008).

## Conclusion

Thinking back to the Gilegos brothers (and others like them), I wonder which of the strategies I have outlined in this chapter might have been helpful to them. How might being connected to 'glocal' organisations (e.g. those that work with Mexicans for better conditions either in Mexico or in the US southwest, or organisations that address immigrant rights) have been beneficial? Would participating in research about 'pathways' to the US and legal protection, or about how different types of documents function have been beneficial? What issues might they have chosen to focus on? Would language/literacy pedagogy that was situated within glocal movements or struggles have been beneficial? Could language classes that provided a context for exploring issues of migration and mobility have given them insight as well as skills to address the challenges facing them? What other strategies or models that I have not even begun to consider here could have enabled them to address the challenges of mobility? How, for example, might social media be harnessed in flattening hierarchies, addressing inequities and fostering dialogue?

I am mindful of Michael James' admonition that there are limits to what educationists can do. None of the models I have explored are panaceas; nor can they be enacted unproblematically. Despite the constraints, my hope is that the questions I have outlined are useful in helping researchers, educators and academics to step outside of our taken-for-granted positioning and roles. My own research encounters suggest that we need to be attentive to the potential for reproducing colonising relationships through research practices and projects. A starting point may be to reconceptualise the relationship between the local and the global as symbiotic and reciprocal, rather than unidirectional in terms of global impacts on the local. This reconceptualisation may enable us to find spaces to align ourselves with glocalisation struggles and movements. Another step may be to consciously consider whose interests our practice serves and to hold ourselves to high standards of ethical rigour. Repositioning ourselves entails engaging those we are researching and/or teaching as co-participants in conversations about mobility, migration, language and literacy. This means expanding the circle of who is involved in setting research agendas, in determining the content and functions of pedagogical practice, and in considering how this work will be used.

# References

Alternative Information Development Centre (AIDC) (no date). http://www.aidc. org.za

Anderson, G. (1989). Critical ethnography in education: origins, current status, and new directions. *Review of Educational Research*, 59 (3): 249–70.

Auerbach, E. and Wallerstein, N. (2004). *Problem-posing at work: English for action.* Edmonton, Alberta: Grass Roots Press.

Barton, D. (1994). *Literacy: an introduction to the ecology of written language.* Oxford and Cambridge: Blackwell.

Baynham, M. (2007). Transnational literacies: immigration, language learning and identity. *Linguistics and Education*, 18(3): 335–8.

Ciobanu, C. and Naidoo, K. (2009). Q&A: global economic apartheid is obstacle to fair climate deal. *Interpress Service*, 17 December 2009. http://www.ipsnews. net/2009/12/qa-global-economic-apartheid-is-obstacle-to-fair-climate-deal/.

Freire, P. (2007). *Pedagogy of the oppressed.* New York: Continuum.

Gómez, G. (2007). Computer technology and native literacy in the Amazon rain forest. Chapter Thirteen. In L. Dyson, M. Hendriks and S. Grant (eds), *Information technology and indigenous people* (pp. 117–19). Hershey: Information Science Publishing.

Horton, M. (1998). *The long haul: an autobiography.* New York: Teachers College Press.

Hurtig, J. (2008). Community writing, participatory research, and an anthropological sensibility. *Anthropology and Education Quarterly*, 39 (1): 92–106.

James, M. (1990). Demystifying literacy: reading, writing, and the struggle for liberation. *Convergence*, 23(1): 14–25.

Kerfoot, C. (1993). Participatory education in a South African context. *TESOL Quarterly*, 27 (3): 431–47.

Lin, A. (2005). Critical transdisciplinary perspectives on language-in-education policy and practice in post-colonial contexts: the case of Hong Kong. In A. Lin and P. Martin (eds), *Decolonisation, globalisation: language-in-education policy and practice* (pp. 38–54). Clevedon: Multilingual Matters.

Lin, A. and Martin, P. (eds) (2005). *Decolonisation, globalisation: language-in-education policy and practice.* Clevedon: Multilingual Matters.

Luke, A. (2005). Foreword: On the possibilities of a post-postcolonial education. In A. Lin and P. Martin (eds), *Decolonisation, globalisation: language-in-education policy and practice* (pp. xiv–xix). Clevedon: Multilingual Matters.

Makoni, S. and Makoni, B. (2007). 'I am starving with no hope to survive': Southern African perspectives on pedagogies of globalisation. *International Multilingual Research Journal*, 1(2): 105–18.

Martin, L. (2012. Whose knowledge is it anyway? *Mail and Guardian Online*, 9 November 2012, http://mg.co.za/article/2012-11-09-whose-knowledge-is-it-anyway. Downloaded March 2013.

Nevins, J. (2008). *Dying to live: a story of U.S. immigration in an age of global apart-heid*. San Francisco: Open Media/City Lights Books.

Sen, R. with Mamdouh, F. (2008). *The accidental American: immigration and citizen-ship in the age of globalisation*. San Francisco: Berrett-Koehler Publishers, Inc.

Via Campesina (no date). http://viacampesina.org/en/index.php/organisation-mainmenu-44

Wallerstein, N. and Auerbach, E. (2004). *Problem-posing at work: popular educator's guide*. Edmonton, Alberta: Grass Roots Press.

Wang, C. (2003). Using photovoice as a participatory assessment and issue selec-tion tool. In M. Minkler and N. Wallerstein (eds), *Community-based participatory research for health* (Ch. 9). San Francisco: Jossey-Bass.

Warshauer, M. (2000). The changing global economy and the future of English teaching. *TESOL Quarterly*, 34 (3): 511–35.

# 9
# Xenophobia and Constructions of the Other

*Hilary Janks*

## Introduction

*Makwerekwere* is the hostile term commonly used to construct foreign Africans living in South Africa as Other. It carries with it the undercurrent of emotions – such as loathing, outrage, fear and rejection – that result in ongoing and repeated xenophobic attacks, the worst and most widespread of which occurred in 2008. The term is an onomatopoeic representation of the 'unintelligible' sounds of the languages spoken by foreign Africans, highlighting language as a significant marker of identity. In an analysis of the 'ideology of makwerekwere', Matsinhe (2011: 298) confronts the question: 'How did it come to pass that in the imagination of an African nation [South Africa], Africa and Africans represent the negativity of Otherness?'

He considers the role played by colonial and apartheid discourses on the inferiority of blackness in the production of 'collective afrophobic self-contempt' (p. 299). When the ongoing negative representation of foreign Africans in the South African press (Adegoke, 1999; Harris, 2002) and the 'criminalisation of African foreign nationals as "illegals", "illegal aliens", "illegal immigrants", "criminals" and "drug traffickers"' (Matsinhe, 2011: 298) by the Department of Home Affairs and the South African police are added to the mix, there can be no doubt that language and discourse are implicated in the production of xenophobia.

Over a decade ago, Adegoke (1999: 114) found that discourses circulating in the South African press pertaining to foreign African nationals and their countries were 'systematically negative'. This led her to conclude that xenophobia should be addressed in schools. She recommended inclusion within the critical literacy curriculum, where other oppressive discourses such as those pertaining to race, gender, class, sexual orientation and age, for example, are given attention. With the subsequent ongoing and widespread attacks on foreign Africans in South Africa, her recommendation appears prescient.

The chapter begins with competing explanations of xenophobia in South Africa and theory related to Othering. The link between apartheid discourses and xenophobic Othering is brought to bear on an exploration of *District 9*, a science fiction movie set in South Africa. All these ideas come together in a the final section of the chapter which offers an example of critical literacy activities relating to *District 9* and the role of movies, language and discourse in the construction of the dangerous Other.

## Xenophobia in South Africa

The literature on xenophobia offers different theses to account for xenophobia in South Africa. An overview of these is provided by Matsinhe (2011: 297–8). Xenophobia is attributed to the

- need to find a scapegoat that can be blamed for crime, unemployment and the spread of HIV/AIDS (Morris, 1998, in Matsinhe, 2011: 297)
- 'sudden and intense exposure to strangers' after extended lack of contact with the rest of Africa during apartheid (Morris, 1998, in Matsinhe, 2011: 297)
- 'alleged visible Otherness' of foreign Africans (Harris, 2002 in Matsinhe, 2011: 298)
- negative representations of Africa in the South African media which produced discourses that position foreign Africans as a dangerous Other (Harris, 2002 in Matsinhe, 2011: 298; also Adegoke, 1999)
- state's criminalisation of Africans as 'illegal aliens' (Matsinhe, 2011: 298)
- perceived inferiority of Africans compared to South Africans (Neocosmos, 1998 in Matsinhe, 2011: 298).

Matsinhe argues that, while all of these ideas have some purchase, none of them is able to explain why the xenophobia is directed specifically at black African foreigners. Using theories developed by Fanon (1967) and Elias (1994), Matsinhe offers an account that attributes xenophobia to the unconscious projection onto others of the discourses that produced 'internalised self-loathing in colonised and apartheid subjects in South Africa', that he describes as 'the disgrace of blackness' (2011: 300). With reference to Fanon and Freud, Matsinhe argues that 'in self loathing, the self loathers also loathe those who most resemble themselves' (p. 302).

Because the real differences with the Other are slight they are magnified to render the outsider within, visible. 'Physical self-presentation is put under scrutiny, graded and coded, eg in terms of dress style and hair-cuts. ... Attention is also paid to the shades of skin colour. The idea that foreigners are "too dark" or "too black" is part of the collective South African unconscious.' Language is exaggerated as a marker of difference. Even where foreign Africans are able to speak an indigenous South African language, the extent of their knowledge is tested and their accents are carefully examined for signs of South African authenticity.

What Matsinhe does not appear to consider are the material conditions of unemployment and competition for scarce resources that poor, largely black, South Africans believe to be exacerbated by both legal and illegal immigration. This is expressed in the widespread discourse of 'foreigners coming to steal our jobs'. Because access to good education and qualifications is unavailable to the majority of black South Africans, they are the most vulnerable in relation to competition for work. Because poverty and unemployment in South Africa are over-determined by race, Matsinhe might have overestimated the effect of internalised racial inferiority.

While theories of the production of the Other are rooted in post-colonial theory (Fanon, 1967; Bhabha, 2004; Said, 1978), Thompson (1990) uses Othering as one of the cornerstones of his critical theory of ideology. In discussing the modes of operation of ideology, Thompson sees the mode of *unification*, which works to establish an 'us', and the mode of *fragmentation*, the operation that splits others off from this constructed 'we', as central to the operation of power and the dividing practices of inclusion and exclusion. According to Thompson (1990: 64) power works by 'constructing at the symbolic level, a form of unity which embraces individuals in a collective identity, irrespective of the differences and divisions which may separate them'.

Fragmentation, on the other hand, works to emphasise 'distinctions, differences and divisions between individuals and groups' (Thompson, 1990: 65). The Other is demonised and dehumanised. As a threat to an imagined 'us', the dangerous Other has to be restricted, suppressed, controlled and even eliminated. Barbaric acts of violence are born in these constructions of an alien Other.

A particularly vivid and recent example is the murder of a 27-year-old Mozambican taxi driver, Mido Macia, on 27 February 2013 which was recorded on amateur video and disseminated through social networks. After he allegedly assaulted a police officer and took his firearm, the police tied him to the back of their van and dragged him through the streets for about 400 metres. Macia was subsequently taken to the Daveyton police station, where he died from internal bleeding caused by injuries to his head. It is widely believed that police beat him to death and the policeman involved has been charged with murder. This is just one example of the many inhumane and ongoing acts of violence directed at foreign African nationals in a climate of increasing distrust, as reflected in the Afrobarometer attitudinal survey report (Citizen Surveys, 2012).

The link between apartheid discourses of 'die swart gevaar' [literally, the black danger] and current discourses of xenophobia come together in the movie *District 9*. Because xenophobia is spread across the globe, the movie's relevance has not been restricted to South Africa.

## District 9

Neill Blomkamp's film, *District 9*, was originally intended as an allegory of apartheid. It was released in South Africa shortly after the 2008 xenophobic attacks in which 67 foreign Africans were killed, hundreds were injured and thousands were forcibly driven out of their homes. The ease with which the film can also be read as an allegory of xenophobia speaks to the continuities of black Othering across both these discourses. This supports Matsinhe's thesis. In South Africa both of the discourses of apartheid and xenophobia are overtly racist. In xenophobic discourses elsewhere, racism is thinly disguised: Australia constructs asylum seekers as the threat, France – women who wear the veil, Europe – migrant workers, the US – illegal immigrants. The list is endless. Foucault (1970) argues that discourse is 'the power which is to be seized' (p. 110), precisely because of its power to shape identities. As educators we have to produce resistant readers who understand the social effects of all forms of semiotics. The film *District 9* provides a way of entering this difficult space.

*District 9* is science fiction: the story of human beings' first encounter with an alien species, which is set in Johannesburg, South Africa. Neill Blomkamp, the director who grew up in South Africa during apartheid, wanted to make a film about segregation and the dehumanisation of the racialised Other. He uses satire to do so with a light touch, and his choice of genre enables him to play with the multiple connotations of the word 'aliens' (strangers, foreigners, beings from outer space). The use of humour lowers our defences, enabling us to laugh simultaneously at both the characters and ourselves. Lying behind the laughter, however, is our recognition of our own prejudices or inaction and our own complicity when confronted with the unjust use of power.

*District 9* is a film about how we relate to a species very different from our own. It is about human arrogance and intolerance when confronted by the unknown stranger. It is about fear for an *us* that justifies violence against *them*, a *they* who are different. It is about corporate greed and ruthlessness. It is about two fathers: one (the human father) willing to destroy his daughter and son-in-law to serve his own selfish ends; the other (the alien father) striving to give his child a meaningful future. In the end it is about our ability to transcend our naturalised prejudices and to understand and appreciate the Other. As Wikus, the main character and anti-hero, comes to know the alien so do we; his transformation becomes our transformation.

The aliens are depicted as large and insect-like. They resemble the 'Parktown prawn' (*Libanasidus vittatus*, a monotypic king cricket), which although harmless instils fear in many South Africans. Frightening as the aliens' size and appearance are, the Prawns nevertheless have human features that enable us to empathise with them. Their eyes are expressive, their facial movements reveal tenderness, and they act with an intelligence that surpasses our own.

The script is explicit about the naming of the aliens and the following sequence is presented as a collage of news reports and the opinions of ordinary South Africans (each dash represents the start of a different speaker):

- The aliens, Prawns, they take my wife away.
- The derogatory term Prawn is used for the aliens and obviously implies something that is a bottom feeder, that scavenges the leftovers. I mean you can't say they don't look like that. That's what they look like, right?
- The aliens made off with an undisclosed amount of cash. One bystander was hurt.
- What for an alien might be seen as recreational, setting fire to a truck, derailing a train, is obviously an extremely destructive act.
- They can take the sneakers you're wearing off you.
- They take whatever you have on you. Your cellphone or anything.
- After that they kill you. (*District 9*, lines 63–73)

Notice how this description ranges across their strange appearance, the assumption of their criminality, their different values and the threat they pose to human life. The conclusion is inevitable – they must be expunged.

- I think they must fix that ship and they must go.
- A virus, a selective virus. Release it near the aliens.

–   They must just go. I don't know where, just go. (*District 9*, lines 57–59)

This is later shown visually when Wikus discovers a large Prawn incubator. After phoning for a 'population control team' he unplugs the nutrition supply to the Prawn eggs and the 'little guys' with glee. In handing part of the disconnected life support system to Thomas, his sidekick, he says

You can take that. You wanna keep it as a souvenir of your first abortion? (*District 9*, line 214)

Wikus' casual manner, as if murdering a new generation is an everyday occurrence, shows complete disregard for the life of the Other. Murder is committed without pause or regret.

The residents riot and the government develops plans to move 1.8 million Prawns to a

safer and better location, 200 kilometers outside of the city ... so that the people of Johannesburg and South Africa are going to live happily and safely, knowing the Prawn is very far away. (Wikus, *District 9*, lines 87–91)

This is an intertextual reminder of the apartheid laws which confined black South Africans to rural Bantustans, the so-called 'homelands', and to urban ghettos. The name 'District 9' evokes memories of evictions from an area in Cape Town known as 'District Six'.

District Six was named the Sixth Municipal District of Cape Town in 1867. Originally established as a mixed community of freed slaves, merchants, artisans, labourers and immigrants, District Six was a vibrant centre with close links to the city and the port. By the beginning of the twentieth century, however, the history of removals and marginalisation had begun.

The first to be 'resettled' were black South Africans, forcibly displaced from the District in 1901. ... In 1966, [District 6] was declared a white area under the Group areas Act of 1950, and by 1982, the life of the community was over. 60 000 people were forcibly removed to barren outlying areas aptly known as the Cape Flats, and their houses in District Six were flattened by bulldozers. (District Six Museum, http://www.districtsix.co.za/frames.htm, downloaded 28 October 2010)

It was only one of many communities to be bulldozed in terms of the Group Areas Act (1950) and in the name of separate development. The use of military vehicles in the film is a visual reminder of the caspers and hippos used to control black townships during periods of insurrection in the struggle for liberation, euphemistically referred to as periods of 'unrest'. African black townships in South Africa, like *District 9*, were built outside of the city with few roads leading in and out, enabling them to be cut off easily by military forces. The aerial shots of *District 9* are images of existing shack settlements which show how the structural effects of segregation and apartheid continue.

The signage in *District 9* holds up a mirror to old apartheid signs. The signs that include alien silhouettes appear in the film *District 9*. Humans are constructed as the unmarked norm for whom privileges are reserved. The Prawns are designated as 'non-humans' who are confined to the slums, denied access to places reserved for humans, and denied the right to simple amenities such as buses and benches. They are also constructed as unclean and corrosive, in both the literal and figurative meanings of the word. The old apartheid signage constructs whites (or *Blankes*, in Afrikaans) as the unmarked form, with blacks marked linguistically with the prefix *non*. Amenities are similarly preserved for whites only. Non-whites who transgress might expect to be shot and devoured by dogs. In these signs we see the pervasive construction of blackness as inferior described by Matsinhe (2011), which produces the 'disgrace of blackness' subsequently projected onto foreign Africans (see the wording of signs in Figure 9.1).

As in the case of South African xenophobic manifestations, Othering has a linguistic dimension. The choice of language, accent and grammar are clear markers of identity in this film. Shot as a quasi-documentary, the action is interspersed with news broadcasts, expert commentary and vox populi. English is the unmarked choice of language with Wikus, the anti-hero, using Afrikaans-English with flat vowels and occasional grammatical inaccuracies. His accent, designed to capture that of an obedient apartheid civil servant, suggests both his white-collar status and his level of education. His father-in-law's accent, by way of contrast, is a university-educated variety of Afrikaans-English and suggests his wealth and his power. Posh Anglo-varieties of South African English are given to the expert commentators and news readers, while African languages and second language errors are reserved for Africans on the street. The Nigerian criminals speak in a subtitled foreign African tongue. This echoes the ideology of *makwerekwere* where the word references the sounds of foreign African languages experienced as

| Wording of the signs in *District 9* | Wording on apartheid signs |
|---|---|
| **BUS BENCH FOR HUMANS ONLY**<br>REPORT NON-HUMANS<br>1-866-666-6001<br><br>**BEWARE**: NON-HUMAN SECRETIONS MAY<br>CORRODE METAL<br>D-9.COM<br><br>**PICKING UP NON-HUMANS**<br>**IS FORBIDDEN**<br>$10,000 FINE<br>**INTO THE SLUMS**<br><br>**FOR HUMANS ONLY**<br>NON-HUMANS BANNED | **NIE-BLANKES – NON WHITES ONLY**<br><br>**WHITES ONLY**<br><br>**FOR USE BY WHITE PERSONS**<br>THESE PUBLIC PREMISES HAVE BEEN RESERVED<br>FOR THE EXCLUSIVE USE OF WHITE PERSONS<br>By Order Provincial Secretary<br>**VIR GEBRUIK DEUR BLANKES**<br><br>**DANGER!** *NATIVES,INDIANS &*<br>*COLOUREDS.*<br>*IF YOU ENTER THESE*<br>*PREMISES AT NIGHT*<br>Picture of a *YOU WILL BE LISTED AS*<br>skull and *MISSING.*<br>crossbones *ARMED GUARDS SHOOT*<br>*ON SIGHT. SAVAGE DOGS*<br>*DEVOUR THE CORPSE.*<br><br>*YOU HAVE BEEN WARNED !* |

*Figure 9.1*   Sign wordings

incomprehensible to local Africans. The use of subtitles when the aliens speak shows that the sounds they are making constitute an intelligible language of an intelligent species.

The linguistic choices in the script are directed at constructing the Prawns as primitive, incapable of understanding 'the concept of private property' and 'unable to think for themselves'. The following sequence shows the ways in which Wikus infantilises the Prawn:

Prawn:       No, it's not my house. I don't live here.
Wikus:       Well, that's a pity because, you know, this ... This is nice cat food, you know. But of course it's not your house. So, we'll just have to go and give it to someone else. ...
News reader: The creatures became terribly obsessed with cat food.
(*District 9*, lines 194–198)

This use of language appears subtle when contrasted with the use of images which portray the aliens as ugly savages hacking off chunks of raw meat to cart away in wheelbarrows.

But negative constructions are not reserved for the aliens alone. Traces of old-style apartheid interaction appear in Wikus' relation to Thomas, his black partner. Wikus assumes the right to wear the only protective vest, while Thomas' fears for himself and consequently for his family are trivialised. Thomas addresses Wikus as 'boss', which creates an intertextual reference to apartheid forms of address. Finally, the film is framed within current xenophobic discourses which construct Nigerians as drug dealers and criminals:

| | |
|---|---|
| Sociologist: | The Nigerians had various scams going. One of them was the cat food scam. Where they sold cat food to the aliens for exorbitant prices.... Not to mention interspecies prostitution. And they also dealt in alien weaponry. |
| Wikus: | You have car high-jacking, there's a chop shop there, you can see that, that's somebody's car in there.... |
| News commentator: | The Nigerians in District 9 are headed by a man called Obesandjo. He's a very powerful underground figure in Johannesburg. |
| Wikus: | You don't want to play with these boys. They will cut you in pieces. |
| | (*District 9*, lines 213–224) |

Many of the high-frequency tropes relating to foreign Africans that Adegoke (1999) found in her research can be seen in *District 9*'s construction of the Nigerians: war and violence, foreign relations, dictatorship, civil unrest and riots, economic advancement (their own), corruption and crime. In addition, Adegoke's analysis by country shows a negative evaluation of Nigeria, particularly within the frames of crime and dictatorship (Adegoke, 1999: 91). Even as the film moves towards reconstructing the 'Prawns' as an intelligent and compassionate species, and towards transforming Wikus into a more sympathetic human being, the Nigerians continue to be constructed as unremittingly evil. This works to reinforce xenophobic discourses of foreign Africans in South Africa. Janks (2010: 183) describes the process of design, deconstruction and redesign as cyclical (Figure 9.2).

*District 9* is designed to deconstruct and satirise apartheid's practices of segregation, exclusion and Othering and the violence used to enforce

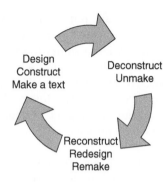

*Figure 9.2*   Janks' redesign cycle

racist policies. The treatment of the Prawns acts as a mirror to apartheid policies and practices. It is therefore ironic that in doing so, it produces a text which, when deconstructed, shows its own forms of Othering, this time of Nigerians.

## Conclusion

Stories often require heroes and villains, but who is chosen for which role has everything to do with the discourses from which they emerge. These choices reflect the relations of power that exist in specific sociohistorical contexts, who counts as the enemy and the patterns of naming and representation. It is important for students to understand the discourses that are instantiated in these texts and the ways in which they form our understanding of the Other, often below the level of our consciousness. In the same way movies are a product of their place and time. Figure 9.3 is an activity taken from *Doing Critical Literacy* (Janks, 2014). It is designed to help students read Hollywood films in relation to the social, political and historical shape-shifting of the enemy. Discussions of the Other in Hollywood movies abound in the literature (e.g. Small, 1973; Steinmetz, 2011; Shaheen, 2009).

The following pedagogical moves (see Figure 9.3) underpin the activities in 'Us and Them' (see Figure 9.4):

Questions like those in Figure 9.4 can be asked of *District 9*. The film reminds us powerfully that beauty and evil are in the eye of the beholder. The positions we take in relation to Others tell as much about who we are and the discourses that we inhabit as they do about those

1. Students are required to uncover both the history and the ideology that lead to particular constructions of Otherness.

2. They have to deconstruct negative naming practices.

3. They have to describe the stereotypes of successive enemies portrayed by Hollywood.

4. They have to consider the possible social effects of repeated negative representations of the Other.

5. They have to find and interrogate representations of the Other in their own communities. They have to make a collage that can be displayed, compared and discussed.

*Figure 9.3*  Extract from *Doing Critical Literacy* (Janks, 2014)

we construct as irreconcilably different. *District 9* invites us to consider what is lost by our refusal to engage with those who are different from us. It is clear that there is much humankind could have learnt from the technologically sophisticated 'Prawns'. We have a sense too, that Wikus' learning about himself, the human race and the Prawns is only just beginning. To the extent that he is everyman and everywoman, our journey into Otherness, like his, is just beginning. Perhaps we will have arrived when we accept that as with the Prawns, we have a lot to learn about Nigerians.

The literature suggests that xenophobia is reduced as we come to know those whom we fear. Education has an important role to play in helping students come to terms with difference and to recognise that diversity is a resource for seeing and thinking in new ways, as is suggested by the teaching exercise in Figure 9.4. Knowing and accepting ourselves is a good place to begin.

## References

Adegoke, R. (1999). Media discourse on foreign Africans and the implications for education. Unpublished master's dissertation, University of the Witwatersrand, Johannesburg.

Bhabha, H. (2004). *The location of culture*. London and New York: Routledge.

Citizen Surveys (2012). *Afrobarometer round 5: survey in South Africa. A comparative series of national public attitude surveys on democracy, market and civil society in Africa*. Cape Town: The Institute for Democracy in South Africa.

Elias, N. (1994). Introduction: a theoretical essay on established and outsider relations. In N. Elias and J. Scotson, *The established and the outsiders*. London: Sage.

Fanon, F. (1967). *Black skin white masks*. New York: Grove Press.

204

**US AND THEM**

Anyone who has watched mainstream Hollywood movies understands the difference between the 'good guys' and the 'bad guys'. Who the bad guys are changes according to whom America sees as its 'enemy' at different moments of history. The enemy is often given an offensive or derogatory name. To whom do these names refer? When and why were they seen as a threat to the US? How are they typically portrayed?

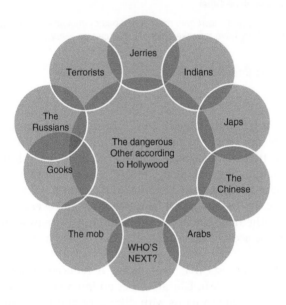

It is a pity that people tend to construct a sense of who they are in contrast to people who are different (however insignificantly) from them. Too often the Other is seen as a dangerous threat. Look at your own country: read your newspapers; listen to the news on TV. Who in your country is portrayed as a threat to society? Is it 'the youth'? Is it immigrants? Is it women who wear the veil? Is it a racial group? Is it foreigners? Is it criminals? Is it unemployed people? Is it people with HIV-AIDS? Design a collage – using photographs, headlines, words, cartoons – of the people or types of people currently constructed as the 'bad guys' in your own country or community. Compare your collages.

Adapted from Janks (2014)

*Figure 9.4* Extract from *Doing Critical Literacy* (Janks, 2014)

Foucault, M. (1970). The order of discourse. Inaugural lecture at the Collège de France. In M. Shapiro (ed.), *Language and politics*. Oxford: Basil Blackwell.

Harris, B. (2002). Xenophobia: a new pathology for a new South Africa? In D. Hook and J. Eagle (eds), *Psychopathology and social prejudice*. Cape Town: University of Cape Town Press.

Jackson, P. (2009). *District 9*. Directed by Neill Blomkamp, TriStar Pictures.

Jackson, P. *District 9*. Script downloaded 12 August 2010 at http://www.mymoviescripts. com/?id=District+9

Janks, H. (2010). *Literacy and power*. London and New York: Routledge.

Janks, H. (ed.) (2014). *Doing critical literacy*. New York and London: Routledge.

Matsinhe, D. M. (2011). Africa's fear of itself: the ideology of *Makwerekwere* in South Africa. *Third World Quarterly*, 32 (2): 295–313.

Morris, A. (1998). 'Our fellow Africans make our lives hell': the lives of Congolese and Nigerians living in Johannesburg. *Ethnic and Racial Studies*, 21(6).

Neocosmos, M. (2008). The politics of fear and the fear of politics. 12 June 2008 at http://www.pambazuki.org/en/category/features/48712 in Matsinhe (2011).

Said, E. (1978). *Orientalism. Western conceptions of the Orient*. London: Penguin Books.

Shaheen, J. (2009). *Reel bad Arabs: how Hollywood vilifies a people*. Northampton, Mass.: Olive Branch Press.

Small, M. (1973). Buffoons and bravehearts: Hollywood portrays the Russians 1939–1944. *California History Quarterly*, 52 (4): 326.

Steinmetz, J. (2011) *Schindler's List, Inglourious Basterds*, and the problem of evil in American cinema. Downloaded 22 April 2013, from http://papers.ssrn.com/sol3/papers.cfm? abstract_id=1803986

Thompson, J. B. (1990). *Ideology and modern culture*. Oxford: Basil Blackwell.

# 10
## Bodies of Language and Languages of Bodies: South African Puzzles and Opportunities

*Crain Soudien*

### Introduction

A somewhat esoteric discussion around the question of the relation-ship between modern subjectivity or its weaker expression of identity, and citizenship and human rights is playing itself out in contempo-rary social theory circles (see Malabou, 2011). In this discussion, not quite at its heart, is the question of the nature of the *unconscious* and its ontological anchorings. In one version of this discussion Žižek (1999: 301) takes issue with the important work of Butler (1997) on *resistance* to imposed ideas of subjectivity and identity. He says that Butler appears to suggest that resistance to 'disciplinary power mechanisms', and he is referring to the mechanisms which produce gender, culture and other forms of subjectivity, is grounded in the idea of an ontological 'pre-existing positive body'. At issue for him is not Butler's explanation of the constituted nature of subjectivity but the fixity imputed to it ontologically in and through the unconscious. In this brief essay, I do not engage with the specificities of this debate. I retrieve its general substance to suggest that it highlights the signifi-cance that South Africa, as a particular place in history and in time, holds for thinking through the puzzles of how language as a resource for imagining and taking upon subjecthood and the active processes of ontological fashioning, or less discursively, identity-making, works. I argue that a recognition of the dynamics of this puzzle places us in a position to engage with the meaning and indeed possibilities of what it means to be human beyond our historically constructed understandings of who we are. South Africa is in this sense a deeply important site for the politics, and the scholarship surrounding this politics, of social difference.

## South Africa and its significance for social difference

What makes South Africa a special site for understanding the relationship between language and the body? It is a place where the contradictions and the possibilities around subjecthood that arise through language find powerful expression. How the body is interpellated through language and comes to be ontologised in South Africa in the course of both the everyday and critical engagements with the everyday in the academy and the world of politics makes the country a site of productive possibility for thinking about identity in ways that reject hierarchy and emphasise connectedness. This possibility arises, of course, out of the distinctive place South Africa, along with the United States and Brazil, has in modern world history as a key site for both the production of and undoing of racialised forms of difference. Possibly more so than Brazil and the United States, it is here that the enunciation and justification of a particular kind of racialised language of the self and the *other* take official form. And it is here now, and the hubris around such claims needs to be acknowledged, that the opportunity for devising new languages of self and *other* presents itself with greater potential than it might elsewhere in the world. With respect to the instantiation of 'race' it is in South Africa, first in the encounter of Dutch-speaking Europeans and Khoisan people, and then later that of settlers from Europe and Bantu-speaking people, that ontology as an area of empirical study is most deeply invested with and substantiated in the enduring language of 'race'. Jan van Riebeeck, the first Dutch East India Company Commander of the Cape, used the expression 'stinkende nasie' (stinking nation), when he first met the Khoikhoi people on the shores of what came to be known as Table Bay in 1652. The language he used was, of course, not *born* in South Africa,[1] but the circumstances surrounding its practice, pushed it towards, as it did also in the United States around the Lockean conjugation of native American identity, a deeply consequential naturalisation or biologisation of identity. A philological syntax evolved which fused language and the body and left disciplines such as anthropology mired in complete logical confusion.[2] This process of naturalisation took shape over a long period after the first contact between Europeans and the local people of Africa. In terms of the undoing of 'race', it is necessary, therefore, to emphasise how present the idea of *biologised* difference is at the very beginning of the encounter of difference, but how much its historical evolution takes place in the presence and often incorporation of other forms of difference. 'Race' derives its complexity from the fact that it is never separate from other forms through which people identify. It is not necessarily the point of departure for human beings when they explain and manage their difference. In the beginning of the encounter between the first settlers and the indigenous people awareness of difference pivoted on religious affiliation – of Christians versus heathens – but rapidly took a turn to the somatic when indigenous people, based on and because of what they looked like, became the objects of genocidal campaigns (see Elphick, 1985; Adhikari, 2010). Even, however, when 'looks' came to be the primary signifier of difference, as in the period, for example, of the Great Trek into the interior of South Africa when the Trek-Boers regularly shot black people on sight (see Schoon, 1972: 103), they were always in the presence of countervailing forces. Present amongst the Europeans in this period, to emphasise the point, were extraordinary individuals and groups who used religion to articulate an argument about the unity of humankind. It is the complexity of this making and remaking of 'race' which makes South Africa such an important case study for understanding the relationship between language and the body.

How does the importance of South Africa for understanding this relationship now present itself? The country is going through intense experiences at the personal and the social level of loss and displacement, and of recuperation and renewal around identity and belonging. These experiences are stimulating intense debates about solidarity and social difference. Interestingly, passionate as the debates are, they are not, however, equal to the complexity and even the advances through which South Africans are going experientially. An important reason for this, I argue, is that the debates have not yet connected, on the one hand, the domains of language and language practice and, on the other, the domains of the body and the ways in which bodies are entering, engaging with and negotiating the question of their very physicality, singly and in connection. The question of what are historically perceived as *black* bodies in historically *white* spaces, and vice versa, and the new embodied spaces that are emerging as sociological developments, where people are having to learn how to manage their historically inscribed bodies in new ways is a deeply important phenomenon on the South African landscape. Because this connection is not materialised, the significance which South Africa portends for the discussion of an expansive and inclusive sense of what it means to be human remains unrealised. It is the possibility that is imminent in this realisation that I seek to explore in this essay.

## An ontological hotspot

What human *possibility* is and where it presents itself is important to understand. The possibility that South Africa represents lies in the melange and intensity of everyday experiences through which its subjects are going. These experiences test to the limit the question of what it means to be human and how one sees the humanity of others. It tests the significance and the meanings of words and terms and the ways these have been habituated and embodied. What are these experiences?

On the one hand the country has 'opened up' in all kinds of ways. Sealed off from the rest of the world as it had been during the apartheid era, it has entered and been thrust into the full complexity of global life. Lifestyles have evolved rapidly. Significant has been the intensely quick absorption of parts of the country that would have been shielded from hypermodernity into new modes of consumption that have placed stress on growing up, becoming an adult and exercising responsibility around one's relationships, one's sexuality and one's sense of citizenship, sense of self, and sense of solidarity with others. Urgent new questions have been posed by these developments. Illustrative of these are the challenges of living out new transgressive gendered identities – of thinking of oneself, for example, as being both gay and Zulu – and of fulfilling traditional roles of responsibility to families in contexts and circumstances where the logics of blood and tradition have been broken down by new market forces. I think here of the deeply poignant story of Mbuyiselo Botha, a Sonke Gender Justice activist who refused to pay the bail costs of a brother who had been arrested for rape (Soudien, 2012: 237). It was the logic of what was *right*. Filiality and blood were immaterial against the urgency of doing what his conscience demanded. Strikingly, one is seeing critical new appropriations of the self developing in the country. Individuals are emerging on the margins who are beginning to articulate their identities and their relationships with their ecologies in powerfully new ways (see Ndlovu, 2012). On the other hand, as the country has opened up, old fractures have either hardened or taken on new dimensions. Inequality in the country has become more complex. South Africa has become the world's most unequal society (Benjamin, 2013: 5). Infant and maternal mortality remain high at respectively 47 per 1000 births for children and 300 per 100,000 deaths for mothers (Smallhorne, 2013: 35). The Health eNews Service (2013: 13) reports that South Africa is now one of the most violent countries in the world, with South Africans being 30 per cent more likely to die violently than those in other sub-Saharan countries. Entangled in these experiences are the factors of race and racism, of gender and sexism, class and classism, belief and non-belief, and a multiplication of other forces and influences. And overlaying these factors, moreover, are the almost ineffable questions of past and present, of what individuals and groups consider to be their traditions and what is so intrinsically theirs that they will not brook any kind of critique of it, or even the possibility of critique. Critically in this past and present, precipitating a vortex of desires and resentments, are the anxieties South Africans constantly confront of personal safety and harm to their persons that rampant criminality brings about, of being ill or well, of dying in the prime of their lives through HIV-AIDS, of seeing amongst themselves intense pathologies of self-destruction through substance abuse, through material greed, through the kind of narcissism that is the bread and butter of the everyday in economically resourced parts of the world. How to recognise a fellow human and to extend to him or her unconditional respect is an ontological challenge of immense proportions.

The mainstream of intellectual life, however, is struggling with the challenge before it. Epistemologically, the country appears to be in some difficulty in describing and analysing the hothouse that it is. Its languages of description, its intellectual framings, its theories of what the country is going through and how its subjects come to relate to one another – the intellectual recuperation of all of this – are not quite equal to the experience. And so there is a crisis in some ways. Academic disciplines have not yet been able to step into the density of this social experience. Their instinct is to work in the tired categories of yesterday. The country is busy reinventing itself. But the deliberative equipment it has at its disposal to make sense of this is wanting.

And so, by and large, South Africa finds itself intellectually in thrall to old narrations of its past, present and future. One narrative strand emanates from sections of those who previously ran the country and is represented by a crude but vituperative sense of loss for what had been – a kind of white supremacist resentment (see Steyn, 2001). It amounts to a very particular kind of nostalgia. While this is for many an intensely personal experience, its psychosocial significance is great in so far as nostalgia not only inhibits the capacity to venture into difficult areas of engagement but constantly, in an Althusserian way, from the habit of established identities hails South Africans back into their insecurities and so makes them complicit in reproducing the country's fractures. Out of this, and in response to it, have emerged counter-narratives about how hegemonies are constituted and reconstituted. At the extreme end of these counter-narratives is a version of black consciousness which is angry and impatient. Recently, Andile Mngxitama, a prominent intellectual, wrote on his Facebook page that a critic should be beaten up: 'real bikoists (followers of Steve Biko, the Black Consciousness leader) out there, whenever we see that white little bastard called _____, we must beat the s... out of him' (Abahlali baseMjondolo et al., 2013: 30). In between these exist explanations which depend, in an almost default mode, on frameworks of analysis and explanation that reproduce the categories of domination out of which the country has come.

## Where possibility lies: concluding thoughts

In the midst of this rapidly changing world, what *new* explanations for what is going on are emerging? Important work is emerging at universities as I have tried to explain elsewhere (Soudien, 2011). These include the History Seminar at the University of the Western Cape which seeks to reimagine the humanities in South Africa, the Wits Institute for Social and Economic Research (WISER) which seeks to understand the social nature of South Africa and a host of other initiatives such as the Centre for Humanities Research (CHR) in 2006, a successor structure to the Institute for Historical Research, the Institute for Humanities in Africa (HUMA) at the University of Cape Town in 2010, the Centre for Critical Research on Race and Identity (CCRRI), based at the University of Kwa-Zulu Natal, the Apartheid Archive Project at the University of the Witwatersrand and the Centre for the Advancement of Non-Racism and Democracy (CANRAD) at the Nelson Mandela Metropolitan University (NMMU). The primary interest of the CCRRI, to emphasise the point, is to study 'race thinking and changing identities', for the purpose of understanding and discussing 'the epistemological, moral, cultural and other bases for perceptions of human diversity and difference' (http://ccri.ukzn.ac.za/). Important about these initiatives is their interest in what it means to be human and how this humanity is to be indexed, marked, symbolically framed and, ultimately described. A fundamental constant in all of these projects is the idea of the *constructed* nature of social identity, whatever social identity is under discussion. Buttressing the arguments of scholars in these spaces is what one might now describe as our *better* knowledge that *race* and *gender*, inter alia, are notions that we have elaborately constructed as naturalised markers of difference – that they have no scientific or empirical substantiation. Two features of these intellectual developments are important to note. The first is that as narratives of social difference they continue to exist on the margins. The second, more pertinent for this essay, is that while language is at the heart of these developments, paradoxically, its relationship with the body and with identity is absent and largely unexplored.

What is now the opportunity? While important work has been done by scholars such as Jacob Nhlapo and Neville Alexander, with the latter proposing in 1944 that the spoken varieties of Nguni and Sotho 'respectively be standardised in a written form as the first step to a possible standardised indigenous African language, in order *to help to overcome tribal and ethnic divisions'* (Alexander, 1989: 32) and Alexander again taking this up in his *Great Garieb* metaphor. In the Garieb metaphor Alexander argues for an approach to identity which begins with the premise that South African identity is fluid, 'that no single current dominates, that all the tributaries in their ever-changing forms continue to exist as such, even as they continue to constitute and reconstitutute the mainstream' (Alexander, 2002: 107). For this to happen, multilingual capacity is essential. At the heart of these proposals is a conscious and deliberate process of language planning. Important as this emphasis on planning the learning experience of South Africa in the direction of *harmonisation* of their communicative opportunities is, I would like to suggest that underexamined in this focus is a concern with the ways in which these very languages to be harmonised have had embedded in them racial properties. I am not sufficiently educated in the philological character of the languages of the region to talk about their socially constructed gendered, raced and other *othering* dimensions, which would take us back to the Žizek and Butler debate. This is essential. Less ambitious, but still deeply important, is using the South African experience to understand the ways languages have come to be attached to racial identity. This concern takes its foundation out of the grouping philologically of languages into terms such as Semitic and Hamitic. As Augstein (1997: 5) has argued, these terms were 'unfortunate'. They were unfortunate to the degree that they conflated languages and bodies, and, indeed, problematically, by extension, languages, *minds* and bodies to produce the racial image of a *Semitic* or a *Bantu* mind. The premise upon which these explanations began was physical isolation and separateness, isolation which produced both phenotypical and cultural distinctivenesses. At its root, argued Prichard (Augstein, 1997: 10), was the conventional wisdom that had settled within the linguistic community of the distinctiveness and even the superiority of the Germanic and Aryan contribution to language formation and civilisation. As Augstein (1997: 12) says, 'Prichard would have none of this. He abhorred racial arguments and observed with dismay how "races are made the groundwork of political coalitions and a difference in stock and lineage becomes a plea for separation and hostility".' And so he went out of his way to demonstrate the links between languages and from these '(linguistic arguments) to deduce the unity of (hu)mankind' (Augstein, 1997: 10).

In South Africa the differentiating instinct prevailed – of embodying languages in racial concepts – and was taken a step further with the almost complete conflation of language and body in the term *Bantu*. Meaning *people* the term has its origins in philology and was essentially used to describe the related languages of the western, eastern, central and southern parts of Africa. Critically, during the apartheid era, it was taken beyond its philological compass and incorporated into anthropology, ethnology and social policy as a scientific term to describe the cultural and *raced* identities of people and came to be used by the apartheid government in its official documentation during the 1960s in place of the word *native*. *Native* was defined as anybody who was a member of an 'aboriginal race or tribe of Africa' (South Africa, 1950: 1). This was the meaning inherited by the term *Bantu* – a member of an aboriginal race or tribe of Africa. Important in understanding the dynamics surrounding terms such as these are the measures and instruments used by the state to enforce them. In the height of the apartheid era the government established an agency to ensure the *integrity* of its classificatory definitions and structures. This agency constantly sought to 'improve' itself, to 'tighten loopholes' and 'assisting people by removing uncertainty and unease and the "clouds which hovered over them"' by establishing a Race Classification Board (Valentine, c.2006: 1). The sole function of this board was to devise and implement mechanisms that would scientifically ascertain the 'race' of people around whom there was doubt. There was, of course, no science on which to draw. Racial determination was arbitrary and depended on *intuition* and opinion.

The explicit instruments and mechanisms of classification no longer, as is to be expected, exist in the post-apartheid era. But its classificatory impetus and the naturalised assumptions on which it depended have persisted in the ways in which apartheid-era understandings of *race* continue to be used. The state, in seeking to engage with the racial legacy of the past, continues to invoke *race* as the operational means through which to effect redress. But more critically its discursive reach remains evident in both the everyday and the languages of description to make sense of the everyday. Both bodies and languages continue to be referenced in these ways – *black* is now interestingly used as the preferred way of describing people who would have been in the past described as *native* and then as *Bantu.* The languages associated with them have come to be described as *black. Black* is now a term of embodiment. The discourse of the popular is such that that the indistinguishability of body and language persists.

The challenge and the opportunity that South Africa represents it seems, are to think of how its transgressive post-apartheid experience, in the presence of our *better knowledge* of the constructed nature of social difference and especially that of *race*, makes possible new ways in which one might come to understand the constituted body and to release descriptions of the body from their biologised moorings. How, therefore, might we begin to use and deploy language in ways that open us up to possibilities of our humanness that are not limited by the syntaxes that currently define these languages. It is, I suggest, in exploring the rigorous methodologies of philology, in seeking and making sense of the pathways of the connectedness of our languages and uncovering their histories, and, thereby helping us to keep at bay our inclination to reach for the seductive explanations of embodied cultures and languages, that an important opportunity lies before us. It is this struggle and opportunity that makes the country so important for the global discussion and practice of social difference.

## Notes

1. See the extraordinary work of a contemporary of Charles Darwin, James Prichard (1843), *A Natural History of Man.* While Prichard is known for monogenism, the argument of the 'unity of mankind' (see Augstein, 1997: 2), he distinguishes in this work between 'men' and 'tribes':

   > while the lower tribes live everywhere resistless slaves to the agencies of material nature, the mere sport of their destiny, or the lot which external conditions impose on them, without making an effort to modify the circumstances which limit their capability of existence, man, on the contrary, gains victories over the elements, and turns the most powerful and even the most formidable of their agencies to the promotion of his own pleasure and advantage. (Prichard, 1843: 3)

2. The most dramatic example of this confusion was the splitting of the anthropology department at Stanford University in the late 1990s into two departments, one which was to argue for the 'hard-wiring' of identity and the other for its social constructedness.

## References

Abahlali baseMjondolo, Achmat, Z., Buthulezi, B., Duncan, J., Depelchin, J., Geffen, N., Good, K., Huchzermeyer, M., Jagarnath, V., Kota, A., Manji, F., Mokoape, A., Neocosmos, M., Onceya, T., Pithouse, R. and Unemployed

People's Movement (2013). Mngxitama the bully. *Mail and Guardian,* Letters to the Editor, 28 March–4 April 2013, p. 30.

Adhikari, M. (2010). *The anatomy of a South African genocide: the extermination of the Cape San peoples.* Cape Town: UCT Press.

Alexander, N. (1989). *Language policy and national unity in South Africa/Azania.* Cape Town: Buchu Books.

Augstein, H. (1997). Linguistics and politics in the early 19th century: James Cowles Prichard's moral philology. *History of European Ideas,* 23 (1): 1–18.

Benjamin, C. (2013). With influence growing on world stage, Brics flex their muscles. *Mail and Guardian, Business,* 28 March–4 April 2013, p. 5.

Butler, J. (1997). *The psychic life of power: theories in subjection.* Stanford, Calif.: Stanford University Press.

Elphick, R. (1985). *Khoikhoi and the founding of white South Africa.* Johannesburg: Ravan Press.

Malabou, C. (2011). *The Heidegger change: on the fantastic in philosophy.* Albany, NY: SUNY Press.

Ndlovu, S. (2012). Portfolio of doctoral work. Submitted in partial fulfilment of the requirements for the PhD degree, University of KwaZulu-Natal, November 2012, Durban.

Prichard, James (1843). *A natural history of man.* London: Bailliere.

Schoon, H. (ed.) (1972). *The diary of Erasmus Smit.* Cape Town: Struik.

Smallhorne, M. (2013). A collective responsibility. *Mail and Guardian,* 28 March–4 April 2013, p. 35.

Soudien, C. (2011). The arhythmic pulse of transformation in higher education. *Alternation,* 18 (2): 15–34.

Soudien, C. (2012). *Realising the dream: unlearning the logic of race.* Cape Town: HSRC Press.

South Africa (1950). Population registration Act No. 30. Cape Town: South Africa.

Steyn, M. (2001). *'Whiteness just isn't what it used to be': white identity in a changing South Africa.* Albany, NY: SUNY Press.

The Health eNews Service (2013). Violence, alcohol and mental disorders: in need of an integrated approach. *The Star,* 3 April 2013, p. 13.

Valentine, S. (c.2006). An appalling science. Sunday Times Heritage Project. http://heritage.thetimes.co.za/memorials/wc/RaceClassificationBoard/article.aspx?id=591128

Žižek, S. (1999). *The ticklish subject: an essay in political ontology.* New York: Verso.

# Index

Printed and bound by CPI Group (UK) Ltd, Croydon, CR0 4YY